EATING
from the
White House
to the
Jailhouse

Louise Dodd

Copyright © 2004

Louise Dodd
Courier Herald
115 South Jefferson Street
Dublin, GA 31021

ISBN: 0-9572965-0-7

First Printing   May 2004

3000 copies

For additional copies see order form on page 295.

The author of this book has taken every precaution to ensure that all recipes have been tested and are accurate. Contributors' recipes may have been changed slightly upon testing.

WIMMER
COOKBOOKS
ConsolidatedGraphics
800.548.2537
wimmerco.com

DEDICATION

This book is lovingly dedicated to

My mother-Kathleen (Kitty) Shearouse Futrelle

My daughter-Carol Dodd Porter

My sister-Elizabeth (Libby) Futrelle Richardson

My daughter-in-law-Pamela (Pam) Green Dodd

My sister-in-law-Sybil Newton Futrelle

All wonderful cooks!

FOREWORD

Louise Dodd was born and reared in Guyton, Georgia, near Savannah, in 1929. At the young age of 16, she enrolled at Wesleyan College in Macon, Georgia, the oldest chartered college for women in the world. After her marriage in 1950, she lived in Wrightsville, Georgia for 35 years where her husband practiced medicine and where two children, Carol and Bill, were born.

While in Wrightsville, Louise became affiliated with The Courier Herald *in Dublin where she was an award-winning writer and the creator of a weekly food column, From the Kitchen of Louise Dodd, that she has done for 25 years.*

Elected Mrs. Macon in 1967, Louise represented Macon in the Mrs. Georgia contest while still living in Wrightsville. During her tenure she was presented the keys to the city both in Wrightsville and Macon.

In 1986, Louise moved to Macon where she was immediately hired to do food writing for Macon Magazine. *Her writing appeared in their first issue and she has written for every issue since then.*

Louise has enthusiastically explored the cuisine of many diverse people in places all over the United States and abroad. Her quest for and excitement about good food stories is almost unparalleled.

Louise's travels have included almost every major city in this country. Her dining experiences include such fantastic places as the Pakistan and Indonesian Embassies in Washington and a biscuit factory in rural Candler County, Georgia. Which was more exciting? They're all exciting to Louise.

She has checked out huge John Deere tea pickers in the field on the only tea plantation in America near Charleston, S.C., and has attended the Gilroy Garlic Festival in Gilroy, California. She has gathered fall leaves at Lake Placid, New York "to make decorations for her Thanksgiving table" and has gathered Spanish Bayonet blooms in Cashiers, North Carolina to make a pretty presentation on her plates like she learned about at Jane Butel's Southwestern Cooking School in Albuquerque.

Visiting the Governor's Mansion in Little Rock before Clinton was elected president gave her the opportunity to meet all the Clintons as well as their marvelous cook, Liza Ashley, who had just published a cookbook about her cooking for eight of Arkansas' governors. Louise spent an interesting afternoon at the Governor's Mansion in Atlanta, interviewing their chef and being hosted by Elizabeth Harris, the (then) First Lady of the state. Again, just before he was elected to the presidency, George W's mansion was the site of a lovely luncheon and tour of the mansion in Austin that Louise enjoyed. At another governor's mansion in Jackson, Mississippi, Louise was with a group of food writers who were entertained by Junior League members touting their new cookbook.

From the White House to the jail house, Louise has dined and from the House of Lords in London to the house of the Lord in many Georgia towns. Could she say which was most interesting. Probably not. Louise can always find the intrigue in any situation and enjoys sharing her experiences with her loyal readers at the newspaper and magazine.

The First Lady's Luncheon at the Shoreham Hotel, honoring Nancy Reagan, in Washington, was a marvelous experience for Louise when she was the guest of her congressman and his wife. Rubbing elbows with Ernest Hemingway and Susan Hayward in Miami are among her treasured memories and she writes interestingly of her being with the great movie producer, John Houston, on several occasions. She also writes of meeting the celebrated author and former jockey for the Queen, Dick Francis, at a steeplechase in Columbus.

The steeplechase didn't outshine her day at the Kentucky Derby, though, nor at Belmont in New York. She might not remember the winning horses but she still covets the recipes she gathered at both places.

The wedding of television cook and cookbook author, Nathalie Dupree, on the beach at Jamaica is among Louise's favorite memories along with her close friendship with Jim Fobel of New York, cookbook author, test kitchen director and contributor to many of the national food magazines.

Touring the Amish country with her 92-year-old mother and her sister and sister-in-law brought Louise untold pleasure and a lot of recipes. So have her several visits to the Masters with her sister-in-law. She also had an extraordinary visit to Disney World when Epcot was closed to the public and turned over to food and travel writers from all over the world. It was their 15th anniversary and there were such guests as Dolly Parton and Buddy Rich. All the celebrities were available for press conferences.

A treasured letter from William F. Buckley who had seen Louise's column will always be high on the list. An interview with the Major League batting champion, Wade Boggs, was fun too and especially interesting because he had just published a cookbook on his lucky food—chicken.

The day and half the night, spent at the White House during the Carter administration was an unforgettable experience and later a visit to Plains, Georgia to hear Carter teach his Sunday School class was also special.

Cooking schools have always intrigued Louise and she writes interestingly of her attendance at classes in Atlanta; Albuquerque; Austin; Charleston; Laguna Beach, California; Pinehurst, North Carolina; Las Vegas; New Orleans; and the prestigious school at the Greenbrier in West Virginia-not once but twice. Once she studied there with Julie Dannenbaum, and later with Ann Willan from Normandy, France. She also attended cooking classes taught by Jacques Pepin at Georgia's Sea Island Cloister Hotel and had a brief class with Graham Kerr in Sacramento.

A special trip to the Culinary Institute of America in Hyde Park, New York holds wonderful memories and so does an in-depth look at Johnson and Wales Culinary School in Charleston.

Chefs, not movie stars, are Louise's idols and she has been able to meet many and extract recipes from all of them. John Folse of television fame entertained foodwriters in Seattle with a most interesting cooking demonstration. Dean Fearing of Mansion on Turtle Creek, Dallas' only 5-Star restaurant, ranks high on the list as well as Paul Prudhomme, the great New Orleans chef and cookbook author. Princess Marie de Broglie of Normandy did a cooking class for Macon's Cherry Blossom Festival. Louise was chairman of this cooking event and also of one done for the Cherry Blossom Festival by representatives from the Republic of China. Wolfgang Puck spoke to an enthusiastic group at his fabulous restaurant in Las Vegas and served a special dinner too. Louise writes about all of this in her book.

A lovely day at the desert home of Gladys Knight in the Las Vegas desert produced recipes from the Bellagio chefs who were there to do the meal and also from Gladys' personal recipe files. Sharing a dinner party with wine country's Robert Mondavi gave Louise her first exposure to buffalo on the plate, and Breakfast at Tiffany's had Louise pretending to rehearse as Audrey Hepburn for this special occasion where she still managed to secure recipes.

With a southern drawl as slow as the cane syrup that Georgians pour on their biscuits, Louise is fiercely loyal to her native Georgia. She grew up under the tutelage of good cooks, her mother and grandmother and aunts, and has written, sometimes comically, about many of her small town experiences. She has explored many of the historic restaurants in nearby Savannah and has had many fabulous meals at the Cloister on Sea Island, host to the World 2004 G-8 Summit. Atlanta has been the site of many of Louise's write-about experiences, including a meal at the Coca Cola headquarters and an old-fashioned southern barbecue at Lovejoy Plantation, the home of Betty Talmadge. She also did an in-depth interview with Lynda and Herman Talmadge at their Lake Talmadge home and treasures Lynda's gift to her of her cookbook with a wedding picture of Lynda and Herman tucked quietly inside. Louise was a guest at the grand opening of Atlanta's lovely High Museum and tells of meeting its architect, Richard Maier, at the reception.

You'll enjoy Louise's exciting and exuberant descriptions of dining experiences in Aspen; Cape Cod; Hawaii; Hollywood; Martha's Vineyard; Kennebunkport, Maine; and the Opryland Hotel in Nashville. Barbecue on a Texas ranch ranks high on Louise's list too. Sumptuous meals in several well-known art museums are also quite memorable.

The National Chicken Cooking Contest and the Pillsbury Bake-Off® Contest have been destinations for Louise through the years and she can hardly ever wait to get back home to share with her readers the great excitement that is generated by these huge cooking events. Who wouldn't be excited to see a winner pick up $1,000,000 at Pillsbury? Meeting celebrities at these contests has been fun for Louise too. Alex Trebec, Willard Scott, and Phylicia Rashad, who plays Bill Cosby's wife on television are some of them. Dinners for the writers at these contests are always works of art, both decoratively and culinarily and Louise captures it all.

Traveling in Brussels, Luxembourg, London, Dublin, Ireland and Paris are great memories for this writer who has shared them all including an unforgettable meal at Paris' Tour d'Argent, the oldest restaurant in Paris with a beautiful view of the Seine and a list almost as long as the river of famous people who have eaten there.

Judging cooking contests makes for interesting accounts in the cookbook with recipes gleaned at these occasions. A certified Memphis in May judge, Louise enjoyed judging the world's most famous barbecue contest held along a mile of the Mississippi River in Memphis. She has also enjoyed many times judging Georgia's Barbecue Contest in Vienna, the Big Pig Jig. She writes of other contests she has judged, everywhere from schools to churches.

Among the exciting adventures that Louise writes about on her trips to New York are a twilight dinner at Windows on the World in the now destroyed World Trade Center; a scrumptious spread at the Belmont horse races; a college trip to the Russian Tea Room and Lindy's; and dining at the Waldorf Astoria which caused Louise to research and write about their famous Waldorf Salad.

For the local chapter of the American Cancer Society, Louise has done several television cooking shows. She also did a cooking demonstration for Macon's contribution to the Olympics, Georgia on my Plate, and she served on the board that planned for this big event in Macon's Centreplex. Louise filled the Dublin Theatre when she did a cooking demonstration there.

It's all there and much more. Really delicious recipes, some plain down-home cooking and others sophisticated and involved, make up this quite diverse collection. Over 60 years of culinary experiences and collection of recipes, reveal a part of the food memories of this Georgia native, descended from its first settlers-there's even a recipe from them.

TABLE OF CONTENTS

BEVERAGES AND APPETIZERS

Louise, Dr. Jim Marion, and Clara Eschmann enjoy drinks on Bellagio Terrace in Las Vegas.

BANANA FREEZE

My mother, sister, and sister-in-law and I still enjoy reminiscing about our trip to Pennsylvania to the Amish Country. Mother was about 92 at the time and such a good trooper you never saw. On our return we took the ferry that crossed from the Outer Banks to Ocracoke in North Carolina. There was nothing but water as far as you could see. But since my sister had put a quick claim on a booth we were able to pass the hours away with a nice game of bridge. Thinking seriously and concentrated, Mother said, "I don't know if you girls know it or not but I cannot swim." We had a good laugh because we doubted that anybody could swim out of that large body of water-much less a 92 year old.

This is a recipe for a refreshing drink that I found somewhere when we were at the Outer Banks. It is delicious and so refreshing on a hot summer day.

3	bananas	1	(12-ounce) can frozen orange juice concentrate
1	(6-ounce) can frozen lemonade concentrate	3	cups pineapple juice
3	quarts lemon-lime soda	3	cups water
		2	cups sugar

Combine bananas and lemonade concentrate in container of electric blender; process until smooth. Add remaining ingredients; mix well. Pour into plastic freezer containers; freeze 3 to 4 hours or until slushy. To serve, spoon into chilled glasses. Garnish with a piece of fruit.

GINGER TEA

In a little tea room near the Lick Observatory in San Jose, California we were intrigued with their Ginger Tea. We were intrigued with the great seismograph in the observatory, too, but since we couldn't bring it home we brought home the tea recipe that has no tea but you will vow it's the real thing.

4	(¼-inch thick) slices gingerroot	6	cups boiling water
¼	cup light brown sugar		

Bruise ginger slices with the flat side of a large knife blade. Place in a 6-cup teapot with brown sugar and boiling water. Steep 5 minutes.

BEVERAGES AND APPETIZERS

IRISH COFFEE

Johnson County played Mt. de Sales from Macon in 1967 and many of our friends drove down to Wrightsville for the football game, played on a really cold and icy night. Afterward lots of friends came by for Irish Coffee, which seemed to be an appropriate drink for Irish friends, on a cold night.

1	teaspoon sugar	5	ounces hot coffee
1½	ounces Irish whiskey	1	tablespoon whipped cream

Rinse out a large wine glass or Irish coffee glass with hot water. Put sugar, whiskey and coffee into glass and stir well. Top with whipped cream.

EGGNOG

My neighbor and one of my all-time favorite friends, the late Rita Pryor, and I served this delicious Eggnog at a Christmas party in the '50s before raw eggs became a terrible no! no! Some people say the whiskey cooks the eggs but I say, "Travel at your own risk." This is really delicious though if you like eggnog. (Makes a punch cup full for 6 and then half again.)

6	eggs	1	tablespoon sugar to each egg
1	tablespoon whiskey to each egg		Nutmeg
½	pint whipping cream		

Separate the eggs and beat yolks. Add whiskey. Cover tightly and refrigerate. (Can be done night before.) When ready, beat the cream and put back in refrigerator. Whip the egg whites but don't begin adding sugar until they are stiff; then add sugar very gradually, about 1 tablespoon or less at a time and keep beating until it makes a very stiff meringue. Now here's the trick. Keep beating the whites, while somebody helps you by folding the egg and whiskey mixture into the whipped cream. Then pour it over the beaten whites and gently fold it in. The point is to keep your whites going and stiff and add everything to them; don't go adding them to anything else. Sprinkle with nutmeg in the bowl or on each cup as served.

HOT SPICED CRANBERRY PUNCH

It was a really cold night in the '50s when Gay Chamlee introduced this warming, delicious punch at bridge club one night in Wrightsville. Cranberry juice cocktail was sort of new to all of us at the time so we were anxious to get this recipe so we could make it too. I've served it many times at club meetings and it always goes over well and makes the house smell festive.

2¼	cups pineapple juice	1	tablespoon whole cloves
1¾	cups water	3	sticks cinnamon (broken)
2	cups cranberry juice cocktail	1	tablespoon whole allspice
½	cup brown sugar	¼	teaspoon salt

Put pineapple juice, water and cranberry juice in bottom of an 8 cup percolator. Put the rest of the ingredients in the top. Perk 10 minutes. Serve hot in punch cups.

ORANGE JULIUS

It was always fun to go to Savannah shopping when I was a young girl. Sometimes a photographer would station himself on Broughton Street and make for sale pictures of the shoppers. I treasure the candid shots of mother and me—always all dressed up like we were going to a wedding or something. There was a place near the Globe Shoe Company, (one of Savannah's landmarks), called *Orange Julius and if I could talk Mother into dipping in there, I always bought the most glorious drink, Orange Julius. Some time ago the recipe appeared in a newspaper and I have clipped and saved with a vengeance this treasured recipe.*

❖ Mother and Louise in Savannah ❖

6	ounces frozen orange juice concentrate
4	tablespoons sugar
2	cups milk, divided use
16	ice cubes
1	teaspoon vanilla

Put orange juice, sugar, 1 cup milk, ice cubes and vanilla in blender and blend well. Add second cup milk and serve at once.

BEVERAGES AND APPETIZERS

MIMOSAS

We were mighty excited to be invited into a private home in Seattle for lunch. The home was a Lake Union houseboat and reminiscent of Sleepless in Seattle, the movie that featured lake living in Seattle. We also had a lovely dinner in an exquisite home on Pudget Sound and were all adither when Prince Andrew was staying at our hotel, the Four Seasons. We had a great brunch at Kiana Lodge reached by ferry boat, where television's famous Chef John Folse introduced us to the very first use of olestra in potato chips. As native Americans danced on the side lawn among some of the richest looking flowers imaginable, we sipped Mimosas incomparable.

1	fifth champagne, chilled	Strawberries for garnish
25	ounces orange juice, chilled	Mint sprigs for garnish

Mix champagne and juice. Serve immediately.

GRACE MCKENNEY'S BRANDY ALEXANDER FRAPPÉ

Going through Atlanta on the way to Highlands, Betty Ballard and I became concerned when we missed our Spaghetti Junction exit because the rain was so hard we couldn't see. We renegotiated it and finally were on our way—not able to see two feet ahead of the car. Little did we know that Hurricane Opal was bearing down on us and becoming constantly more and more severe. Our place was on the side of a mountain and I just knew the frame house was going into the valley with the next gust of wind. Betty later laughingly reminded me that I put on my jewelry so that when they found my body in the valley they could identify me. Lights went out, trees went down and we were confined to our premises for several days. Thank goodness, our hostess, Grace McKenney had stored in a lot of good food—and drink. Her Brandy Alexander Frappe served us nicely as we played bridge, and played bridge and played bridge—with lots of candle light to help us see the spots. You'll like this delicious libation.

4	jiggers brandy		Sprinkle of nutmeg
1	jigger crème de cacao	1	pint vanilla ice cream

Pour into blender and blend until smooth. Pour into wine or old-fashioned glasses.

RUSSIAN TEA

Mrs. Mary Hicks was winding up her school teaching career just as I was beginning mine in Wrightsville. She and I shared some special moments as we stood on the playground and supervised the young children. "Miss Mary" was a great hostess and prepared the most delicious little sandwiches and snacks for bridge. I liked her Russian Tea and still make it on an especially cold winter day. It's the best recipe for Russian Tea that I know.

2	quarts strong tea	2	cloves
2	lemons	1½	cups sugar
3	oranges		

Extract juice from lemons and oranges. Boil rinds and cloves in 1 quart water for about 5 minutes. Strain and add to tea and juices. Add sugar or sweeten to taste.

TROPICAL PUNCH WITH FRUITED ICE RING

As I returned to my room at a lovely San Francisco hotel, I heard someone down the hall calling my name. It was my friend Charlotte Lyons, food editor of Ebony Magazine. *She had brought me, all the way from Chicago, a copy of her new book,* The New Ebony Cookbook. *She didn't know it was my birthday but it surely was a lovely present.*

I like her Tropical Punch with a Fruited Ice Ring and find it to be beautiful for a tea, a club meeting, or reception.

❖ Louise beside replica of Golden Gate Bridge on her birthday in San Francisco. ❖

1	(46-ounce) can red fruit punch	2	cups canned pineapple juice
1	(6-ounce) can frozen lemonade concentrate	4	cups water
		½	cup sugar
1	(6-ounce) can frozen orange juice concentrate		Ice
		1	(28-ounce) bottle ginger ale, chilled

Combine all ingredients except ice and ginger ale. Place ice in large punch bowl; pour fruit punch mixture over ice. Carefully pour in ginger ale, stirring to mix. Garnish with fruit or ice ring if desired.

BEVERAGES AND APPETIZERS

CHARLESTON TEA PLANTATION WEDDING PUNCH

On a lovely oak covered sea island deep in South Carolina low country, tea plants were growing over 100 years ago. Now, two tea growers have revived the plantation on Wadmalaw Island and are producing at the Charleston Tea Plantation some of the finest tea in the world. As I stood in the tea fields one Sunday checking out the John Deere tea picker especially made for them, I realized I was seeing something for the very first time, a real-live tea-growing farm. It's a trip that you, too, would enjoy. You'll enjoy, too, a refreshing glass of iced tea made with American Classic Tea. Tea is the world's most popular drink, next to water. It's good in this punch too.

4	cups American Classic Tea, brewed then chilled	2	bottles club soda
4	cups apple juice, chilled		Fresh orange and lemon slices, fresh mint for garnish
2	cups unsweetened pineapple juice, chilled		

Combine the tea, apple and pineapple juices and refrigerate until ready to serve. Add the club soda, fruit slices and mint immediately before serving. Serve iced from a large punch bowl.

MINT JULEP

In the '50s we were invited to a Mint Julep party at the lovely old home of Dr. and Mrs. Corn on College Street in Macon. My only knowledge of mint juleps was the romantic aura that surrounds mint julep drinking in southern novels. I was so excited to be experiencing this great southern tradition on the back lawn of a gorgeous southern home. Well, Mint Juleps are not my drink. I had to surreptitiously water the shrubbery with it. But let's do preserve this great southern tradition—it might be your favorite drink.

1½	ounces Mint Syrup per serving (see below)	Crushed ice
2	ounces bourbon per serving	Mint sprigs

Pour mint syrup and bourbon into each silver julep cup. Fill with crushed ice, add a straw, and garnish with mint sprigs.

Mint Syrup:

4	cups water	4	cups mint sprigs
2	cups sugar		

Boil water and sugar over medium heat for 10 minutes. Add mint sprigs and simmer 30 minutes. Set aside overnight. Strain.

PEACH FUZZY

When Fuzzy Navels were first introduced, I had one at a lovely old plantation in Thomasville and thought it was so good. This is about the same, and the name much more dignified and so-o-o good.

1	(16-ounce) package frozen peaches		1	jigger peach brandy
1	(6-ounce) can pink lemonade		2	cups crushed ice
1	juice can vodka		2	seeded, unpeeled peaches (optional)

Mix all ingredients in blender. When in season, 2 seeded, unpeeled peaches may be added.

HOT BUTTERED RUM MIX

A group of friends and I were at the famous Greenbrier Hotel in White Sulphur Springs, West Virginia. Although we could see nothing but dry and sear-looking grass and bushes from the airplane window (and it was cold January) we were told there'd be no snow for our visit. Not to be outdone, Iris Gillis reserved the snow sleigh for the next morning and then retreated to the spa for a steam bath. Unbelievably, the snow came down softly all night long and when we realized we had first divvys on the sleigh the next day we were delighted. Two horses, red plaid wool blankets and a jovial driver and we were cheerfully on our way. Then afterward, not because we so much wanted it, but because it's a long tradition, we sipped on Hot Buttered Rum in the library.

1	stick margarine (not butter)		¼	teaspoon ground allspice
1	pound light brown sugar		½	teaspoon angostura bitters
1	heaping teaspoon cinnamon		¼	teaspoon ground ginger
1	heaping teaspoon nutmeg			Dark rum

Mix all ingredients except rum thoroughly. Refrigerate until ready to use. For drink, combine 1 heaping teaspoon mix, 2 ounces dark rum and about 4 ounces boiling water. Mix well; keep in refrigerator for several months.

BEVERAGES AND APPETIZERS

MOCK CHAMPAGNE PUNCH

I was in high cotton when my late friend Sally Smith and I attended the grand opening of the High Museum in Atlanta. Richard Meier, the architect of this magnificent building was there along with all the top socialites of Atlanta. They were all dressed in their finest outfits, most of them black, as I made my grand entrance all in white. I never get it right.

One of the impressive drinks was a Mock Champagne Punch that regularly makes the rounds at Atlanta parties. It's not too sweet and really does taste like champagne.

2	quarts ginger ale	1	quart apple juice

Chill ingredients in refrigerator the day before opening them. Mold an ice ring with slices of lemon and lime and sprigs of mint. Combine ginger ale and apple juice. Center the mold in a punch bowl and pour in the punch.

CHATHAM ARTILLERY PUNCH

In 1791, George Washington made a visit to Savannah and was served their memorable Chatham Artillery Punch. And although my grandchildren probably think I was there too, let it be recorded that I was not. My mother got this recipe from a Savannah friend, Mrs. Shelby Myrick, years ago. It's a keeper—a truly famous recipe.

2	gallons Catawba wine	2	quarts maraschino cherries
½	gallon St. Croix rum	36	lemons, juiced and sweetened to taste
8	cans sliced pineapple, cut in small cubes	6	oranges, cut in small pieces
1	quart strong tea (green tea)	6	quarts champagne

Combine wine, rum, cut pineapple, tea, cherries, and lemon juice. This is the stock and should be mixed and allowed to stand as long as possible; 2 weeks is not too long. When ready to serve, add the oranges and the champagne. Place block of ice in the punch bowl. If the bowl will not hold the entire mixture, divide the champagne in proportion to the stock. Do not put the lemon peels in the stock.

PERFECT MARGARITAS

❖ Class at Jane Butel's Southwestern Cooking School in Albuquerque celebrates margaritas. ❖

My sister in law, Sybil, and I had just graduated from Jane Butel's Southwestern Cooking School in Albuquerque when the call came for us to do a Southwestern dinner in Augusta. I knew all the time our newly acquired culinary skills were going to be in great demand.

Syb's son and my nephew, Jeff Futrelle, and his wife Lisa had offered to host a southwest dinner for eight as a charity benefit for their children's school. And of course they knew all the time that Mom and Aunt Louise were off studying on just how to put on the perfect southwest dinner.

Well! Never have we had more fun. Syb and I were in communication via AT&T for weeks in preparation for the big event, while Lisa was spending her time (and Jeff's money) getting all the beautiful Mexican china and crystal that we needed to set a gorgeous table-complete with a flower arrangement that just spoke to you, in Spanish, of course.

Jeff was busy setting up his Margarita Machine, one of only two like it in the world because the maker made only two and quit. One for himself, one for Jeff. The Margaritas were truly sensational.

The computer-savvy children contributed by making adorable southwest place cards and a beautifully done menu that included: Appetizers: guacamole, tostados, chile conqueso, and quesadillas with Margaritas; Soup: sopa garlic with tortillas; Salad: Acapulco with jicama and walnut vinaigrette; Main course: Roast pork loin with green chile sauce, chile rellenos with red chile sauce, peppered rice, blue corn muffins: Dessert: Classic flan; After dinner: Mexican chocolate.

Jane Butel offers one of her secrets for the perfect Margarita. You can use a small amount of egg white in each batch. It helps to sustain the foam. Also she says they are best when made with fresh lime juice and a word of warning: Be careful—they are strong!

Coarse or Kosher salt (optional)	6	ounces tequila
Juice of 4 or 5 limes, save halves after juicing	2	ounces Triple Sec
		Ice cubes

If salted rims are desired, place salt in a small, dry saucer. About an hour before serving. Squeeze limes; then rub the rims of each of 4 goblets with a lime half to moisten; then dip into the salt to generously coat the rims. Place glasses in freezer to frost. Combine lime juice, tequila, Triple Sec, and ice in a blender or cocktail shaker. Blend or shake well. Taste and add more lime juice or Triple Sec, if desired. Pour into the frosted goblets and serve.

HOTEL VICKSBURG PUNCH

Ike (President Eisenhower) liked the punch so much that he was served in Vicksburg, Mississippi, he took the recipe home to Mamie. Although his visit to Mississippi in 1946 preceded mine in 1987, I enjoyed the same famous punch served at the Governor's Mansion in Jackson by the Junior Service League of Vicksburg. They were touting their recipe book, Vintage Vicksburg *and from it served us lots of their favorite recipes including* Down in Dixie Bourbon Pie *and* Sis's Pralines. *You'll like their punch that makes approximately 1 gallon.*

2	cups boiling water	1	(46-ounce) can pineapple juice
1	cup sugar	1	(20-ounce) can crushed pineapple
½-1	cup lemon juice	1	(6-ounce) jar cherries
3	(12-ounce) cans frozen orange juice–diluted	1	(32-ounce) ginger ale

To boiling water add sugar and lemon juice. Boil for 5 minutes. Set aside to cool When cooled, add orange juice, pineapple juice, pineapple and cherries. Chill. Just before serving, add ginger ale.

SPANISH BAYONET BLOOMS

Spanish Bayonets grow everywhere in the south and send up their tall stalks of many white buds at different times of the year. Just site some plants and watch them. Take each individual bud and spread it open, handling gently. These make lovely plate decorations alone or in combination with some kind of greenery.

CHEESE DIP

At Taffy Beall's lovely new country home in Brewton, Cissy Beall Kight served this fantastic cheese dip that had everybody dipping into it all night—when they could nudge me away from the trough. This is so-o-o good it's unreal.

2	pounds Velveeta cheese	1	pound sausage meat
1	(10-ounce) can Ro-tel tomatoes	1	pound ground beef

Cut up cheese in crock pot. Brown meat and put in crock pot with tomatoes. Serve with salsa and tortilla chips.

TEX MEX DIP

This deliciously simple little appetizer wins my vote every time. You can whip it up in just minutes and refrigerate it until time to pull it out for a family surprise or for guests.

Layer in a 3-quart casserole:
2   cans refried beans

Layer 2: In a small bowl mash:
3   avocados
2   tablespoons lemon juice

½   teaspoon salt
¼   teaspoon pepper

Layer 3: In a small bowl mix:
1   cup sour cream
½   cup mayonnaise

1   package taco seasoning

Layer 4:
1   bunch of green onions, chopped

Layer 6:
2   medium tomatoes–seeded and chopped

Layer 5:
2   small cans black olives, chopped

Layer 7:
1   pound Cheddar cheese, grated

Chill and serve with tortilla chips.

DRIED BEEF DIP

My neighbor in Wrightsville during our children's growing up years was and is a true friend, Mary Ann Norris. When she served this at a party one night, I ate so much that she finally handed me a soup bowl and a spoon. I love it!

3   cans cream of mushroom soup
1   cup mild cheese
1   large (8-ounce) can sliced mushrooms

3   (2½-ounce) jars dried beef, shredded
½   cup Sauterne

Warm undiluted soup. Stir in cheese until melted. Add mushrooms, beef and Sauterne. Serve hot from chafing dish with Triscuits. Also delicious over baked potatoes or toasted English muffins. Eat it straight from a bowl if you wish.

BEVERAGES AND APPETIZERS

SARDINE AND CHEESE DIP

Years ago as I was exploring the cookbooks left in a lake house we had just bought, I found The Famous Chef Cookbook. My cleaning and setting the house in order came to a screeching halt as I found recipe after recipe that I wanted to try. This dip sounds so much like one that Mother used to make and is delicious-even if you don't eat sardines, it's delicious.

2	small cans sardines	¼	teaspoon salt
2	(3-ounce) packages cream cheese	1	tablespoon Worcestershire sauce
1	clove garlic, finely minced	1	teaspoon lemon juice
3	teaspoons onion, minced		

Drain and mash sardines; blend with cream cheese; blend with garlic, onion, salt and Worcestershire sauce, and lemon juice. Chill for several hours before serving to blend flavors. Serve garnished with pimento strips. Use as a dip for crackers, or potato chips.

SURPRISE SANDWICH SPREAD

At bridge at Marjorie Massenburg's one night—she, Carolyn Henderson, and Bettye Sims were discussing the Surprise Sandwiches and how great they are—"kinda like shrimp salad—but nobody every knows quite what it is."

Carolyn said use Duke's mayonnaise. They all said use Capt. John Derst's Old-Fashioned Bread.

2	hard-cooked eggs	1	cup pecans, chopped
1	medium jar olives, drained	2	cups Hellmann's mayonnaise
1	small onion, chopped		

Put eggs, onions, olives, and pecans in food processor and chop until mixture is thoroughly minced. Mix well with mayonnaise. Delicious with brown bread.

GLADYS KNIGHT'S VERY SPECIAL APPETIZER

A short drive out into the desert from Las Vegas and we were at the lovely contemporary home of the famous singer, Gladys Knight. She was there with all her graciousness to tout prevention and control of diabetes with which her mother had recently died. They were very close; her pictures were prominent in the house as well as those of Gladys' two children who were also at home that day.

The lunch, the ambiance, the hospitality, were all overwhelming but perhaps most overwhelming of all was their gorgeous and delicious appetizer served in tall stemmed compotes like champagne flutes.

❖ Louise and Shanga Henderson, Gladys Knight's son, at her desert home. ❖

The rims of the glasses were dipped in lime juice, then encrusted with herbs and salt. Guacamole filled the bottom half of the glass and Gazpacho filled the rest. Dollops of sour cream were on top, sprinkled with lime zest with two pieces of chives stuck into the sour cream.

I have re-created this special appetizer several times for guests and I love serving it. Do I tell the origin? Well, of course.

Guacamole:

4	medium avocados, chopped not mashed	8	drops Tabasco sauce
2	tablespoons lime juice	½	teaspoon salt
1	teaspoon grated onion	½	teaspoon garlic salt
2	teaspoons olive oil	1	tablespoon Worcestershire sauce

Combine all ingredients.

Gazpacho:

1	carrot, peeled	6	garlic cloves, minced
2	cucumbers, halved and seeded, but not peeled	46	ounces tomato juice (6 cups)
3	red bell peppers, cored and seeded	½	cup white wine vinegar
8	plum tomatoes	½	cup good olive oil
2	red onions	1	tablespoon kosher salt
		1½	teaspoons black pepper

Roughly chop cucumbers, carrot, peppers, tomatoes and red onions into 1-inch cubes. Put each vegetable separately into a food processor fitted with a steel blade and puree until it is coarsely chopped. Do not overprocess! Then, combine processed vegetables in a large bowl; add garlic, tomato juice, vinegar, olive oil, salt and pepper. Mix well and chill before serving. The longer Gazpacho sits, the more the flavors develop.

BREADS AND ROLLS

Louise in basement
kitchen of
French Chateau Chenonceau.

HOT ROLLS BY LIZA

Liza Ashley started her cooking career at the Arkansas Governor's Mansion in 1955 right on through the Clinton years when I met her. Over 30 years she worked for seven governors so you know she was doing it right.

This is her greatly requested recipe for Hot Rolls by Liza that she has served to hundreds of guests at the Governor's table. One legislator used to go back to the kitchen and ask Liza if he could take home the leftover rolls!

¾	cup shortening	1	cup cold water
1	cup boiling water or scalded milk	¼	cup lukewarm water
2	eggs, beaten	2	cakes yeast (or 2 packages dry yeast)
¾	cup sugar	7½	cups sifted flour
2	teaspoons salt		

Combine shortening and boiling water; stir until shortening is melted. Combine eggs, sugar, and salt and beat in cold water. Soften yeast in ¼ cup lukewarm water. Combine the three mixtures and add the flour. If dough is too soft to hold shape add ¼ cup more flour. Cover and let stand in a warm (but not hot) place for 2 hours or until it doubles in bulk. Shape into rolls and allow to rise again until double in bulk. Bake at 400 degrees for 20 to 30 minutes.

DILLY GARLIC ROLLS

What a wonderful experience it was to go to California in July of 1998 with my sister Libby, who had lived there at one time. We were visiting her friend (and mine too) Jill Bragga in San Jose but we coincided the trip with the Gilroy Garlic Festival that I had long dreamed of attending. What an experience! People were there from everywhere sampling the garlicky food that included everything from chili to ice cream. There was a garlic cooking contest that generated a lot of interest and a garlic cookbook The Garlic Lovers' Cookbook *that was appealing, though I really didn't want a recipe for the ice cream. Dilly Garlic Rolls are a snap to make because the rolls are already made. You just add the embellishments.*

¼	cup softened butter	¼	teaspoon garlic powder
½	teaspoon dill weed	6	ready-to-serve pull apart rolls

Cream together butter, dill weed, and garlic powder. Break rolls apart from the top and spread butter mixture between sections. Wrap in aluminum foil and place on grill and heat 10 minutes, turning once or twice.

BREADS AND ROLLS

ICEBOX ROLLS

I've never been more shocked than when early in my marriage I tried Icebox Rolls and they were an overwhelming success. I had never attempted yeast breads because a red flag always came up when I even thought about it. Our home demonstration agent in Johnson County, Martha Butts, did a weekly recipe column in the Wrightsville Headlight and on one occasion gave the recipe for Icebox Rolls. Feeling quite brave, I tried the recipe and since then this has been my very favorite yeast roll recipe. A note in the margin says "Made for Jazz Festival in 1982. Made dough on Tuesday—left in fridge. Made out rolls on Sunday and put back in fridge. Then took out 1 hour ahead of dinner which was Sunday night."

1	cup vegetable shortening	¼	cup lukewarm water
¾	cup sugar	2	packages yeast
2	teaspoons salt	2	eggs
1	cup boiling water	7	cups plain flour (unsifted)
1	cup cool water		

In mixing bowl combine shortening, sugar and salt. Beat well. Add boiling water to mixture, beat well. Add tap water and beat well. Dissolve yeast in ¼ cup lukewarm water 105 degrees. Check to see that shortening mixture is not too hot, then add dissolved yeast. Beat eggs and add to mixture. Add flour a little at a time to form soft dough. (Use more or less.) Refrigerate in large container for at least 4 hours. When ready to bake, set dough out at room temperature for 1 hour. Shape into rolls. Let rise for about 2 hours or until doubled in bulk. Bake at 450 degrees for 15 to 20 minutes. (Can leave dough in mixing bowl.)

ORANGE CRUNCH ROLLS

Sometimes my notes grow dim through the years and my memory even dimmer. If I remember correctly, Lydia Woods from Dublin gave me this recipe at my friend's Iris Gillis' house. If you want them to be a little daintier than Brown n' Serve rolls, cut them in half or even into four pieces.

Place Brown n' Serve rolls on a well-greased baking sheet. Butter them. Dip in following mixture.

2	tablespoons grated orange rind	Enough orange juice to moisten
1	cup sugar	

Coat the top of each roll well. Bake at 350 degrees until done.

STRAWBERRY ORANGE MUFFINS

"A friend in need is a friend indeed." Well, maybe so, but a friend who brings good food when you're feeling low, is a friend indeed. My precious friend, Becky Bowdre, came with a week's supply of gourmet food when I was feeling "under the weather" and it did me so much good, I was soon on top of the weather. It would be hard to decide what was best from the great bounty but these muffins (made in miniature tins) were absolutely wonderful. They are perfect to serve at a luncheon but also mighty good for breakfast.

Put them on a tray for someone sick and they'll do more good than medicine—guaranteed.

1¼	cups halved strawberries	1¼	cups sugar
3	tablespoons butter or margarine, melted	1	teaspoon baking powder
2	teaspoons grated orange rind	½	teaspoon salt
2	large eggs		Cooking spray
1½	cups all-purpose flour	2	teaspoons sugar

Preheat oven to 400 degrees. Combine first 4 ingredients in a blender, and process just until blended. Lightly spoon flour into dry measuring cups; level with a knife. Combine flour, 1¼ cups sugar, baking powder, and salt. Add strawberry mixture to flour mixture, stirring just until moist. Spoon batter into 12 muffin cups coated with cooking spray. Sprinkle with 2 teaspoons sugar. Bake at 400 degrees for 20 minutes or until muffins spring back when touched lightly in center. Remove from pan immediately.

KELLOGG'S ALL-BRAN ORIGINAL MUFFINS

Part of writing is an ego trip; no one denies. Perhaps one of the biggest boosts to my ego was years ago when the Rev. Lotis McAfee of Wrightsville, a greatly beloved elderly local preacher and abattoir owner called me and said he wanted their cook to make some All-Bran Muffins but she needed a recipe. Now I never dreamed that "Brother Lotis" read my column but he started off his request by saying he did. You may be sure I was quick to fill this request. This is the original Bran Muffin by Kellogg's and is a recipe to save forever. I go right by the recipe but I do add about ¾ cup raisins.

1¼	cups all-purpose flour	1¼	cups milk
½	cup sugar	1	egg
1	tablespoon baking powder	¼	cup vegetable oil
¼	teaspoon salt		Vegetable cooking spray
2	cups All-Bran		

Stir together flour, sugar, baking powder and salt. Set aside. In large mixing bowl, combine All-Brand and milk. Let stand about 5 minutes or until cereal softens. Add egg and oil. Beat well. Add flour mixture stirring only until combined. Portion batter evenly into twelve 2½-inch muffin pan cups coated with cooking spray. Bake at 400 degrees about 20 minutes or until lightly browned. Serve warm.

BROCCOLI MUFFINS

This is a recipe that nearly knocked my socks off a few years ago. The Dublin Service League invited me to a lovely luncheon at Ann Curry's house and this was one of the recipes that they were presenting for the Antique Fair Tearoom that year. I gave it an overwhelming A+ at that time and went on to select it as the Recipe of the Year in the Courier Herald. It's just so simple and just as good as it is simple. I strongly suggest that you use paper liners in your muffin tins because the muffins tend to stick.

1	box (8½-ounces) cornbread mix	1	stick melted margarine
4	eggs, beaten	1	package (10-ounce) frozen chopped broccoli, thawed, and chopped fine
1	(8-ounce) carton small curd cottage cheese		

Preheat oven to 350 degrees. Mix all ingredients together. Line muffin tins with paper liners. Pour batter into liners. Bake muffins until brown on top.

POPOVERS AT TIFFANY'S

"Maybe I'll go as Audrey Hepburn," I thought as I whirled around the room, taking a quick peek or two in the mirror to see if maybe stays and straps and a couple of good corsets might give me back my 24-inch waist. The invitation had come from the Atlanta Chapter of the Wesleyan Alumnae Club for Breakfast at Tiffany's in Atlanta, their third store outside New York. I couldn't believe it nor could hardly contain my enthusiasm.

In a talk to us in the store, the marketing manager, alluded to the fact that Tiffany's was such a historic institution (1837), very like Wesleyan (1836).

Many celebrities have either shopped at Tiffany's or been the recipients of Tiffany gifts. Abe Lincoln bought a pearl necklace for Mary Todd Lincoln; Eleanor Roosevelt's engagement ring was from Tiffany's; Lyndon Johnson's White House china was from Tiffany's and Diamond Jim Brady dropped in regularly to buy jewelry.

None of the celebrities have been more interesting than the ones with whom I shopped side by side in the flagship store at Fifth Avenue and 57th Street in New York City—the Japanese Sumo Wrestlers who incidentally took over the store with their fat bodies and matching wallets.

Among the delicious breakfast items at Breakfast at Tiffany's was Popovers—so good hot (and though not at Tiffany's) with fig preserves they'll wow you just like Tiffanys.

2	eggs	½	teaspoon salt
1	cup milk	1	tablespoon melted butter
1	cup sifted flour		

Beat ingredients 1 to 2 minutes. Do not over-beat! Fill 6 or 8 well greased custard cups ½ full. Bake in a hot oven, 475 degrees, for 15 minutes. Reduce the heat to 350 degrees and continue baking for 25 to 30 minutes. A few minutes before removing from the oven, prick each popover with a fork to allow the steam to escape. Serve with plenty of butter.

STUFFED FRENCH TOAST

It was a thrill beyond words to be at Disney World for their 15th anniversary when they had invited food writers and travel journalists from all over the world to be their guests. I mean all expenses paid! Epcot was turned over to us completely with the gates closed to the public. We wandered from one ethnic restaurant to another with great abandon, trying to get at least a taste of every foreign country represented. Food writers were given a special tour of the enormous underground kitchens and there we were privileged to meet Johnny Rivers the Executive Chef of Walt Disney World Resorts.

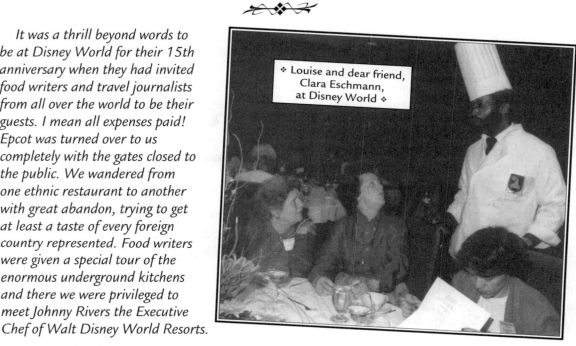

❖ Louise and dear friend, Clara Eschmann, at Disney World ❖

He was no doubt intrigued with the "Southerness" of my friend Clara and me because he spent a good deal of time at our table discussing our southern recipes. This is one of his recipes that is often served at Disney World.

2-4 slices sourdough bread, depending on size, cut 1-inch thick	⅓ cup sugar
1 banana	1 teaspoon cinnamon
1 egg	Oil or shortening for frying
¼ cup milk	Whipped butter (optional)
½ teaspoon vanilla	Maple syrup (optional)

Cut 2-inch pocket in one side of each bread slice. Cut bananas in half crosswise. Split each piece lengthwise. Remove peel. Stuff 2 pieces in each pocket of bread, depending on size. (If bread slices are small, use 4 and stuff one piece banana in each pocket.) Mix egg, milk and vanilla until well blended. Mix sugar and cinnamon. Heat about 4 inches of oil in deep fryer or deep saucepan to 350 degrees. Dip stuffed bread into egg and milk mixture, soaking a few minutes to penetrate into bread. Fry about 3 minutes until lightly browned, turning to brown both sides. Drain on paper towels on cake rack. Sprinkle with sugar and cinnamon. Serve immediately. Spread with whipped butter and serve with maple syrup, if desired.

SCONES

No cookbook would be complete without the inclusion of my dermatologist and friend, Dr. Jenny Allen. Sometimes we just have to curb our culinary discussions in order for her to get to the next patient. Jenny knows food though, and has traveled all over the world and it is so tempting for me to keep on-and on-and on. On one of her visits to Wales she brought me A Taste of Wales that has some of the most extraordinary recipes. This one is from Cyfie Farm in Powys, a 17th Century farm sitting high on a hillside overlooking the beautiful Meifod Valley. It you've been to Wales you know it is breathtakingly lovely and you know too that their scones are a specialty. This recipe has Welsh measurements but the equivalent is given also.

225 g	(8-ounce) flour		50 g	(2-ounces) margarine or butter
2	level teaspoons cream of tartar		25 g	(1-ounce) sugar
1	level teaspoon bicarbonate of soda		1	egg beaten and made up to 125 ml
	Pinch of salt			(¼ pint) with milk

In a medium-sized mixing bowl, sift together flour, cream of tartar, bicarbonate of soda and salt. Rub in margarine until the mixture resembles bread crumbs. Add sugar and mix to a soft dough with egg and milk mixture. Turn dough onto a floured board and roll to ½ to ¾-inches thick. Cut into circles using 2-inch cutter. Place scones on greased baking sheet. Bake at 425 degrees for 10 minutes. Cool on cooling trays, with a tea towel thrown over them to retain moisture. Eat scones as fresh as possible, slit and spread with strawberry jam and clotted cream, or butter.

❖ Louise, Lord Mayor of Tenby, and Lord Parry discuss recipes over drinks at Lord Parry's home in Wales. ❖

BREADS AND ROLLS

SALLY LUNN

Years ago a delegation from Dublin visited The White House and subsequently many of the places of interest in and around Washington. With June and Arnold Adams and Dot and Malcolm Towson we lunched at the historic Gadsby's Tavern in Alexandria where George and Martha Washington once dined and danced. All my life I had heard of Sally Lunn but had never tasted it nor seen it. It is probably their signature dish and is outstanding. Serve it warm with plenty of butter and you'll understand why George and Martha were dancing.

1	cup milk	⅓	cup sugar
½	cup solid shortening	2	teaspoons salt
¼	cup water	1	envelope dry yeast
4	cups flour, sifted	3	eggs

Generously grease 9- or 10-inch tube pan. Warm milk, shortening and water in small saucepan over low heat to 120 degrees (shortening does not have to melt). Combine 1⅓ cups flour, sugar, salt and yeast in large mixing bowl. Add warm milk mixture and beat at medium speed 2 minutes, scraping sides of bowl several times. Continuing to beat, gradually add ⅔ cup flour and eggs. When mixed in, beat at high speed 2 minutes. Add remaining flour and blend thoroughly. Cover bowl lightly and let dough rise in warm draft-free area (85 degrees) until doubled in bulk, about 1¼ hours. Beat dough down with spatula or use lowest speed on mixer. Turn into baking pan. Cover lightly and let dough rise until increased in bulk by ⅓ to ½ about 30 minutes.

Meanwhile, preheat oven to 350 degrees. When dough has risen, bake 40 to 50 minutes. Carefully remove bread from pan and let cool slightly. Slice with serrated knife.

PANCAKE NONPAREIL

Pancake Nonpareil is a treat that my good friend Mary Ann Norris of Wrightsville shared with me years ago. The nonpareil means that it has no comparison and I'll attest to that. This is a great breakfast surprise or can be served at a luncheon right from the skillet with jam or syrup or even berries and whipped cream or sour cream.

2	eggs			Powdered sugar
½	cup milk			Lemon juice
¼	cup flour		½	cup butter
	Nutmeg			

Put all ingredients except butter, powdered sugar, and lemon juice into blender. Then heat butter until bubbling in 10 or 12-inch skillet (one that goes to the table). Blend the other ingredients for 1 or 2 seconds. Pour this batter into skillet and bake in 425 degree oven for 15 minutes. Sprinkle with sifted powdered sugar and lemon juice. Bake 5 minutes more.

ANGEL BISCUITS

Mother always said "Angel Biscuits" with a different inflection than she used for most foods, as if she were the inventor. Angel Biscuits were something she liked to do and she loved the compliments that always were sure to come after someone sank their molars into one of these light and fluffy, cloud-like Angel breads. This recipe will make about 4 dozen 2-inch biscuits. Don't worry if that sounds like too many. The dough keeps well in the refrigerator for almost a week.

5	cups sifted self-rising flour		2	packages yeast dissolved in ¼ cup warm water
½	cup sugar			
1	teaspoon baking soda		2	cups buttermilk
1	cup shortening			

Combine flour, soda, and sugar; cut in shortening and stir in yeast and buttermilk. Be sure to mix well. Keep covered in refrigerator at least 1 hour or 2 before using. Roll out and cut as desired. Place on greased pan. Let rise for 2 hours. Bake at 450 degrees for about 10 minutes.

BISCUITS À LA CUILLER

It was an exciting time for me when I was chair of a committee to bring Princess Marie-Blanche de Broglie from Normandy, France to do a cooking class for The Cherry Blossom Festival. Months of planning went into the event, all of it fun. Perhaps the most fun of all though, was when the committee was whisked to Atlanta in the Fickling Company limousine to meet the princess at the airport. I had never met a real live princess and I didn't know whether she'd have a wand and a tiara or what. Of course she was just like us and just as charming and wonderful as you could ever hope for a princess to be. All the way home in the limo we laughed and had great fun, while at the same time getting in brief discussion about the upcoming cooking class. The princess was greatly impressed when we started seeing Macon's gorgeous cherry trees in full bloom and could hardly contain her excitement. Her class was quite informative and interesting and her recipes certainly collectible. This Ladyfinger recipe, known in France as Biscuits à la Cuiller, is one that I particularly enjoy because at some times of the year Ladyfingers are almost impossible to find in the store. I have a Ladyfinger pan that I bought years ago at an antique store but if you don't have one just use a pastry bag.

1	cup cake flour	4	egg whites
4	egg yolks		Pinch of salt
¾	cup sugar		Powdered sugar (for dusting)
1	teaspoon vanilla extract		

Sift the flour onto a piece of wax paper. With an electric mixer or by hand, beat the egg yolks with all but 2 tablespoons of the sugar in a large bowl for several minutes, until they are thick and light in color. Add the vanilla and mix well.

In another bowl, beat the egg whites with a pinch of salt until they form soft peaks. Sprinkle with the remaining 2 tablespoons of sugar and continue beating until they form stiff peaks. Fold the egg whites gently into the yolk mixture, one-third at a time, alternating with the sifted flour. Don't worry if the mixture is not completely homogeneous.

Using a pastry bag fitted with a large round tip, pipe the batter in 4-inch "fingers" onto a greased and floured baking sheet, spacing them at least 1-inch apart. Dust them lightly with powdered sugar.

AILEY BUTTERMILK BISCUITS

No one could ever be dearer and more vital than my precious friend, Joann Floyd. We've shared a lot of good times—some as far away as Paris—some as near by as Ailey, Georgia, her hometown. Joann and her husband, Waldo, both have a great love for Ailey and although there's no immediate family there anymore, they still go regularly to spend time and enjoy the small town life. They have converted the old drug store building which was family property, into what Joann laughingly calls her New York apartment. Actually New York would be so proud because it really is darling. Joann is a lovely, lovely hostess and knows just what to do to entertain her guests no matter in which of her several homes she's entertaining. When you go to Ailey, she's sure to take you somewhere you wouldn't want to miss, The Ailey Cafe, where they serve the most delicious country breakfast and their biscuits are wonderful. But so are the ones Joann makes at home by this recipe.

¼ cup shortening	½-¾ cup milk, buttermilk is best
2 cups sifted enriched self-rising flour	

Cut shortening into flour until mixture resembles coarse crumbs. Blend in enough milk to make a soft dough. Turn out onto lightly floured board or pastry cloth. Knead gently 30 seconds. Roll out ½-inch thick. Cut out biscuits with floured 2-inch biscuit cutter. Place on ungreased baking sheet. Bake in preheated 450 degree oven for 10 to 12 minutes, or until lightly browned.

❖ Good friends in the Ailey Cafe. Carolyn Henderson, Joann Floyd, Sybil Futrelle and Louise. ❖

RED LOBSTER BISCUITS

You haven't ever tasted biscuits if you haven't tasted those to-die-for creations that come out of the kitchen at Red Lobster. At one time there was a recipe printed that said it was much-like the Red Lobster's biscuits. It was good but not quite THE recipe. Then Linda Cicero, whom I have met at seminars and who is a syndicated food columnist, published what she calls Red Lobster Biscuits—no "much-like"—just Red Lobster Biscuits. This is wonderful. Now if I can just find out how they make that delicious Cole Slaw I'll be fulfilled—or maybe just filled because I can eat a big bowlful of it.

2	cups all-purpose flour	⅔	cup cold milk
½	teaspoon salt	8	ounces shredded Cheddar cheese
4	teaspoons baking powder	1	stick (8 tablespoons) butter or margarine
3	tablespoons confectioners' sugar	1	teaspoon minced garlic
½	cup shortening	¼	cup minced fresh parsley

Preheat the oven to 450 degrees. Stir together the flour, salt, baking powder and confectioners' sugar in a large bowl. Cut in the shortening with two knives (or use a food processor) until the mixture looks like small peas. Stir the milk in with a fork just until the dough cleans the sides of the bowl. Stir in the cheese. Place butter and garlic in a 9x13-inch pan and place in the preheated oven until butter melts and garlic is fragrant. Remove pan from oven and stir in the parsley. Form about ¼ cup dough at a time into a ball. Drop balls of dough into melted butter mixture and turn to coat well. Shape into biscuits. Bake for 10 to 12 minutes, until golden brown. Spoon any remaining butter on top. Serve warm.

BISCUITS

This is the first biscuit recipe I ever used when I started housekeeping and cooking seriously. It calls for Obelisk flour that I vaguely remember but if we still have it, I don't know where it is. The recipe is cut from the side of the flour box. This is good and simple—I guess all biscuit recipes are. This makes about 16 medium-sized biscuits. For guests I like to cut them smaller—about the size of a quarter.

2	cups Obelisk flour	3	tablespoons shortening
2	teaspoons baking powder	⅔	cup sweet milk
1	teaspoon salt		

Light oven and adjust temperature to 475 degrees (hot oven). Sift together the flour, baking powder and salt into mixing bowl then cut or rub in shortening. Add milk and mix with a spoon to get a soft dough. With lightly floured hands, pat or gently knead the dough into a small ball. Roll dough ⅜-inch thick, cut and place biscuits on a flat ungreased baking sheet. Bake to a golden brown color in 8 to 10 minutes.

ROQUEFORT BISCUITS

Betty Ragland wins the gold prize for enthusiasm. No matter what project she has going, she gives it more than 100%. It's just fun to watch her. Recently she and her husband Max had a dinner for their Gourmet Club and since it wasn't too long after 9-11-01, Betty wanted to carry out a patriotic theme. She brought me a picture of her dining table and it really was festive and beautiful. She even asked her guests to wear patriotic-looking outfits and she carried out the theme with red, white and blue food. Her menu included Shrimp Pâté, Tomato Bisque, Blueberry Salad, Deviled Chicken, French Potato Gratin, Potted Red Cabbage, Roquefort Biscuits and Red Velvet Cake. She was sweet to share her ideas and recipes with me and said that the Roquefort Biscuits are truly different.

¼	pound Roquefort or blue cheese	1	egg yolk
¼	pound softened butter	1⅓	cups sifted all-purpose flour
2	tablespoons whipping cream		

Mash cheese in bowl with fork. Beat in butter, cream, and egg yolk, then knead in flour. Shape into a ball and wrap with waxed paper. Chill until firm. Roll out ¼-inch thick and cut into 1½-inch rounds. Brush with egg and bake at 425 degrees for 10 to 15 minutes.

MAMMY'S CRACKLIN CORNBREAD

Lovejoy Plantation was our destination and all the food writers were eagerly anticipating an interview with the hostess, Betty Talmadge. She was indeed the gracious lady that we had hoped she would be and we had free run of the house and the yard where a huge white tent was set up for the barbecue. I was fortunate to catch Mrs. Talmadge in her study when everybody else was in the yard and we had a very pleasant little visit. It was after the bitter divorce from Senator Herman Talmadge and I couldn't help but laugh out loud at one of her needlepoint pillows that said, "A woman needs a man like a fish needs a bicycle." Well, that's debatable but if was funny. Mrs. Talmadge did fabulous needlework and her home was filled with many gorgeous pieces as well as lovely oil paintings and a great collection of autographed photographs of political celebrities—Herman noticeably missing. Betty Talmadge is a great cook and knows food, having for years been in the country ham business. What better to go with a meal featuring country ham than her recipe for Mammy's Cracklin Cornbread.

4	cups cornmeal	1	tablespoon salt
⅔	cup flour	2	eggs
⅔	cup sugar	4	cups buttermilk
1	teaspoon soda	2	cups cracklins, finely chopped

Sift dry ingredients together. Beat eggs with buttermilk. Mix all ingredients. Pour into well-greased and papered loaf pans. Bake at 400 degrees for 1 hour, or until done. Slice and serve with country butter.

SPIDER CAKE (CUSTARD CORN BREAD)

For many years Jean Thwaite was food editor of the Atlanta Constitution *and she and I became friends by attending seminars together. I'll never forget one particular adventure that we had together in Savannah. We were attending a meeting sponsored by the Savannah Sugar Refinery and were staying at the (then) new Hyatt Hotel on Bay Street. Just a few doors down the street the great Emma Kelley, who played a role in* Midnight in the Garden of Good and Evil, *was playing the blues in her own nightclub and since Emma and I were acquainted, I asked Jean and several of the other girls to go hear her. There were some businessmen at the next table who wanted to talk to us and although two of them were Japanese, we exchanged tidbits of light conversation. Finally they pulled their chairs up to our table and we learned that they were shipping executives, here from Japan on a ship harbored nearby. "Would we like to go aboard in the morning and have a tour of the ship?" Considering myself a great judge of character, I had already perceived that they were nice men so with a little encouragement from Jean we decided to go. We actually walked a gang plank to get into the ship. A new experience for all of us. We had a wonderful tour; learned a lot about the ship and even went to the galley and interviewed the Japanese cooks who could speak NO English. What fun! In remembering Jean, who died several years ago, I always remember one of her very favorite recipes out of the thousands she dealt with every year.*

¼	cup sugar	2	eggs
1½	cups cornmeal	2	cups milk
½	cup flour	2	tablespoons butter
1	teaspoon salt	1	cup whipping cream
1	teaspoon (heaping) baking powder		

Combine dry ingredients. Add eggs, mix, then add milk. Melt butter in casserole in 400 degree oven. Pour in ingredients. Add 1 cup cream poured gently in center after dish is on rack in oven. Bake at least 30 minutes.

BREADS AND ROLLS

JOYCE MANN'S MEXICAN CORNBREAD

In November of 1985, just after our move from Wrightsville (where we lived 35 years) to Macon, my longtime friend Joyce Mann entertained for us with a Mexican party. Joyce had "put the big pot in the little one," as the old cliche goes, and had decorated both the house and the dining table with festive Mexican doings. The entire meal was super but it was the Mexican Cornbread that caused me to call for the recipe.

1	cup self-rising meal		1⅓	cups salad oil
1	cup plain flour		1	large onion chopped fine
4	eggs		1	small bell pepper, chopped fine
4-6	jalapeño peppers (chopped fine)		½	teaspoon salt
2	cups sour cream		1	tablespoon sugar
2	cups creamed corn		4	cups sharp cheese

Mix all ingredients together (except 2 cups cheese) Pour ¼ of mixture into a well greased hot, iron skillet (about 9-inch in diameter.) Sprinkle cheese on top and bake in 350 oven until brown. Cool slightly and slice into 6 pie shaped wedges. Serve warm. Joyce says "It is good to have two iron skillets so that more can be baked at once. May be halved for fewer people."

❖ THE Bridge Club
Dean, Mary Helen, Beverly, Pat,
Helen, Lucille, Marguerite, Louise and Joyce ❖

KUGELHOPF (RAISIN BREAD)

This is one of the family's favorite, most favorite, recipes. My mother was still making this bread when she was 95 years old to take to "old" and sick people. She would always bring it when she visited and now I'm taking it when I visit my children. The recipe is said to be Austrian and brought to this country in 1734 when my ancestors, the Salzburgers, came to Georgia to settle. I'm not sure about that because for sure they didn't have any Crisco and probably no dry yeast but I do know that it's a specialty of the Salzburger people who still live in Effingham County near Savannah. One source says that brewer's yeast was used in Austria years before Marie Antoinette, who was very fond of Kugelhopf. This is easy to make; is always a success; and wows the grandchildren as well as the adults. Be sure to save enough to butter and toast for breakfast. It's just so good that merely writing about it sends me to the kitchen to make a couple of loaves. It also makes 6 miniature loaves that are wonderful to take to friends.

1½	packages dry yeast	1¾	cups water
¼	cup warm water	¼	cup evaporated milk
1	tablespoon Crisco	4½	cups plain flour plus 2 cups plain flour
½	teaspoon salt	1½	cups raisins
1	cup sugar		

Mix together yeast and ¼ cup warm water. In a large mixing bowl put Crisco, salt, sugar, 1¾ cups water and milk. Add yeast mixture and mix well. Add 4½ cups flour and blend in well. Cover bowl with tea towel and let dough rise in warm place for 2 hours. Add 2 cups flour and raisins. Mix well. Grease 2 loaf pans and divide dough into them. Brush tops with melted butter. Let rise about 45 minutes. Bake at 325 degrees for 25 to 30 minutes.

TROPICAL BANANA BREAD

Esther Rolle, the television actress of Good Times, *contributed one of her favorite recipes to the* Black Family Reunion Cookbook *edited by my friend Libby Clark from Los Angeles who did the book for the* National Council of Negro Women, Inc. *Esther related her story of growing up with 18 children in the house and the importance that was put on mealtimes. It was expected that they all appear at the table for meals to share joys and sorrows and just to become close. Close it must have been with 20 of them at the same table but what wonderful memories she has—"My most vivid memories are of meal times," she said. This Tropical Banana Bread is one of her recipes—probably not from childhood days because it only makes one loaf.*

½	cup Crisco shortening	2	cups all-purpose flour
1	cup sugar	1	teaspoon baking soda
2	eggs, well beaten	½	teaspoon salt
1	cup mashed bananas (2 to 3 medium)	½	cup chopped pecans or walnuts
½	cup dairy sour cream		

Heat oven to 350 degrees. Grease and flour 8½x4½x2½-inch loaf pan. Combine Crisco and sugar in large bowl. Beat at medium speed of electric mixer until creamed. Add eggs, bananas and sour cream. Beat until well blended. Combine flour, baking soda and salt. Add at low speed of electric mixer. Mix just until blended. Stir in nuts. Spread in pan. Bake at 350 degrees for 50 to 60 minutes or until toothpick inserted in center comes out clean. Cool in pan 10 minutes. Remove from pan to cooling rack. Cool completely before slicing.

BRITTLE BREAD

When the grand old De Soto Hotel was in its heyday in Savannah, it was always a treat to dip in for a meal on one of our excursions "to town." Although we lived 29 miles away, we always said we were going "to town" when we headed toward the coastal city. The hotel was right across the street from our dentist and I always crossed my fingers that I wouldn't have a filling to keep me from enjoying lunch at the De Soto. They had many menu items worth preserving but their Brittle Bread, set on the table as soon as you were seated, has to be the best.

2¾	cups flour, unsifted		½	teaspoon soda
¼	cup sugar		½	cup butter
½	teaspoon salt		8	ounces plain yogurt or sour cream

Blend flour, sugar, salt and soda. Cut butter into the dry mixture. Add yogurt and mix to a soft dough. Break off marble size pieces of the dough and roll very thinly on a floured board. Sprinkle with salt or sugar. Bake at 400 degrees for 5 to 8 minutes on ungreased cookie sheet. Turn off heat and allow to crisp in oven. Can be mixed in food processor.

PUMPKIN BREAD

This Pumpkin Bread was the hit of the Lake Rabun Cooking Class that a friend and I did one year. The recipe is one from Nina Beth Sheppard Terrell who was in my sister's class at Wesleyan and who has been my friend through the years. This makes three loaves and you'll need them all. Be sure to serve some Maple Leaf Butter with the bread. If you have butter molds in the shape of a maple leaf, just mix together softened butter with a small amount of maple syrup until well blended. Put the butter into the leaf mold, and place it in the freezer for a few minutes. Unmold onto plate and refrigerate while making other molds. When ready to serve, place all butter "leaves" on a plate and decorate with a few very small fall leaves—(assuming it's fall—) really a good time to serve this bread and butter.

2	cups sugar		1	teaspoon baking soda
1	cup oil		1	teaspoon ground cloves
3	eggs		1	teaspoon ground cinnamon
1	(16-ounce) can pumpkin		1	teaspoon ground nutmeg
3	cups plain flour		1	cup pecans, chopped
½	teaspoon salt		¾-1	cup dates, chopped
½	teaspoon baking powder			

Mix sugar, oil, eggs and pumpkin. Add dry ingredients and spices. Mix thoroughly. Fold in nuts and dates. Divide mixture among 3 (4½x8½-inch) loaf pans which have been greased and floured. Bake at 350 degrees for 40 to 45 minutes.

IRISH SODA BREAD

When we moved into a new home and neighborhood in Macon at Christmas time in 1986, a couple down the street sent a delicious loaf of Irish Soda Bread. Along with it they sent the recipe, typed on green paper in keeping with the Irish theme. Later we had a couple from Dublin to come for dinner during St. Patrick's Festival and I made and served the Irish bread. They were impressed. You will be too because this is a delicious loaf of bread. Don't dare omit the caraway seeds and raisins. They are integral.

4	cups sifted flour		¼	cup butter or margarine
¼	cup granulated sugar		2	cups seedless raisins
1	teaspoon salt		1	egg
1	teaspoon baking powder		1⅓	cups buttermilk
3	tablespoons caraway seeds		1	teaspoon baking soda

Sift together dry ingredients, except soda. Sift in caraway seeds. Cut in butter until mixture resembles cornmeal. Stir in raisins, separating and coating each. Combine egg, buttermilk and soda in separate bowl. Beat well, and let stand until thickened and bubbly. Stir into flour mixture. Turn onto well-floured board or counter and knead dough until smooth. (If dough is sticking to hands, rub them with a little extra flour.) Shape dough into ball and place in greased 8-inch cake pan. Cut a cross in top and fill cut with butter. Bake in preheated 375 degree oven for 1 hour and check for doneness with a straw or skewer. Cool before cutting.

To serve: Cut loaf in half at cross. Take one half and slice about ¾-inch thick. Butter both sides, and broil each side until golden. This bread is very filling, and is delicious with cream cheese, marmalade, or just plain "barefoot"!

Blarney Castle
in the Village of Blarney
and the county of Cork
Ireland

I hereby certify

that Louise Dodd
of The Courier Herald, of Dublin
visited this Castle and, having kissed
The Blarney Stone
is now sent forth with the
Gift of Eloquence
which this Stone bestows

Dated this 28 day of February 1984
Signed M. P. Hillyard
Keeper of the Castle

❖ Plaque of kissing the Blarney Stone ❖

JUSTUM ET TENACEM

WAFFLES

When the four grandsons were just little boys, one of my greatest pleasures was to see them all sitting around my breakfast table in their pajamas eagerly awaiting the cooking of the "heart waffles." You see, I have a waffle iron that makes the waffles in the shapes of hearts and that made them very special to the boys. Carol (their mother) told me that one day the boys were discussing with their friends what they liked to eat at Grandmother's house. Asa topped all the comments by saying, "You don't know anything until you've tasted my grandmother's heart waffles." That's what makes life wonderful! My waffle recipe is from my college home ec. cooking textbook (1947) and I always enjoy opening it and seeing the smears on page 127—many a waffle made from that page.

1½	cups flour	2	eggs, separated
½	teaspoon salt	1	cup milk
2	teaspoons baking powder	4	tablespoons melted shortening

Sift flour, salt, and baking powder together. Beat egg yolks and add milk and shortening. Add flour and beat with rotary beater until smooth. Fold in stiffly beaten egg whites. Bake in hot waffle iron. Makes 4 (9-inch) waffles.

SOUPS

*Louise stirs
"My Own Vegetable Soup"*

COLD TOMATO AND BASIL SOUP

So many good restaurants feature a Tomato and Basil Soup, almost all of them different. Here's one that is served cold in chilled bowls that will make your summer days happy. Be sure to garnish the soup with small basil leaves, and if you don't have any, there's no better time than now to start cultivating some so that you're ready when you get an urge for this delicious soup.

4½	cups sliced tomatoes		3	cups chicken broth
2	cups chopped onions		2	tablespoons flour (preferably potato flour)
¼	cup olive oil			
1	tablespoon tomato paste		2	cups water
1½	teaspoons salt		⅓	cup lightly-packed fresh basil leaves
1	teaspoon minced garlic			Salt and white pepper to taste
1	teaspoon sugar		¼	cup olive oil

In a heavy saucepan simmer the first 7 ingredients over low heat for 20 minutes, stirring frequently. In a bowl combine ½ cup chicken broth with the 2 tablespoons flour and stir in the remaining chicken broth, water and basil leaves. Add the liquid to the tomato mixture. Simmer and stir for 2 minutes. Put mixture through fine disc of a food grinder over a bowl; add salt and pepper and chill for several hours. Stir in olive oil in a stream.

LO-CAL DELICIOUS SUMMER SOUP

This one has made the rounds several times and keeps on revolving by. Everybody likes it but unless you tell them, they cannot figure out what's in it. People who don't like buttermilk often come back for seconds.

1	can tomato soup		1	teaspoon Worcestershire sauce
2	soup cans buttermilk			Dash Tabasco sauce
1	teaspoon curry powder			

Blend all together in blender. Chill overnight or all day. Garnish with parsley sprig.

TOMATO BISQUE

One of my favorite grandchildren stories concerns Greenville, S. C., and their close proximity to the mountains. Once, when visiting my close friend, Carolyn Henderson, in her Greenville condo where she stayed sometimes during her mother's last years, she invited some of her Greenville friends over to play bridge. "And where in Greenville do you live!" I asked the new acquaintance whose name I could remember, Martha.

"Oh, I live out by the monadnock," she said as if she were certain everyone knew what that was. Admitting my ignorance, she explained to me that it is the first hill of the mountains. Webster says a single remnant of a former highland which rises as an isolated rock mass above a plain.

I was so intrigued to add a new word to my vocabulary that I told the grandsons about it, taught them how to spell it and what it meant. We drilled and drilled.

At the end of Inman's fourth grade when the teacher asked the children to write about something they had learned during the year, Inman wrote, "I learned what a monadnock is." Wonder what in the world the teacher thought.

And I learned how to make Tomato Bisque from a dinner party on Paris Mountain which forms a dramatic backdrop to the northwest area of Greenville, site of many beautiful mansions.

¾	cup butter	3	tablespoons tomato paste
2	tablespoons olive oil	¼	cup plain flour
1	large onion, thinly sliced	3¾	cups chicken broth
½	teaspoon dried thyme	1	teaspoon sugar
¾	teaspoon salt	1	cup heavy cream
½	teaspoon pepper		Fresh dill
3	fresh ripe tomatoes, crushed		

Heat ½ cup butter and oil together in Dutch oven. Add onion, thyme, salt and pepper. Cook until onion is wilted. Add tomatoes and tomato paste; stir to blend. Simmer for 10 minutes. Put flour into small bowl. Add 5 tablespoons broth to flour; blend well. Stir flour paste into tomato mixture. Add remaining broth. Simmer for 30 minutes, stirring frequently. Remove from heat and cool. Pour cooled mixture into blender or processor; blend well. Strain mixture. Add sugar and cream to strained mixture and simmer for 5 minutes. Add remaining butter. May be served hot or cold. If serving cold, sprinkle with fresh dill.

ICED CUCUMBER AND MINT SOUP

It was such a treat for me and my friend and former food editor, Clara Eschmann, to drive up to Social Circle to have lunch with Nathalie Dupree, of television fame, and her college professor/ author husband Jack Bass. Clara and I had attended their on-the-beach wedding in Jamaica, and we were eagerly anticipating seeing our old friends again.

For the lunch, which was truly inspired, we started off with an Iced Cucumber and Mint Soup. Nathalie gave both of us her latest cookbook as we departed, and in it we found the recipe for this delicious dish. It was a hot July day when we were there so this was a cooling and soothing soup to serve.

3	cucumbers, peeled and diced		2	cloves garlic, finely chopped
	Salt		1	hard-cooked egg, grated or chopped
½	cup tomato juice		¼	pound fresh shrimp, cooked, peeled and chopped
½	cup chicken stock, fresh or canned			
2½	cups plain yogurt			Fresh mint, finely chopped (optional)
½	cup heavy cream			

Put the cucumbers in a colander, sprinkle with salt, and allow to drain for 30 minutes to remove the bitter juices. Rinse well, and set aside or refrigerate until needed. Meanwhile, stir together the tomato juice, stock, yogurt, cream, garlic and egg until well blended. Just before serving, add cucumbers, mint and shrimp. Serve in iced bowls.

❖ Eric Owens (apprentice with Nathalie) and Nathalie Dupree in Social Circle. ❖

COLD AVOCADO BISQUE

Say "The Cloister" and Georgians know. It's one of the most highly rated resorts in America and the place you go when you need pampering in elegant surroundings. Dining at the Cloister is relaxed, yet sophisticated with enough pleasant waiters to make everything easy even when you're in the dining room or the more informal Beach Club. Here's one of their popular recipes with a note that says, "Save the seeds from the avocados and add to the soup until serving time. This prevents discoloration."

1	pint fresh chicken stock, cold	1	cup milk
2	small ripe avocados		Salt, pepper and curry powder to taste
1	cup sour cream		

Puree all ingredients in blender. Chill and serve.

CRAB STEW

A favorite of our entire family is Mrs. Saida Lewis' Crab Stew. The Lewises were retired G. E. executives who left the "Nawth" and settled years ago in my hometown, Guyton. Mrs. Lewis did extensive entertaining in her lovely, country home and in her lake house, both across the road from where we lived. Mother managed to assemble a nice collection of her recipes, but this has always been the favorite.

4	tablespoons butter	3	hard-cooked eggs, finely chopped
1	quart milk	1	lemon, sliced paper thin
1	pound fresh crabmeat		White pepper
2	tablespoons cornstarch, stirred into ¼ cup of the milk		Salt

Combine the butter, milk, and crabmeat. Add the cornstarch mixture. Add the finely chopped eggs. Heat and simmer for several minutes. Do not boil. Add the lemon slices, salt and pepper, and heat through. Serve very hot with a lemon slice in each bowl.

CRAB CHOWDER SUPREME

What fun it is to go to Beverly's house—whether in Macon or Hilton Head. Beverly Meadors is the quintessential hostess who does everything so beautifully yet is so gracious, calm and composed that you'd never dream she's been to a lot of trouble. We always have a great time at Beverly's and when Mort blesses us with some of his specialty, roasted peanuts, it's even more special. This is one of Beverly's signature dishes—a really very special chowder.

½   cup chopped celery

½   cup chopped onions

3   tablespoons butter

Cook these in a large saucepan until tender. Add the following:

1   (10¾-ounce) can condensed potato soup

1   (7½-ounce) can crabmeat or fresh is best

1   (8-ounce) can creamed corn

2   tablespoons chopped pimento

¼   teaspoon salt

Dash of white pepper

¼   teaspoon thyme

1   bay leaf

1   dash of accent

¼   cup dry sherry

Cook until heated thoroughly, stirring often- about 15 minutes. Stir in sherry. Heat 2 minutes. Remove bay leaf. Garnish with parsley.

TUNA BISQUE

I really don't know of any recipe that gets rave reviews more than this Tuna Bisque, which is my Mother's recipe. I have made it so many times I don't really need to look at the recipe any more. I carry it to an older friend of mine, and she empties the container, hands it back, and says, "Make me some more." And I do because it's so delicious I always want to save out a bowl or two for myself.

1   small can button mushrooms

½   cup finely chopped onions

2   tablespoons butter

1   (10½-ounce) can mushroom soup

1   soup can filled with milk

1   (7-ounce) can tuna–drained and flaked

1   tablespoon chopped parsley

1   teaspoon curry powder

1   (2-ounce) jar chopped pimento

½   teaspoon salt

Sauté onions and mushrooms in butter until tender. Add remaining ingredients. Simmer over low heat for 10 minutes. A good bit more milk may be added if desired. This is delicious served hot immediately or can be refrigerated and heated and served later.

WINTER SHRIMP SOUP

It was cold wintertime, and as is our custom, our bridge club was celebrating still one more birthday. Always it's a luncheon with everybody but the honoree bringing a specific covered dish. This time we were doing a soup for the main course, which suited me fine; I was assigned the soup. Immediately, I searched through some of my favorite soup dishes and found this which I made with crab instead of shrimp simply because I had a pint of nice crabmeat in the freezer. It serves 8 people but is so good you might serve fewer.

3	cans mushroom soup		1	small can button mushrooms
2	soup cans milk		1½	pounds raw peeled shrimp, cut into small pieces
4	green onions and tops, chopped			
¼	cup finely chopped celery		3	tablespoons dry sherry
	Small bud garlic, pressed			Salt
	Worcestershire sauce			Pepper
	Tabasco sauce, to taste			

Stir mushroom soup and milk until smooth on low fire; add finely chopped green onions, celery and pressed garlic. Season with Worcestershire sauce and Tabasco sauce. Add 1 can small button mushrooms and 1½ pounds raw shrimp. When shrimp are done, add sherry. Season to taste with salt and pepper. Crabmeat may be used instead of shrimp.

SHE CRAB SOUP

Lots of places serve She Crab Soup, but if you haven't had it at The Mills House *in Charleston, you haven't experienced the ultimate. This recipe might not be theirs but I think it's mighty close and the one I like to use.*

2	tablespoons butter		½	teaspoon mace
1	tablespoon flour		1	tablespoon Worcestershire sauce
3	cups milk		1	teaspoon salt
1	cup cream		½	teaspoon pepper, freshly ground
½	pound crabmeat		4	tablespoons dry sherry
¼	cup crab roe*			Sprinkle of paprika
1	small onion, grated			

Melt the butter in top of double boiler and blend in the flour until smooth. Add the milk and cream gradually and stir constantly with a wire whisk. Add crabmeat, roe, onion, mace, Worcestershire sauce, salt and pepper. Cook slowly in double boiler for 25 minutes. Just before serving, put 1 tablespoon of warm sherry in each soup cup and sprinkle the top with paprika.

*If crab roe is not available in your fish market, crumble the yolk of hard-boiled eggs in the bottom of each soup cup.

CRAB AND CORN BISQUE

When I think back on possibly the ten most memorable dining experiences I've ever had, I have to include lunch at Commander's Palace in New Orleans. We were with a group of about ten people, some friends from Thomasville and some from Wrightsville. We were seated upstairs where our long table looked out at exquisite old oaks hanging in moss, highlighted by the noonday sun and shadows. The jazz player, Alvin Alcorn, whom we knew quite well, lingered long at our table lightly pumping the valves on his shiny brass trumpet and making the greatest music you almost ever heard. The wine kicked in, and then there was food. This famous New Orleans restaurant is known for its great cuisine, and we were not disappointed. It was superb. I like their Crab and Corn Bisque a whole lot, and you will too.

½	cup (1 stick) butter	1	quart (4 cups) crab stock, available in specialty food stores
1½	cups chopped green onion tops		
2	tablespoons all-purpose flour	2	(12-ounce) cans whole kernel corn, drained
1¼	teaspoons Creole Seafood Seasoning		
1	teaspoon granulated garlic	1½	cups whipping cream
	Pinch thyme	1	pound lump crabmeat

Melt butter in 3-quart saucepan over medium heat. Add onion, and sauté until wilted. Stir in flour, Creole Seafood Seasoning, garlic and thyme and continue cooking until flour begins to stick to pan. Blend in crab stock, reduce heat and simmer until stock thickens, about 15 minutes. Add corn and simmer an additional 15 minutes. Slowly stir in cream and blend well. Gently add crabmeat. Remove from heat and let stand 30 minutes. Reheat gently over very low heat, being careful crabmeat does not break up into flakes and cream does not curdle. Serve immediately.

AFRICAN CHICKEN PEANUT SOUP

This recipe is from one of Macon's best chefs and restaurateurs, Allan Bass, who owns Bert's downtown. Allan is innovative with his food and wine, always having menu items that you enjoy immensely. His African Soup is so delicious that you will not believe it. It's fun to make, too, because of the combination of African ingredients—whoever heard of sweet potatoes and peanut butter in soup? It's sensational. I can't get enough and if I can't get to Bert's I just make up a batch at home.

2	(8-ounce) boneless chicken breasts (about 2 cups diced)	1	cup homemade salsa (you may substitute bottled)
2	cups cooked rice	1	teaspoon cumin
1½	cups peeled and cubed sweet potatoes	¼	teaspoon ground red pepper
½	cup yellow onion, chopped	4	cups chicken stock (or substitute canned chicken broth)
½	cup red bell pepper, chopped		
2	garlic cloves, minced	1	can black beans, drained (15-ounces)
1	jalapeño pepper, seeded and minced	⅓	cup creamy peanut butter

Bake or grill the chicken until just done. Chop into small pieces. Cook the rice in a separate pan and set aside. Sauté first 5 ingredients 5 minutes, or until sweet potato is tender, over medium heat with a little olive oil. Stir in cooked chicken and next 6 ingredients and bring to a boil. Reduce heat and simmer 10 minutes. Add peanut butter and stir well.

PEANUT SOUP

Several times Willard Scott, radio and TV personality, was chosen to emcee the Pillsbury Bake-Off® contest which I attended. He was always jovial and entertaining and just as friendly as he could be. I even had my picture taken with him, and it hangs in my office just as if we were good friends. This is Willard's recipe for Peanut Soup and a whole lot more predictable than the weather he has announced for so many years.

❖ Louise and Willard Scott ❖

3	cups chicken or turkey stock	1	carrot, diced		Pepper
1	onion, chopped	1	cup peanut butter	1	pint milk or cream
2	stalks celery, diced		Salt		

Simmer stock with onion, celery, and carrots. Add peanut butter. Add milk or cream and seasonings to taste. Blend thoroughly and heat.

PORTUGUESE WHITE TURNIP SOUP

Christ Church in Macon has published one of the finest cookbooks called With Our Blessings. *Begun in 1825, two years after the founding of Macon, the church is Macon's oldest congregation and one of the most influential. They have all kinds of outreach programs, including the weekend lunch program and Meals-on-Wheels. Probably the most important thing they ever had, though, was my dear and precious friend, Clara Eschmann, long-time food editor of the Macon Telegraph. Clara provided her Portuguese White Turnip Soup for the church's cookbook, and it is superb.*

(Note: Clara died in the spring of 2002 before this book was published.)

❖ Clara and Louise in Aspen ❖

2	pounds white turnips		Salt
1	pound sweet onions		Pepper
¼	stick butter	2-3	shots dry sherry
1	pint chicken broth	3	cups half-and-half
5	cups milk		

Slice and chop turnips and onions. Cook in butter until tender. Add chicken broth and continue cooking until very tender. Set aside. Remove about 2 cups of the vegetables and puree the remaining vegetables. Put pureed mixture and milk into 3-quart pan. Add seasonings, sherry and half-and-half. Simmer until soup thickens. Add reserved vegetables; heat to hard simmer; serve at once. Top with chopped green onions and paprika or parsley and croutons.

NANCY REAGAN'S ONION WINE SOUP

❖ Nancy Reagan waves to crowd at First Lady's Luncheon ❖

This will always rank as one of my life's most memorable and treasured experiences. Luella and J. Roy Rowland, when he was in Congress, invited me to Washington for a week of superlative entertaining. J. Roy would have a list every night of what was going on the next day that might interest me and Ann Kirkland who also went. There were such things as a Gershwin concert, attended by members of the Gershwin family, held in the Library of Congress, and it was a treat so rare tears of joy spilled down my face. Then there was a wonderful chicken fest put on by the Alabama Congressional delegation. But perhaps best of all was the First Lady's Luncheon in the spacious ballroom of the Shoreham Hotel. Nancy Reagan was making her final appearance as First Lady at the First Lady's Luncheon and was lovely all dressed in red to blend in with the red and black decor in the immense room. Red Anthurium lilies adorned every table, and a huge red Liz Claiborne tote bag hung on each chair, filled with interesting gifts like a hair dryer and a black and red scarf with the words: "First Lady's Luncheon June 22, 1988."

That should have been enough for almost anybody, but we were entertained by the incomparable United States Marine Band and Marvin Hamlish tickled the ivories all in between.

Barbara Bush was there. Sandra Day O'Connor—almost any woman in Washington with political involvement. It was a day to always remember and Nancy Reagan's Onion Wine Soup is also to long remember.

❖ Ann Kirkland, Louise and Luella Rowland at First Lady's Luncheon ❖

¼	cup butter	1	large potato, sliced	1	cup light cream
5	large onions, chopped	1	cup dry white wine	1	tablespoon minced parsley
5	cups beef broth	1	tablespoon vinegar		Salt
½	cup celery leaves	2	tablespoons sugar		Pepper

Melt butter in large saucepan. Add chopped onion and mix well. Add beef broth, celery leaves and potato. Bring to boiling. Cover and simmer for 30 minutes. Puree mixture in a blender. Return to saucepan and blend in wine and sugar and vinegar. Bring to boiling and simmer 5 minutes. Stir in cream, parsley and salt and pepper to taste. Heat thoroughly but do not boil.

SOUPS

CURRIED PUMPKIN SOUP

My darling friend from college days, Becky Bowdre, and I were commissioned to do cooking classes in the mountains. What a good time we had planning and implementing all our ideas. It was autumn and the leaves were a glorious profusion of color, so we decided on a theme to complement the weather. I made little cookbooks of all the recipes shaped like pumpkins with orange cardboard for the cover. The Curried Pumpkin Soup was a real crowd pleaser and one that I call upon quite often in the fall.

2 tablespoons butter	¼ teaspoon salt
¼ cup finely chopped onion	Freshly ground pepper
1 tablespoon all-purpose flour	¼ teaspoon freshly ground nutmeg
1½ teaspoons curry powder	1 cup milk
2 (10¾-ounce) cans chicken broth	Minced chives or parsley
1 (16-ounce) can pumpkin	Lowfat plain yogurt (garnish)
1 teaspoon brown sugar	

Melt butter in 3-quart saucepan over medium high heat. Add onion and sauté until translucent, about 5 minutes. Mix in flour and curry powder and cook until bubbly, about 2 minutes. Remove from heat and gradually stir in broth. Add pumpkin, brown sugar, salt, pepper and nutmeg. Cook over medium heat, stirring constantly until thickened. Blend in milk and continue cooking until warmed through; do not boil. Ladle into individual pumpkins that have been hollowed out and put tops back on before serving or ladle into bowls. Sprinkle with chives or parsley. Garnish with yogurt. Serve immediately.

❖ Martha Gaddis, Pat Childs, Becky Bowdre and Louise at Lake Rabun ❖

AUTUMN PUMPKIN BISQUE

A visit to Americus, Georgia, and nearby Plains always includes a meal at the lovely old Windsor Hotel in Americus, open seven days a week. It was built in 1890 for $1,000,000 from investors. In 1986, the restoration of the historic landmark was over $5,000,000. This Pumpkin Bisque, when in season, is one of their best recipes.

2	pounds pumpkin, peeled, in 1-inch cubes	¼	cup chopped parsley
1	pound bacon, diced	4	cups half-and-half cream
1	medium onion, diced fine		Salt and pepper
½	teaspoon cumin	1½	cups grated Gruyère or Swiss cheese

In large pot over low heat, sweat pumpkin in small amount of water 40 minutes; test for tenderness. Remove from heat and cool slightly; mash and set aside. In the pot, render bacon over medium heat. Add onion and sauté until translucent. Combine with pumpkin pulp and stir in remaining ingredients except cheese. Simmer until slightly thickened. Divide into bowls and top with cheese.

POTATO-CHILI SOUP

Lifestyles of the Rich and Famous was the name given to the luncheon sponsored by the National Broiler Council *and the* National Potato Board. *High atop a mountain that overlooked the valley of Aspen, Colorado, in a home that is rumored to be valued at 10 million, the food editors had a very tempting glance at the Rich and Famous.*

Perhaps the biggest hit of all, at the several courses meal, was the scrumptious soup course, Potato-Chili Soup. Hardly able to divert our attention from the magnificent surroundings, we did manage to enjoy this soup tremendously.

1	medium onion, diced	6	russet potatoes (about 9-ounces each), peeled and medium dice
2	roasted poblano chiles, stemmed and seeded	1	cup heavy cream
1	teaspoon ground cumin	¼	cup fresh lime juice
3	tablespoons butter	2	tablespoons chopped cilantro
9	cups chicken or vegetable stock		Salt and pepper to taste

Sauté onions, chiles and cumin in the butter. In a separate pot, heat stock. Add potato to onion and add hot stock. Cook until potato is soft: puree in batches and strain. Return to heat; add cream and lime juice and cilantro. Adjust seasoning and serve.

CREAM OF CARROT SOUP

My friend, Beryl Hicks, knew exactly what to do to entertain me when I was visiting in Laguna Beach, California. She took me to a cooking school. Yes, she made reservations for the two of us at Robert's, and away we went just full of gleeful anticipation.

It wasn't exactly what we had expected. It was just Robert and all his cronies, and at first we thought maybe we'd make our exit at the break, but before we ever got to the break, we were having such a fabulous, good time that you couldn't have pulled us away with a twenty-mule team. Robert was an actor like none I've ever seen and a comedian too. All of his friends were comics, and Beryl and I just joined right in. I can remember so well Robert's rendition of Caesar's Salad, complete with the raw egg, long before Caesar Salad became a household word. And his Carrot Soup was out-of-this world. Beryl and I learned a lot, but most of all we laughed a lot, and that's so important in today's world.

6	medium carrots, peeled and chopped	1	teaspoon sugar
1	small onion, chopped		Salt and pepper to taste
1	small bay leaf	1	tablespoon grated lemon rind
2	tablespoons butter or margarine	1	tablespoon chopped parsley
3	cups chicken stock, divided		

Combine carrots, onion, bay leaf and butter in heavy pan with a lid. Cook over low heat until carrots are tender, keeping the lid on to create condensation. The moisture will help to prevent burning, but a little stock may be added if it looks as if may be burning. Cook approximately 8 minutes. Cool slightly and remove bay leaf; add 1 cup chicken stock. Pour into an electric blender; turn to low and then high. Blend 1 minute. Return to pan in which the carrots were cooked. Add remaining stock and sugar. Season with salt and pepper. Serve hot and garnish with a little grated lemon rind and parsley.

SOTO AYAM-CHICKEN GINGER SOUP

Can you imagine a little girl from a tiny, tiny town, all grown up and dining at the Republic of Indonesia Embassy in Washington? It was a meal to remember forever, and a night we shall cherish all our lives. Our hosts were so lovely and gracious, dressed so beautifully in their native garb and exuding warmth and welcome.

Since we were guests, too, of the National Broiler Council, *the Indonesians were heavy on chicken recipes, including this unusual and delicious soup. I think you'd have to live on an Indonesian Island to have time for this complex, yet delicious, recipe.*

❖ Indonesian Hostesses ❖

1	whole chicken, cut-up	1	(2-inch) piece fresh ginger peeled
1	tablespoon vinegar	1	teaspoon pepper
	Salt to taste	2	medium onions, quartered
5	candle nuts or unsalted macadamia nuts	1	(2-inch) piece fresh lemon grass or juice of 2 lemons
1	teaspoon turmeric		Sambal Kemeri (see next page)
3	cloves garlic		

Put the chicken pieces in a pot with water to cover. Add the vinegar, and salt. Bring to a boil. Put the nuts, turmeric, garlic, ginger, pepper and onions into a food processor or blender and bring to a fine paste. Add salt as needed. Add the spice paste and the lemon grass or lemon juice to the boiling soup and cook over medium heat until the meat separates from the bones- about 1 hour. Remove the chicken pieces- scrape chicken from the bones with a fork. Discard the bones and return the chicken to the pot. Remove the lemon grass if used. The soup may be served as is or made into a clear broth by straining through cheesecloth, chilling, and removing the fat. To serve, put the soup in a large tureen on the center of the table and surround it with the various condiments, each in a 4-inch bowl. The guests may serve themselves. The rice or vermicelli and the bean sprouts should be put into the bowls before the soup; the rest of the condiments are stirred into the soup afterward.

Condiments:

2	cups fresh bean sprouts, blanched	1	bunch green onions, finely sliced
2	cups vermicelli, broken into small pieces and soaked in hot water	1	cup dried onion flakes fried in hot oil
5	stalks celery, finely sliced	2	cups potatoes, sliced paper thin and fried in hot oil or 2 cups unsalted potato chips

Serve with 2 cups cooked white rice

Sambal Kemeri-to serve with soup, stirred in:

8	fresh red chiles	Salt to taste
8	unsalted macadamia nuts	Juice of 1 lemon

Put all the ingredients in a blender or food processor and grind to a smooth paste. If necessary add chicken stock to moisten.

CORN AND ACORN SQUASH SOUP

Quick. Let me write it down before I forget it. It is worth saving forever and cooking at frequent intervals. Quite by accident, I invented this delicious soup. It's like when the man was asked why he climbed the mountain. "Because it was there." In my kitchen were three ears of white corn and an acorn squash. There was also some wonderful rosemary I had picked from Carol's country place, Laurens Hill, the day before when I stopped to check on the preliminary fix-up before they moved in the furniture. The rest is history. I made a discovery. This is absolutely delicious.

½	cup chopped sweet onions	1	teaspoon Krazy Jane salt
2	tablespoons butter	½	teaspoon black pepper
2	cans chicken stock	½	cup milk
3	ears corn, cooked and cut off cob	1	pinch red pepper
1	acorn squash, cooked and pureed	1	teaspoon finely chopped rosemary
2	tablespoons cornstarch		

Sauté onion in butter, until tender. Pour chicken stock into saucepan. Add corn, squash, and onions. Stir cornstarch into milk and add to stock. Season with salt, pepper, red pepper and rosemary. Simmer for 20 to 30 minutes. Serve piping hot with buttered toast.

MULLIGATAWNY SOUP

There'll always be a great memory of our incomparable visit to London and to the House of Parliament where we were entertained so lavishly by Lord Parry, who was a frequent visitor to Macon, and a friend of many of us on the trip. We were in Great Britain to invite the people of Ireland to be our special guests at the upcoming Cherry Blossom Festival. Lord Parry, actually from Wales, was hosting us around those beautiful British Isles. We stood on the historic stone terrace of the House of Parliament overlooking the Thames River and had drinks as we visited with members of the House. I was so excited I don't begin to remember who all was there, but I distinctly remember meeting Lord Earl Grey because of his family's connection with the great Earl Grey Tea Company. Later we went upstairs for lunch in a beautiful dining room, with huge oil portraits everywhere. It seems that two peers (members of the House) had to sit at each table of guests, and of all things I was seated to the right of Lord Tonypandy. Shock went through my every vital organ as my brain whirled to wonder what in the world I'd say to a Lord in the House of Parliament. My nervousness was ungrounded because when Lord Tonypandy found out that I was a Methodist, we were off and running. He had spoken many times in this country in the cause of Methodism. We had such great rapport that I hated to see our meal come to an end.

Although I didn't bring home any recipes from the luncheon, I did get a copy of this popular English dish that is a lot easier to eat than pronounce.

This was a very popular dish with British officers serving in India during the British Colonial Period because it was easy to carry along flasks of the hot soup on winter forages into the hills. Here's hoping your consumption of it will be a bit easier- maybe at your own dinner table.

1	large chicken, cut into pieces	2	heaping teaspoons curry powder
¼	pound veal trimmings, cut up	5	tablespoons cornstarch
6	cups water		Juice of 1 lemon
3	tablespoons (⅜ stick) butter		Salt and pepper
4	large onions, chopped	1	cooking apple, peeled and sliced
2	garlic cloves, minced		Boiled rice

Simmer chicken and veal trimmings in 6 cups water for about 1 hour. Melt butter in large skillet and cook garlic and onions until translucent. Mix curry powder and cornstarch with chicken/veal stock to form a paste and blend thoroughly. Stir in lemon juice and cook about 30 minutes. Chill.

Thirty minutes before serving, cut chicken into small pieces, discarding bones. Add chicken to soup. Add lemon juice and salt and pepper to taste and reheat. About 20 minutes before serving; add apple. Serve with boiled rice.

❖ Mary Helen Daniel and Louise on terrace of House of Parliament overlooking Thames River. ❖

SOUPS

BROCCOLI, MUSHROOM, AND LEEK CREAM SOUP

While vacationing in Maine, I managed to eat not only my share of the lobsters but several other people's too. They were so wonderful. But so was this soup that we had in Kennebunkport, the place where the Bushes have a lovely home built out on the rocky coast, yet visible from the road. It's ironic that George Bush publicly demeaned broccoli and yet this recipe is chosen from Kennebunkport.

❖ Sybil Futrelle and Louise in Maine, getting ready to deal with some lobster. ❖

6	tablespoons (¾ stick) butter
2	cups beef stock (homemade preferred)
2	cups chicken stock (homemade preferred)
2	pounds broccoli, coarsely chopped
¾	pound mushrooms, sliced
½	pound leeks, split and coarsely chopped
⅓	cup white wine
½	small shallot, minced
⅛	teaspoon dried basil
1	cup half-and-half
1¼	cups whipping cream
	Salt and freshly ground pepper

Combine 2 tablespoons each butter, beef stock and chicken stock in large skillet. Place over medium-high heat; add broccoli and cook until soft. Puree in blender or food processor in 3 batches adding at least ½ cup stock with each batch. Transfer to large saucepan or Dutch oven and add remaining stocks. Heat through, stirring occasionally. Cover and keep warm over low heat. Heat remaining butter in skillet. Sauté mushrooms and leeks lightly. Add to soup. Combine wine, shallot and basil in heavy-bottomed medium saucepan and reduce over medium heat until all liquid evaporates, watching carefully to avoid scorching. Meanwhile, heat half-and-half and 1 cup whipping cream in small saucepan just until hot. Whisking constantly, add cream in slow steady stream to shallot-basil mixture, and cook over medium heat until reduced by ⅓. Whisk cream mixture into warm soup. (At this point soup can be cooled and frozen for future use.)

When ready to serve, reheat soup just to simmering point. Fold in remaining whipping cream and salt and pepper to taste.

TORTILLA SOUP

When Marguerite Cato and I get together, we have a wonderful time discussing recipes and telling one another about the outstanding ones we've found since our last swap. It's unfortunate that she moved away to Nashville and left us, but we still get in a recipe swap occasionally.

When she was at my house last, we kept the copy machine humming, supplying her with a good many new recipes to take back home. Marguerite doesn't just copy recipes like a lot of people—she puts them to good use. And no better cook could be in the "test kitchen."

She called me back to tell me that this is wonderful. It has sort of a southwestern taste and is a great first course for any meal but especially one with a southwest theme.

1½	pounds boneless skinless chicken breast halves	1	tablespoon hot pepper sauce
1	large onion, chopped	½	cup flour
2	fresh jalapeños, seeded and chopped	1	(14-ounce) can whole tomatoes, crushed
4	cloves garlic, minced	4	(14-ounce) cans chicken broth
2	large carrots, chopped	8	corn tortillas, cut into thin strips
4	teaspoons vegetable oil		Vegetable oil for frying
1	teaspoon ground cumin	½	cup sour cream
1	teaspoon chili powder	1	avocado, chopped
1	teaspoon lemon pepper	1	cup shredded Cheddar cheese
1	teaspoon salt		Chopped fresh cilantro, to taste

Rinse the chicken and pat dry; chop. Sauté the onion, jalapeños, garlic, carrots, and chicken in 4 teaspoons oil in a stock pot for 5 minutes. Stir in the cumin, chili powder, lemon pepper, salt, hot pepper sauce and flour until mixed. Add the tomatoes and chicken broth; mix well. Simmer for 1 hour, stirring frequently. Fry the tortilla strips in ¼-inch oil in a skillet until crisp; drain. Arrange several tortilla strips in each soup bowl. Spoon 1 tablespoon each of the sour cream and chopped avocado over the tortilla strips. Ladle the soup over the layers; sprinkle with cheese and cilantro.

BEER CHEESE SOUP

St. Louis, with its landmark arches, brews more beer than any other American city. It has a wonderful City Art Museum and lovely botanical gardens. It also has a great symphony orchestra, and when I was there, they had just published their Symphony of Cooking, *which I promptly purchased.*

Tying in with the city's beer production, the cookbook carries a splendid recipe for Beer Cheese Soup that you're sure to like.

2	cups dried lentils		2	tablespoons butter
2	inch cube salt pork or ham bone		2	tablespoons flour
1	cup cut-up celery (with tops)			Juice of 1 lemon
½	cup chopped onion		1	tablespoon salt
1	teaspoon sugar		¼	teaspoon pepper
½	teaspoon thyme			Chopped scallions or lemon slices
1	bay leaf			

Cover lentils with water. Soak overnight. Drain and save liquid. Put lentils into large kettle. Add water to saved liquid to make 9 cups. Add to lentils with salt pork or ham bone. Cover and simmer 3 hours. Add celery, onion, sugar, thyme and bay leaf. Cover and simmer ½ hour more. Put soup through a sieve or puree in blender. Melt butter in saucepan. Blend in flour. Add a little of the soup and mix well. Stir mixture back into rest of soup. Stir until it boils, about 3 to 5 minutes. Add lemon juice, salt and pepper. Sprinkle each serving with scallions or lemon slice.

HAM BONE SOUP

Whoever thought I'd have to go all the way to San Antonio to get an authentic Afro-American recipe for Ham Bone Soup? I found a cookbook called The Melting Pot *at the Institute of Texas Culture, and in it are 27 different ethnic group recipes used by cooks today, not old world nor traditional recipes. An accompanying drawing shows the family serving the soup to their pastor, and it makes me want some right now. It is truly delicious.*

1	ham bone with meat	1	cup snap beans, broken
2	large onions, diced	1	cup butter beans
3	stalks of celery	¼	cup diced turnips
3	carrots	½	cup green peas
1	pound tomatoes	1	tablespoon sugar
3	potatoes, cubed		Salt and pepper
2	whole cloves	1	cup fresh corn kernels

Cover the ham bone with water in a large kettle. Boil until meat is almost tender. Add remaining ingredients, except the corn. Cover and cook slowly for 3 to 4 hours. Add corn during the last 15 minutes of cooking.

MY OWN VEGETABLE SOUP

I'm like a vulture on the fence whenever there's a ham bone or turkey carcass left at a dinner party or family get-together. It's always the perfect beginning for stock for vegetable soup and usually I do end up bringing home the bones. This soup is delicious and freezes well. Make up a big pot full and freeze it in 1-quart bags to pull out whenever you hanker for good, hot, homemade vegetable soup.

	Turkey carcass or large cured ham bone (even honey-baked)	2	cans corn, 1 creamed, 1 regular
1	cup onions, chopped	1	can French beans
1	cup celery, chopped	1	can English peas
4-5	carrots, peeled and diced	1	can or 1 small package frozen cut okra
2	cans tomatoes, pulverized in blender		Salt to taste
			Pepper to taste

Cook meat until it all falls off bones. Remove from stock and cut meat into small bite-size pieces. Return to stock. Add all vegetables and simmer for a couple of hours. Season to taste.

U.S. SENATE BEAN SOUP

Martha Green, long a local celebrity in Dublin and a teacher who made indelible, great, positive impressions on her students, shared with the Moore Street Cookbook committee her classic recipe for Bean Soup that is served in the U.S. Senate Restaurant.

I've always remembered that Martha had formal dinner parties arranged for her students in order that they may become comfortable with sophisticated dining. Thanks, Martha, for doing such a wonderful service for tomorrow's leaders and for sharing this recipe that is one to treasure and preserve.

1	pound dry navy beans	¼	cup parsley, chopped
1	ham hock with some meat	1	cup potatoes, mashed
2	cups onion, chopped		Dash Tabasco sauce
1	cup celery, chopped with leaves	1	teaspoon salt
2	cloves garlic, pressed	⅛	teaspoon white pepper

Cover beans with water and soak overnight. Place ham hock and drained beans in 3 quarts of water in Dutch oven. Bring to a boil. Simmer for 2 hours. Add remaining ingredients and simmer, covered for another hour. Remove ham hock, dice the meat, and return the meat to the pot. Adjust the seasonings and serve.

BLACK BEAN SOUP

My longtime friend, Rose Crockett McRae, now lives in Savannah and pretty well keeps up with the goings on down there. Years ago when Savannah was a part time home for them, Rose sent me a note that said, "As you know, there are cookbooks and cookbooks and more cookbooks but Savannah Style *is such a very special cookbook and since we share a mutual love for* The Port City *and also cookbooks, it is my pleasure to add this one to your collection."*

It was my pleasure to add it too, and I still think about Rose and her generosity every time I see the book. Then when I open it to cook Black Bean Soup, I really get her on my mind—such a dear friend all the way back to the forties.

1	pound black beans	½	teaspoon hot sauce
2	tablespoons olive oil	½	medium onion
1	medium ripe tomato	½	medium green pepper
1	bay leaf	1	garlic clove, peeled and crushed
½	cup olive oil	¼	teaspoon cumin
½	medium onion, chopped	2	tablespoons wine vinegar
½	green pepper, chopped	1	tablespoon salt
1	garlic clove, minced	2	tablespoons dry sherry
1	level teaspoon crushed oregano		

Wash beans and discard imperfect ones. Place in a deep bowl and cover with water 2 inches above beans. Soak overnight. Next day, pour beans into a 3 to 4-quart kettle with the same soaking water. If necessary, add more water so that beans will be covered 1-inch above. Add to the beans 2 tablespoons olive oil, whole tomato, bay leaf, ½ onion, ½ green pepper, crushed garlic clove. Bring to a boil then lower heat to moderate, cover and cook until beans are tender, about 1 hour. Use only a wooden spoon for stirring. Remove the bay leaf and what is left of the half onion, tomato, pepper and garlic.

In a skillet, heat ½ cup olive oil and sauté the chopped onion and green pepper until transparent. Add the garlic, crushed oregano, cumin, wine vinegar and salt. Stir to mix well and cook 2 minutes longer, then add to beans. Stir in hot sauce, cover and cook for a good half hour. Correct seasonings, and add sherry. Serve hot with cooked long grain white rice and raw chopped onions.

SALADS AND
SALAD DRESSINGS

Louise and Sybil Futrelle prepare Jicama Salad for Southwest Dinner.

BACON-BLUE CHEESE DRESSING

On a special trip to Dallas with the National Broiler Council, Dean Fearing, the famous chef at The Mansion on Turtle Creek, Dallas' only 5-star restaurant, was to give a demonstration for the food editors at 3 o'clock. My plane was sitting in Tuscaloosa and I was dining on an $8 airport hot dog at that time.

Not to be outdone, my friend, Betty Ballard, and I stayed over an extra day in Dallas and were able to get reservations at the world-famous restaurant. What a thrill and a treat. We truly dined—in the most elegant meaning of the word.

Here's Dean's recipe for Bacon-Blue Cheese Dressing which is delicious over spinach and Red Onion Salad.

4	slices bacon	1	cup fresh buttermilk
3	shallots	1	tablespoon cornstarch
1	clove garlic, peeled and minced	1	tablespoon water
2	tablespoons white wine vinegar		Salt to taste
¼	cup heavy cream		Fresh cracked black pepper to taste
¼	cup chicken stock	¼	cup blue cheese, crumbled

Julienne bacon across grain into short strips. Place in a medium sauté pan over medium heat and sauté for 6 minutes or until bacon is crisp. Remove and drain on paper towel. Pour off half of bacon fat from pan. Add shallots and garlic and sauté for 2 minutes. Stir in white wine vinegar. Reduce slightly. Bring to a boil, stirring constantly, then add cream, chicken stock, and buttermilk. Return to a boil. Dissolve cornstarch in water. When dressing returns to a boil, stir in cornstarch little by little until dressing is slightly thickened. Simmer 10 minutes. Season with salt and pepper. Add blue cheese and bacon strips. Keep warm.

FRUIT SALAD DRESSING

This little recipe is so simple you might discount it. But don't. It's a quick and easy way to make a great-tasting dressing for fruit. I've had it for years and years.

½	pint orange or rainbow sherbet	½	pint mayonnaise

Blend ingredients together and serve over fresh fruit.

MRS. MCAFEE'S WESLEYAN DRESSING

When I was in college, there was a charming little brick building across the road from the college entrance gates. Called The Pharm, *and run by one of the finest cooks in the world, the spot was a favorite destination for college girls who were always hungry. Mrs. McAfee had so many special recipes but this is the only one that has endured the passage of years (in my possession anyway.) This dressing is so good you are going to want to drink it but please serve it over grapefruit sections on lettuce. It's just marvelous.*

1	small onion		Juice of 1 lemon
½	cup sugar	2	teaspoons salt
½	cup vinegar	2	teaspoons pepper
1	cup chili sauce	2	teaspoons paprika
1	cup oil		

Grate onion. Combine it with all other ingredients in a bottle or jar. Shake well.

ASHEVILLE SALAD

Marge Woodfin, one of our McJaals, brought this delicious salad for Ann Wall's birthday in 1999. It goes really well with Shrimp Salad or you can even add shrimp to this salad. It's easy and it's called Asheville Salad because it was always served at the Old Battery Park Hotel in Asheville for many, many years.

Don't lose this. We all lost it one time and nearly panicked.

1	can tomato soup	½	cup chopped green pepper
6	ounces cream cheese, softened	½	cup chopped celery
2	tablespoons gelatin dissolved in ½ cup cold water	½	cup chopped green onion
		1	cup mayonnaise

Heat tomato soup to boiling point. Add all other ingredients. Pour into 8-inch square pan and chill until firm. Cut into squares and serve on spinach or lettuce leaves. May be garnished with slices of stuffed olive, pimento or red, sweet pepper.

ORANGE SUPREME SALAD

Way back when our children were in school together, Joy Hortman would always bring delicious, new creations for us to sample at school suppers.

Since then Joy and her husband Jimmy, have run a very successful restaurant on the Courthouse Square in Wrightsville. I do not wonder. I just hope she gives her customers the benefit of this delicious salad she introduced to me in the '70s.

1	large box orange Jell-O	1	cup pineapple juice
1	large can crushed pineapple, drained, save juice	2	tablespoons lemon juice
		¾	cup sugar
1	large box Dream Whip	2	tablespoons flour
1	(8-ounce) package cream cheese	2	eggs, beaten

Step 1: Mix Jell-O by directions (less ¼ cup water.) Pour into 9x12-inch casserole dish. Chill until Jell-O begins to thicken; add pineapple and let congeal.

Step 2: Whip Dream Whip. Cream the cheese and combine. Spread over congealed salad and chill.

Step 3: Combine juices, sugar, flour and eggs in double boiler. Cook over low heat until thick. Chill and spread over Dream Whip. Refrigerate at least 2 hours before serving.

SPICED PEACH SALAD

This congealed salad is one of our bridge club's favorites. It goes so wonderfully well with ham, especially, but is a winner any way you serve it.

1	(28-ounce) can spiced peaches	½	teaspoon salt
1	teaspoon cinnamon	1	(6-ounce) can frozen orange juice concentrate
6-8	whole cloves		
1	(6-ounce) package orange gelatin	½	teaspoon ginger
¼	cup sherry	3	ounces cream cheese, broken into pieces

Drain liquid from peaches and measure, adding enough water to dissolve gelatin as the package directs. Boil liquid with cinnamon and cloves for 2 to 3 minutes. Remove cloves and dissolve gelatin in hot liquid. Add sherry, salt, orange juice, ginger, and cream cheese. Put the mixture in blender and whirl until cream cheese is well blended. Remove stones, cut peaches into pieces, and add to the liquid mixture. Pour into a 6-cup mold and refrigerate until set.

SALADS AND SALAD DRESSINGS

CRANBERRY SALAD WITH MAPLE SOUR CREAM SAUCE

There's hardly anything more fun than going on a side trip with my darling friend, Latha Tyson. She knows more about what's going on, and where, than anybody. And she has an indomitable happy spirit that makes her a joy to experience. Thus when she called me in the spring of 2002 to go to Candler County with a van full of friends to the biscuit factory I was getting ready before we hung up.

It was one of those wonderfully pleasant days where you just kept on meeting new people and going to interesting new places, including a wonderful wood carver's in Scott, Georgia where I ended up with several very artistic carvings.

The biscuit factory for many years produced these delicious Miss Marcile's Biscuits. Now it is just used occasionally for special luncheons and what a special lunch Marcile Byrd served us that day. Every one of her recipes was a keeper but this is the one I've already served several times. It's delicious.

6	ounce package of cranberry Jell-O	1	large can (1 pound 4 ounces) crushed pineapple
1½	cups boiling water	1	can jellied cranberry sauce
½	cup blackberry wine	½	cup chopped pecans

Dissolve Jell-O in 1½ cups boiling water. Add ½ cup of wine–(Blackberry is my choice). Add pineapple and juice. Mash cranberry sauce with fork before adding to Jell-O and pineapple mixture. Add pecans. Congeal.

Maple Sour Cream Sauce:

1	cup sour cream	1	tablespoon maple syrup
2	tablespoons sugar	½	teaspoon nutmeg

Mix together and place in refrigerator over night. Serve on top of salad.

SYBIL'S PINK ARCTIC FREEZE

This is another of my sister-in-law's great recipes. I have used it over and over again, especially during the holidays because it's so good with the Thanksgiving turkey or the Christmas ham—or anything, really.

2	(3-ounce) packages cream cheese	1	(9-ounce) can crushed pineapple, drained
2	tablespoons mayonnaise	½	cup chopped pecans
2	tablespoons sugar	½	pint cream, whipped
1	can whole cranberry sauce		

Soften cheese, blend in mayonnaise and sugar. Add fruits and nuts. Fold in whipped cream. Pour in 8½x4½x2½-inch loaf pan. Freeze. To serve, let stand at room temperature 15 minutes. Turn out on lettuce. Slice.

RASPBERRY RING

The only notation on this old recipe says, "Thanksgiving here—1987." Always liking to spring new recipes on the extended family on holidays, I do believe this was a big hit. It just sounds yummy, doesn't it?

1	(10-ounce) package frozen raspberries thawed	1	pint vanilla ice cream
2	(3-ounce) packages raspberry Jell-O	1	(6-ounce) can frozen lemonade
2	cups boiling water	¼	cup chopped pecans

Drain raspberries and reserve syrup. Dissolve gelatin in boiling water and add ice cream gradually until melted. Stir in lemonade and reserved raspberry syrup. Chill until partially set. Fold in raspberries and pecans. Mold in 6 cup containers.

SALADS AND SALAD DRESSINGS

PERFECTION MOLDS

No cookbook could be complete without the old tried-and-true Perfection Salad. This goes way back to my childhood and is just as tasty as ever because it has a little bite to it that goes so well with so many meats.

1	envelope unflavored gelatin	1	tablespoon lemon juice
¼	cup sugar	1	cup chopped celery
½	teaspoon salt	½	cup finely shredded cabbage
4¼	cups cold water, divided	2	tablespoons chopped green pepper
¼	cup vinegar	1	whole pimento, chopped

Combine gelatin, sugar, and salt in a small saucepan. Add ½ cup water; bring to a boil, and stir until gelatin is dissolved. Stir in remaining water, vinegar, and lemon juice. Chill until consistency of unbeaten egg white. Stir vegetables into thickened gelatin mixture. Pour into lightly oiled mold. Chill until firm.

SYB'S TOMATO SALAD

My recipe collection contains an inordinate number of my sister-in-law's, Sybil's, recipes for two reasons: One, Syb is a great cook who likes to try new recipes; two, she and I get together frequently and recipe sharing is our main thing—no, shopping—no, recipe swapping. It's a tie.

2	(3-ounce) packages raspberry Jell-O	2	cans Del Monte stewed tomatoes, crushed
1	cup boiling water	8	drops Tabasco sauce

Combine Jell-O and water, add tomatoes and Tabasco sauce. Congeal. Serve with Sour Cream Dressing.

Sour Cream Dressing:

1	cup sour cream		Worcestershire sauce
1	tablespoon mayonnaise		Lemon juice
	Heaping teaspoon horseradish		(leftover dressing is real good on roast beef)
	Dash of salt		

Combine all ingredients. Mix well.

BLOODY MARY ASPIC

Some of my recipes have no notation as to origin and there's no remembering about them either. This is one that is written on back of a sheet of paper that has an itinerary for a 6-day trip to Branson, Missouri—cost $669. Although, I surely didn't get to go on the trip, I love this recipe.

14	ounces Bloody Mary mix	3	tablespoons minced green pepper
1	small lemon Jell-O	1	tablespoon minced onion
1	tablespoon vinegar	½	teaspoon salt
1	cup minced celery		

Boil Bloody Mary mix. Dissolve Jell-O in it. Stir in vinegar and add celery, pepper, onion and salt. Pour into wet mold and chill at least 3 hours. Unmold–fill center with cottage cheese or cooked frozen peas chilled and tossed with mayonnaise.

MANGO SALAD

Always written on the back of a bridge score sheet, Lucille Pinkston's recipes are legendary. This one for Mango Salad was a real attention-getter at bridge one day—a recipe I like to use because I really like mangoes. They can be bought fresh too—or sealed fresh in a jar.

1	(3-ounce) box lemon Jell-O	½	cup mango juice
1½	cups boiling water	2	tablespoons lemon juice
1	can mangoes drained and mashed (save juice)	1	(3-ounce) package cream cheese

Dissolve Jell-O in boiling water. Add mango juice and lemon juice. Partially congeal. Soften cream cheese and beat slightly. Stir into Jell-O mixture with mangoes. Pour into mold and congeal.

SALADS AND SALAD DRESSINGS

CONGEALED GRAPEFRUIT SALAD

There's hardly anything more beautiful than a trip to my friend's, Clare Dodd's, in Marshallville when the camellias are in bloom. We drive through pretty farm country, always enjoying the numerous peach orchards along the way. At Clare's we sometimes load into the golf cart and take to the woods to see the hundreds of exquisite camellias. Fifteen acres of pines, magnolias and camellias punctuated with bulb flowers—some even from Clare's home garden back in Ireland—make a picture so breathtaking that it's good we're in an open-air cart to catch air. Most all of the camellias are from seedlings propagated by Clare's late husband Dick Dodd who was a camellia lover; an avid hunter and a tennis player of some note. A trip to Clare's is always a day apart—so special in every way. The luncheons that she and Essie serve are always to be recorded. At a '96 luncheon she introduced us to this lovely grapefruit salad that is so pretty on a lettuce leaf and garnished with slices of star fruit. It's delicious too. Clare says if you use sweetened grapefruit to cut the sugar to ½ cup.

2	envelopes unflavored gelatin	1	(8-ounce) package cream cheese, softened
½	cup cold water	¼	cup half-and-half
2	(16-ounce) cans unsweetened grapefruit sections, undrained	½	cup chopped pecans
1½	cups sugar		

Soften gelatin in cold water; let stand 5 minutes.

Drain grapefruit, reserving juice; add enough water to juice to measure 2 cups. Combine liquid and sugar in a saucepan; bring to a boil. Remove from heat; add gelatin, stirring until dissolved. Stir in grapefruit sections.

Combine cream cheese and half-and-half; beat at medium speed of an electric mixer until smooth. Stir in chopped pecans. Pour over half of gelatin mixture into a lightly oiled 8-inch square dish, and chill until partially set. Spread cream cheese mixture evenly over top; spoon on remaining gelatin mixture. Chill until salad is firm.

LIZZIE LEE'S LIME SALAD

When we moved to Wrightsville, Georgia in September of 1950, we had the good fortune to almost be adopted by the town's very best cook, Lizzie Lee Colston. This was one of her favorite recipes, became one of my favorite recipes; is certainly a favorite of my children and grandchildren. This is on the table at all special family meals.

1	(3-ounce) package lime Jell-O	½	pint cream
1	cup miniature marshmallows	½	cup mayonnaise
1	(3-ounce) package cream cheese	1	small can crushed pineapple
2	cups boiling water		

Dissolve Jell-O, marshmallows and cream cheese in water. Let set in refrigerator. Whip cream and add mayonnaise. Fold in pineapple. Beat Jell-O mixture and fold in cream mixture. Pour into Bundt pan or square cake pans. Makes 10 full molds.

JELL-O-PRETZEL SALAD

Years ago I was invited to judge a cooking contest at Hillcrest School in Dublin. I'm always glad to judge but even gladder to taste something new and different. Joyce Driskell who taught the 2nd grade asked me to be sure and taste the Jell-O-Pretzel Salad which I did with great trepidation. It sounded like a strange combination to me but it is positively delicious. You must try it if you haven't already.

¾	cup margarine	9	ounces Cool Whip
3	tablespoons sugar	1	large package Jell-O, strawberry
1⅔	cups pretzels, broken	2	cups boiling water
1	(8-ounce) package cream cheese	1	pint frozen strawberries
1	cup sugar		

Cream margarine and sugar; add pretzel pieces and press into a 13x9-inch pan and bake in a 350 degree oven for 10 minutes.

Cream the cream cheese and the 1 cup sugar; fold in Cool Whip. Spread on pretzel mixture after it cools. Dissolve Jell-O in boiling water. Add strawberries and refrigerate until partially jelled. Pour over cream cheese mixture and chill until firm.

CHERRY SALAD

Whenever I make a good old congealed salad I think of my darling young friend, David Clay, who is an attorney with the Environmental Protection Association. David is a great host and a wonderful cook who studies and knows food quite well.

When stationed in the nation's capital he was invited to a party where everybody was to take a dish. David, with his great Southern heritage (the son of my college roommate Joyce Clay and Clarence Clay) offered to bring a congealed salad but found out rather quickly that the social scene in Washington, didn't deal with "congealed" salads. That's all right, David, I do, and my friends do—don't all good Southerners?

Never do I make a congealed salad that I don't think about David. He can put 'em all to shame. How dare they!

1	package cherry gelatin (3-ounce)		Rind and juice of 1 orange
1	envelope unflavored gelatin	1	cup pecans, chopped
1	No. 2 can crushed pineapple	½	cup sugar
1	No. 2 can red sour cherries	3	cups fruit juice (leftover cherry,
	Rind and juice of 1 lemon		pineapple, and maybe pear juice)

Heat 3 cups fruit juice and dissolve cherry gelatin and sugar. Dissolve unflavored gelatin in ¼ cup cold water and add to cherry gelatin mixture. Add grated rind and juice of orange and lemon. Let mixture begin to congeal then add fruits and pecans. Let congeal and unmold on lettuce cups.

ROAST GARDEN SALAD

A hurried day trip from Brussels over to Luxembourg was worth the extra effort. The small city of Luxembourg is the capital of the country Luxembourg. It is perched on a plateau that is cut steeply on three sides by rivers. As we dined on the terrace of the restaurant we chose for lunch we looked out at one of the beautiful rivers and enjoyed their Roast Garden Salad.

8	ounces olive oil	6	ounces yellow squash, sliced
4	ounces balsamic vinegar	8	mushrooms
½	teaspoon salt	½	sweet red pepper, roasted, skinned, in julienne
½	teaspoon pepper		Romaine lettuce, washed
½	ounce chopped garlic	2	tomatoes, quartered
12	ounces zucchini, sliced	4	ounces Asiago cheese, grated

In bowl, stir together oil, vinegar, and seasonings. Coat squash with oil mixture, lay on hot grill until dark marks appear, repeat on other side, chill. Dip mushrooms in oil mixture, sauté, and chill. To assemble, place lettuce on 4 plates; divide vegetables among plates; and top with grated cheese.

HEARTS OF PALM SALAD

When I am serving a dinner party for eight or ten I need a break! Everything cannot be prepared-from-scratch. Therefore I quite often cheat and serve this salad that is as simple as opening a can. It is an elegant and delicious salad and often gets rave comments.

3	(#1) cans hearts of palms		Rings of red, green and yellow bell pepper
	Lettuce leaves		
1	recipe Vinaigrette Dressing		

Vinaigrette Dressing:

2	tablespoons red wine vinegar	1	teaspoon coarse salt
½	cup olive oil	½	teaspoon freshly ground black pepper

Put all ingredients in bottle and shake well. Arrange lettuce leaves on individual salad plates. Through rings of red, green and yellow (1 each) bell pepper slip several pieces of hearts of palms. Split them longways if too fat. Drizzle vinaigrette over salad.

SALADS AND SALAD DRESSINGS

JICAMA IN CITRUS DRESSING

Do you have any idea how fresh and crispy jicama is for a salad? I learned a lot about jicama (pronounced hi-ca.ma) when I attended Jane Butel's Southwestern Cooking School in Albuquerque and I haven't been able to get enough of it ever since. Try this and I know you'll like it. I did myself a favor and bought a mandoline to do julienne slicing. I had always wanted one and proudly boasted to a close friend that I had finally bought a mandoline. Her answer was, "I didn't know you knew how to play one." If you're a serious cook, do buy a mandoline. I use mine several times a week for slicing, chopping, julienning, or cubing. It saves me hours of time.

| 2 | jicamas–about 1 pound total weight | ½ | cup chopped toasted pecans |

Peel and cut jicamas into julienne strips. Put into a salad bowl with the pecans and dress with the following:

Citrus Dressing:

5	tablespoons lime juice	¾	teaspoon salt
3	tablespoons orange juice	2	teaspoons chopped fresh cilantro
1	tablespoon honey		

Mix together ingredients except for cilantro. Pour over jicama. Add cilantro and toss well. Serve at once over lettuce or watercress.

GREEN JACKET HOUSE SALAD

For a good many years, The Green Jacket Restaurant *in Macon garnered our patronage because all of us were crazy about their House Salad. Finally one day, one of the girls gathered enough courage to beg the delicious recipe. Thus we preserve it for posterity—and for you too because* The Green Jacket *is no longer in operation here.*

4	slices ripe tomato	1	head lettuce, broken into pieces
4	tablespoons oil	2	green onions, chopped
2	tablespoons red wine vinegar	4	teaspoons parsley
½	teaspoon oregano		Pita chips (New York style)
1	teaspoon monosodium glutamate		

Chop tomatoes. Add oil, vinegar and sprinkle with salt. Add oregano, monosodium glutamate (Accent), lettuce, onions and parsley. Break pita chips into salad. Toss lightly and serve immediately. Sprinkle with Parmesan. Do not add lettuce until ready to serve. No good leftover.

THE FIRST SATURDAY IN MAY

Attending the Kentucky Derby had to be a dream come true although "my horse" came in dead last. Well, I always had a special place in my heart for the underdog (I mean underhorse) anyway. The First Saturday in May (the date of the Derby) is a salad that Kentuckians like a lot and so will you.

4	large bunches of watercress	2	(14-ounce) cans heart of palm, drained and sliced
2	cups fresh mushrooms, sliced	1	cup almonds, sliced and toasted

Vinaigrette Dressing:

½	cup best grade olive oil	1	teaspoon dry mustard
2	tablespoons white wine vinegar	⅛	teaspoon fresh ground pepper
1	teaspoon salt		

Combine salad ingredients in a large bowl. Place dressing ingredients in a jar with a tight fitting lid; shake to blend. Toss salad and dressing just before serving. Place on individual chilled plates. Chill plates and forks in the freezer if you really want to do it right.

HELEN SMITH'S BROCCOLI SALAD

This great recipe, given to me by fellow bridge club member, Helen Smith, was the first one of its kind I ever tasted. I nearly flipped it was so good. Other recipes have come and gone but this one to me is the best. Some of the recipes call for bacon and raisins which make it taste great. Recently I have been making the salad with broccoli slaw, found in the prepackaged produce section. That makes it easier and quicker.

1	bunch broccoli–chopped very small	1	small onion–diced fine
1	head cauliflower–chopped very small		

Combine vegetables in salad bowl.

Dressing:

½	cup sugar	1	teaspoon salt
½	cup vinegar	1	cup mayonnaise

Put the ingredients into jar or bottle. Shake well before pouring over salad.

SEVEN LAYER SALAD

It comes back and comes back, causing periodic stirs in the culinary world just as returning fashions do in the world of style. This wonderful recipe not only has a super taste appeal, it is so attractive when made in a footed trifle bowl.

Layer in this order in a trifle bowl:

	Head of lettuce, torn in pieces	1	pint mayonnaise
1	cup diced celery	1	tablespoon sugar
½	cup diced onion	6	ounces Cheddar cheese, grated
½	cup chopped bell pepper	10	slices bacon, cooked and crumbled
1	can garden peas, 10 ounces	2	tablespoons Worcestershire sauce

Do not toss. Refrigerate 10 to 12 hours. When serving, dip from bottom of bowl to get all layers.

AVOCADOS ROMANOFF

Life doesn't get much better than when you're sitting out in the courtyard of the Court of the Two Sisters in New Orleans. There are strolling jazz musicians, who cut loose with the music for which New Orleans is famous. Don't complain if you wait a few minutes for your meal—the ambience is so terrific you need to take it all in before you start eating. It's in the French Quarter and such an integral part of it. Their recipe for Avocado Salad is terrific.

❖ Louise at computer with New Orleans poster ❖

3	ripe avocados
6	lettuce leaves
⅔	cup sour cream
1½-2	ounces black caviar
6	pimento strips

Halve the avocados, remove the pits, and peel. Place each avocado half on lettuce leaf, and fill each cavity with sour cream.

Circle the sour cream in each avocado with a line of caviar. Lay a pimento strip over the sour cream.

WILD INDIGENOUS IRONSTONE GREENS-MINERS LETTUCE, WILD PEA SHOOTS, AND WATERCRESS WITH CHARDONNAY PICKLED CALIFORNIA APRICOTS

When dining at Ironstone Vineyards in Murphys, California we were served the most memorable and delicious salad. It was billed on the menu as Wild Indigenous Ironstone Greens-Miners Lettuce, Wild Pea Shoots, and Watercress with Chardonnay Pickled California Apricots.

The real surprise though, was the ingenious way in which the salad was served. I have tried many times to recapture the container for the greens and I have finally mastered it. I cut strips of unsliced bread (have the bakery to slice the bread long-ways) about 3 inches high. Then I grease well a very clean tuna can. I place the strip around the inside of the can and join the edges together by pressing firmly with my fingers. Toast in oven. Remove; cool; and arrange salad greens inside it. Place a slice of apricot on either side.

SMUT'S SLAW

"With a name like Smuckers, it has to be good." With a name like Smut Frost, it is good. Smut, an unlikely name for a pretty little lady, gave me this recipe years ago and I have made it a hundred times—or more. I consider it one of my favorite recipes and you will too.

1	head cabbage, shredded	1½	cups sugar
1	large onion, thinly sliced	1	cup vinegar
1	cup celery chopped	1	teaspoon mustard seed
2	teaspoons salt	½	cup salad oil
	Black pepper to taste	1	teaspoon celery seed

Combine cabbage, onion, celery, salt and pepper. Heat sugar, vinegar, mustard seed, salad oil and celery seed to boil. Pour over cabbage. Cover and refrigerate. May be kept several days–covered. Add carrots and bell pepper for color.

SALADS AND SALAD DRESSINGS

TACO SALAD

It must have been late '60s or early '70s when our friends Beryl and Skinner Hicks visited from Hollywood with all the glamour and excitement you'd expect. Quite unexpectedly, though, they brought ingredients for Taco Salad and prepared it for us in our kitchen with the children just ogle-eyed. We had not had Tacos before and it was an immediate hit. We still like it so much.

1	package taco shells	1	medium tomato, chopped or cut into wedges
1	pound ground beef		
1	packet taco seasoning mix		Pitted ripe olives
1	medium head lettuce, torn into pieces		Picante sauce-salsa
4	ounces (1 cup) shredded Cheddar cheese		Sour cream and/or guacamole

Bake salad shells as specified on back of package. Prepare ground beef and taco seasoning mix as directed on packet for taco filling. Place each baked shell on a serving plate. Fill shells with lettuce. Top with warm seasoned meat, cheese, tomato, olives and salsa. Serve with sour cream and/or guacamole, if desired. Serve immediately.

LOLA'S BEAN SALAD

This might just be the very first recipe I ever requested from a hostess. Lola and Bill Tyson of Savannah had a country place near Wrightsville and shortly after we settled there in 1950 they invited us to their lodge for a fish fry. Lola was a great cook and served this "then new" dish along with the fried fish and cheese grits. I thought it was sensational then and although it's an old recipe now, it's still mighty good.

1	can waxed beans	1	large onion (chopped)
1	can green beans	1	large bell pepper (chopped)
1	can chili beans		

Heat:

1	cup garlic vinegar	½	teaspoon salt
¼	cup Wesson oil	½	teaspoon pepper
1	tablespoon sugar		

Pour heated mixture over beans, onions, and pepper. Let stand overnight.

WALDORF SALAD

You would think that I'd be satisfied to spend a relaxing weekend at the Waldorf-Astoria with my sister-in-law (1994) and not be concerning myself with hunting recipes. As you can see—not so. This is the Waldorf's famous salad from perhaps the most famous hotel in the world.

1	cup diced apple		4	lettuce leaves
1	cup diced celery		2	tablespoons walnuts or pecans
¼	cup mayonnaise			

Mix apples, celery and mayonnaise; pile in lettuce leaf on individual salad plates. Garnish with nutmeats.

ORIENTAL SALAD

Mary Ida Carpenter Phillips, from Soperton, originally from Guyton, and I grew up together, went off to college together, were in each others weddings and are still mighty good old friends. I'm proud of Mary Ida for a lot of reasons but do think it was outstanding that she was elected to serve out the term of her late husband, Pete Phillips, in the State Legislature.

Her politics didn't keep her from being a domesticated homemaker of the first order though, and on one occasion at a luncheon at her home she served this delicious salad that had all the guests sitting around the living room afterward, copying Oriental Salad.

1	can bean sprouts		1	small can Mandarin oranges
1	can bamboo shoots		1	medium onion, sliced
1	can water chestnuts, sliced		½	cup chopped celery
1	small jar pimento, chopped		½	cup chopped green pepper

Drain vegetables and combine in a large bowl with oranges. Heat and pour the following marinade over the vegetables and refrigerate before serving.

Marinade:

⅓	cup oil		1	teaspoon salt
¾	cup sugar		1	teaspoon pepper
⅔	cup vinegar			

SALADS AND SALAD DRESSINGS

JEWELED RICE SALAD

A trip with my friend Mary Jean Yates to see the beautifully decorated porches in Opelika, Alabama at Christmas time was one of the highlights of the entire holiday season. Two streets of lovely Victorian homes are lighted profusely and on every porch are Christmas scenes with life-sized figures all dressed in their holiday finery. An Opelika artist made a few life-sized figures for her home decorations one Christmas and having one left over, she sneaked it to her neighbor's porch. That's how it all began and it's still going strong as far as I know. Call the Chamber of Commerce to be sure. And be sure to check out some of the local restaurants. We had this delicious salad in Opelika but I don't remember the name of the place even though we went back the next year and took our entire garden club.

For the dressing:

3	tablespoons olive oil
6	tablespoons orange juice
1	tablespoon grated orange zest
1	tablespoon grated lemon zest

1	teaspoon salt
½	teaspoon paprika
¼	cup finely chopped fresh cilantro

For the salad:

1	cup frozen peas
3½	cups cooked white rice
⅔	cup sliced green olives

½	red bell pepper, chopped
½	yellow bell pepper, chopped

To make the dressing: Combine the olive oil, orange juice, orange zest, lemon zest, salt, paprika, and cilantro in a bowl. Beat with a whisk until combined.

To make the salad: Thaw the peas in a colander under hot running water. Combine the rice, peas, green olives, red pepper, and yellow pepper in a serving bowl; mix well. Add the dressing just before serving; toss gently. Serve from the bowl or on individual salad plates.

JAPANESE NOODLE SALAD

Though it's now all gone due to the September 11, 2001 tragedy, Windows on the World *in the* World Trade Center *will remain in my memory forever. Along with several friends from Dublin, we made reservations at the 107-story-high restaurant for the theater seating—early in the evening. The meal was truly marvelous but the view from that awfully high vantage took my breath away. Beautiful buildings, bridges, water, skyline, people crawling like ants on the street, the excitement of New York all came into focus so high in the sky. I yearned to be there when the lights came on in the city and surely enough we lingered long enough over coffee (which I don't even drink) to see the first light and then soon a thousand more and soon a million more. It was one of life's most memorable experiences.*

This is Windows on the World's Japanese Noodle Salad—a real keeper for so many reasons.

½	ounce (about 6) dried Japanese mushrooms*	1	tablespoon rice vinegar or to taste
8	ounces udon (Japanese noodles)*	¼	teaspoon crushed dried hot red pepper flakes
3	tablespoons sesame oil	2	tablespoons chopped green onion
3	tablespoons Japanese soy sauce*	1	tablespoon chopped fresh cilantro (optional)

Soak mushrooms in warm water 1 hour. Squeeze to remove water; discard stems and thinly slice caps. Cook noodles in boiling salted water just until al dente. Drain and rinse with cold water. Combine mushrooms, oil, soy sauce, vinegar and peppers in same pan used for noodles and warm through over medium heat. Add noodles, toss to cook and cook just until heated. Garnish with green onion and cilantro, if desired.

*Available in oriental markets.

MARINATED RICE SALAD

❖ Lynn Cass and Joni Woolf (owners of Macon Magazine) with Louise and Jim Fobel ❖

Several years ago I prepared a six-course dinner for charity bought at an auction by Beverly and Ed Olson. My friend, Jim Fobel, who has been the test kitchen director for Food and Wine *in New York; who has written numerous delightful cookbooks and who also wrote for* Gourmet *came from New York to help me. Well, actually he was in Atlanta at the time. We had a preliminary cooking class in my kitchen, where Jim demonstrated to the guests the first two courses. It was so much fun and the deal was that we'd get up early the next morning to head to Savannah to show Jim the lovely, historical coastal city. When I knocked on his door and said, "Jim, you'd better get up if we're driving to Savannah," the most pitiful voice you ever heard said, "Louise, do we have to go? I don't think I can make it."*

And I couldn't either but I was going anyway. What a break! What a break! (We did get to Savannah a couple of years later.)

This is Beverly Olson's, not Jim's, recipe for Marinated Rice Salad. This is a recipe that can be made a little ahead and is delicious with any meat and side dishes.

1	cup uncooked rice	¼	cup finely chopped onion
6	tablespoons olive oil	1	(2½-ounce) jar sliced mushrooms, drained
3	tablespoons vinegar	½	cup sliced black olives
1	teaspoon salt	½	cup sliced green olives, stuffed with pimento
	Ground pepper to taste		Tomato slices or wedges for garnish, if desired
1	teaspoon tarragon		
⅓	cup chopped green pepper		
¼	cup chopped parsley		

Cook rice according to directions. Combine oil, vinegar, salt, pepper and tarragon. Pour over hot rice and mix well. Cool. Add green pepper, parsley, onion, mushrooms, and olives. Cover and refrigerate at least 4 hours before serving. Just before serving, add tomato slices to garnish, if desired.

ESTELLE CHESTER'S POTATO SALAD

Estelle Chester was one of Wrightsville, Georgia's finest cooks and left a great legacy of wonderful recipes that she always sweetly shared. This recipe is truly one of the all-time great potato salads. I never take it anywhere that I don't get rave reviews and many requests for the recipe. It serves 25 or more people.

5	pounds red potatoes (boil and then peel and dice)	2	cups carrots (coarsely grated)
1	cup chopped onions (chopped fine)	3	cups chopped celery
2	cups chopped bell pepper	1	quart mayonnaise
1	jar olives sliced (10 to 12 ounces)		

Mix together in a very large bowl.

Dressing:

1	tablespoon salt	1	tablespoon celery seed
1	tablespoon pepper	3	tablespoons vinegar
1	tablespoon sugar		

Combine all ingredients and toss with potato mixture.

ARTICHOKE-RICE SALAD

This salad is a Macon favorite and since I introduced it to my sister-in-law while in the mountains, it's probably now an Augusta favorite too. Serve it with shrimp or chicken and you really don't need much more other than a garnish or two on the plate. Maybe a deviled egg or carrot sticks.

2	cups chicken broth	½	cup mayonnaise
1	cup rice	½	teaspoon curry powder or 1 teaspoon dill weed
¼	cup diced green onion		
¼	cup sliced pimento-stuffed olives	1	(8-ounce) can sliced water chestnuts, drained (optional)
2	(6-ounce) jars marinated artichoke hearts, sliced		

Bring chicken broth to boil: stir in rice. Simmer, covered, until done. Cool slightly. Combine with remaining ingredients; chill thoroughly. (One 8-ounce package prepared chicken-flavor rice mix may be used, omitting butter, instead of chicken broth and rice.)

FROZEN CHERRY SALAD

For 19 years, my sweet friend Carolyn Crayton, masterminded Macon's Cherry Blossom Festival, one of the major festivals in the nation. She always seems to be in a happy jovial mood and has been Macon's ambassador all over the nation and in many foreign countries. She has received more awards and accolades than, perhaps, anybody in Macon. You wouldn't think she has time to even think about recipes—but she does. Here's a simple one—and simply delicious from Carolyn. And of course, what else, cherries.

16	marshmallows	12	maraschino cherries, cut up
1	small can crushed pineapple	½	pint whipping cream
½	cup chopped pecans		

Melt marshmallows in top of double boiler. Add pineapple, nuts, and cherries. Cool. Whip cream; fold together and freeze.

FROSTY SALAD LOAF

Clarence Clay, one of our members' husband, accuses our one-table bridge group, the McJaals, of having at least two birthdays each per year. It does seem that we celebrate frequently but this is how we test and swap our new recipes. We always have a wonderful luncheon. This recipe is one that Ann Oxley served at my house for Joyce Clay's birthday in August, 1999. It is a real keeper.

1	(8-ounce) package cream cheese	1	(1-pound) can apricots, drained
1	cup sour cream	1	small can crushed pineapple, drained
¼	cup sugar	2	cups miniature marshmallows
¼	teaspoon salt		Few drops red food coloring
1½	cups pitted dark sweet cherries, drained		

Let cream cheese soften and beat until fluffy. Stir in sour cream, sugar, salt; then fruits and marshmallow. Add red food coloring to tint pale pink. Freeze. Can be molded in Bundt pan.

CORNED BEEF SALAD

This great recipe was given to me by my close friend, Mary Helen Schwartz, who is an excellent cook and a very gracious hostess. She says it makes the rounds every few years and everybody is always thrilled to rediscover it. This can be a main course.

1   (3-ounce) package lemon Jell-O dissolved in:
1   cup boiling water–add:
¾   cup cold water–chill

Add:

1 (12-ounce) can corned beef, shredded	1 small jar chopped pimentos, drained
½ cup chopped celery	2 hard-cooked eggs, chopped
1 small onion, grated	¾ cup mayonnaise

Mix thoroughly–let set and enjoy!

RICH'S CHICKEN SALAD AMANDINE

Only those who are too young, have no memory of the Magnolia Room at Rich's in Atlanta. It just couldn't have been as perfect as we thought it was. Dressed in high heels, hats and white kid gloves, we descended on this Atlanta institution with almost more verve and excitement than we had for the shopping.

Two of the most popular menu items were Chicken Salad served with Frozen Fruit Salad. It was good then and it's good now. Call up the girls and invite them over for a nice nostalgic surprise. Always be sure to serve both salads on the same plate.

3½ pounds chicken breasts	2 cups mayonnaise
6 stalks celery, diced	½ cup pickle relish
2 tablespoons salt	Garnish: ½ cup toasted almond slices
½ tablespoon white pepper	

To make chicken salad: Boil chicken breasts in lightly salted water until meat is tender. Reserve stock for future use. Let chicken cool. Separate meat from bones and skin by pulling. Leave chicken in medium-size strips. Toss remaining ingredients, except almonds, with chicken meat. Cover and refrigerate until serving. Garnish with almonds and serve with Frozen Fruit Salad. The recipes are always kept together.

FROZEN FRUIT SALAD

1	(8-ounce) package cream cheese		1	(26-ounce) can fruit cocktail, well drained
½	cup powdered sugar		1	(13-ounce) can crushed pineapple, well drained
⅓	cup mayonnaise			
2	teaspoons vanilla extract		2	cups miniature marshmallows
1	(6½-ounce) can sliced peaches, well drained		½	cup whipping cream, whipped
½	cup maraschino cherry halves, well drained			Few drops food coloring, if desired

To make frozen fruit salad: Put cream cheese in mixer. Add powdered sugar and blend in mayonnaise. Add vanilla extract. Fold in fruit and marshmallows gently. Whip cream separately and gently fold into fruit mixture. Add food coloring if desired. Ladle into large paper soufflé cups or muffin liners. Freeze immediately. Defrost about 15 minutes before serving. Do not allow to get soft. Remove soufflé cups or muffin liners before serving.

WEST INDIES SALAD

It was fun to stop for lunch years ago with our friends, Drs. George and Nell Lane from Thomasville, at a restaurant in Biloxi, Mississippi that extended on jeddies out into the Gulf. President Gerald Ford had preceded us there and all the details of his first visit were hot on the lips of the restaurateur and staff. The Navy Seals had swum underneath while the President had his meal.

More impressive than all that, though, was the West Indies Salad that is one of my all time favorites. No, to my great disappointment they would not even begin to tell me about it. Years later, after a 20-year search, I found the identical recipe and I treasure it exceedingly. This is perhaps the finest use of crabmeat among the thousands of excellent recipes. Do try it and save it 'cause those folks in Biloxi aren't going to give you a copy for sure.

2	cups crabmeat		1	tablespoon Worcestershire sauce
1	large onion chopped finely			Salt and pepper to taste
1	tablespoon parsley		½	cup oil
1	teaspoon Accent		½	cup vinegar
	Dash of Tabasco sauce			Avocado or tomato slices

Place crabmeat in a bowl. Cover with chopped onion. Add seasonings and pour the oil and vinegar over. Toss to mix. Cover and refrigerate for at least 4 hours or overnight. Serve on avocado or tomato slices.

GRILLED CHICKEN SALAD

What was the old commercial—"When so and so speaks, everybody listens?" I don't remember who was speaking—was it E. F. Hutton? Anyway, when Becky Bowdre cooks, everybody pays attention. A college classmate of mine, Becky has made triumphant culinary strides since college days of making Prune Whip in the home ec. lab. She is one of the area's most respected cooks, and when she gives me a recipe that she said she got from another of the area's most trusted cooks, Claire Smith, I do prize it with all my might. Not only that Becky comments, "This is the best ever." It's fabulous—give it a try.

½ cup olive oil

1 tablespoon fresh lemon juice

1 teaspoon Dijon mustard

Salt to taste

Pepper to taste

2¼ pounds skinned, boneless chicken breasts

½ pound asparagus, stems trimmed and peeled

1 medium red bell pepper, cut into 1½x¼-inch matchsticks

1 medium yellow bell pepper, cut same

1 small red onion, halved lengthwise and thinly sliced lengthwise

2 teaspoons finely chopped rosemary

½ cup oil packed sun-dried tomatoes, patted dry, coarsely chopped

3 ounces water chestnuts, drained and sliced

½ pound Gorgonzola or Stilton cheese, crumbled

½ cup finely diced country ham

3 heads Bibb lettuce

In large bowl, whisk 3 tablespoons of oil with lemon juice, mustard and salt and pepper. Add chicken. Turn. Marinate and let stand at room temperature 1 hour. Blanch asparagus until crisp tender. Drain; rinse in cold water; drain, and cut in to 1½-inch pieces. Grill chicken about 4 minutes each side. Heat 2 tablespoons oil in large skillet. Add bell peppers and onion and cook until tender. Cut chicken into ¼-inch slices. Place in bowl. Add rosemary and toss. Stir in bell peppers, asparagus, tomatoes, water chestnuts, cheese and ham. Add 3 tablespoons oil and toss. Serve on lettuce.

EDIE FERGUSON'S BOMBAY SHRIMP À LA GREYFIELD

On a very special deep-sea-fishing trip, our crowd stayed at the wonderful old Greyfield Inn on Cumberland Island, off the coast of Georgia. The inn was the former home of the great philanthropist Andrew Carnegie and was run by his granddaughter Edie Ferguson and her husband.

One night at dinner, after a day in the hot sun, we were served this marvelous shrimp dish that I thought was about the best thing I'd ever tasted. I asked Edie for the recipe but got little or no response. As we were saying our final good byes and preparing to load the luggage on the ferryboat to go back to the mainland, Edie surreptitiously slipped the recipe into my hand.

I have treasured it ever since and would list it as one of my top ten all-time recipes. Although the recipe calls for 10 pounds of shrimp I always only use five. It works just as well. I make it in a fish mold and always try to garnish it as beautifully as it deserves.

5	pounds shrimp		1	grated onion (use juice)
	Garlic powder		1	finely chopped bell pepper
	Whole cloves		1	cup Hellmann's mayonnaise
3	cups cooked rice			Curry powder to taste
2	stalks celery (cut small)			

Cook shrimp 3 or 4 minutes in boiling water with garlic powder and cloves. Drain. Cool. Chop or break into pieces. Mix all other ingredients with shrimp, reserving a few whole shrimp for garnishing. Put into a fish mold or other salad mold and let stand in refrigerator overnight. Turn out onto a bed of lettuce. Garnish with shrimp, quartered tomatoes and cucumber slices. Makes an excellent main dish for a summer supper.

SHRIMP SALAD

As popular as Rich's Tea Room was, in downtown Atlanta, it didn't take away from another institution, The Frances Virginia Tea Room. Ladies (and men too) dressed to the nines to visit this popular restaurant, which served delicious Southern food. They had many menu items that you wanted to order but their Shrimp Salad was outstanding.

2½ cups cooked shrimp, cut into bite-size pieces	Salt and pepper
1¼ cups diced celery	Iceberg lettuce
¾-1 cup Special Salad Dressing (see recipe below)	Tomato aspic rings
	Jumbo size green stuffed olives

Mix shrimp and celery with enough special salad dressing to hold shape. Taste. Season with salt and pepper. Serve on crisp lettuce. Garnish with tomato aspic ring and green stuffed olives.

To make Special Salad Dressing: 1 cup mayonnaise, ¼ cup Durkee's famous sauce, ½ cup sandwich spread. Mix together well.

CRANBERRY CHRISTMAS CANDLES

Reluctantly Uncle Osgood Shearouse and Aunt Virginia moved to McLean, Virginia when the great Southern bought out the Central of Georgia. I think he made the transition well. He has been so diligent in keeping in touch with Mother through the years and all the nieces and nephews just adore him. In 1978 he sent Mother the VIP Cookbook that has recipes from many high-ranking Washington dignitaries— (of course we think he is the highest ranking.) This recipe from VIP is unique and delicious and adds to the decoration of the table. Be sure to save up some 6 ounce fruit juice cans before you begin.

1 (16-ounce) can whole berry cranberry sauce	¼ teaspoon salt
3 ounce package red, yellow or orange fruit-flavored gelatin	1 tablespoon lemon juice
	½ cup mayonnaise
1 cup boiling water	1 apple, peeled and diced
	½ cup chopped walnuts

Heat cranberry sauce, strain, set berries aside. Dissolve gelatin in hot juice and water. Add salt and lemon juice. Chill until thickened enough to mound slightly when dropped from a spoon. Beat in real mayonnaise with rotary beater until light and fluffy. Fold in cranberries, fruit, and nuts. Divide mixture evenly into 8 (6-ounce) fruit juice cans. Chill 4 hours or longer, unmold. Garnish with salad greens. To flame; insert small birthday candle, about ¾ of length, into top of cranberry candle. Light just before guests are seated.

VEGETABLES AND SIDE DISHES

Louise prepares English Fare

Louise and Carol prepare demonstration for Macon's Olympic event ~ "Georgia on my Plate."

State Trooper David Damino and Louise cook in White House kitchen.

RISOTTO, MILAN STYLE

Jo Patterson from Millen, Georgia, graduated from Old Wesleyan Conservatory when I was at the college as a sophomore. She was strikingly beautiful and even went on to have a successful modeling career with Vogue in Paris and Rome. The fairy tale progresses as Jo marries an Italian Count and moves into their 18th century hunting lodge near Rome. Jo and her close Italian friend, Anna Cornetto, decided to study cooking with the best cook in Italy and subsequently opened their own school, Lo Scaldavivande, in Rome. They have collected all their wonderful recipes into Italian Cooking in the Grand Tradition. *Jo returned to her alma mater for its Sesquicentennial and presented a wonderful cooking school right in the Taylor Hall Amphitheater. Of course, I was there, on the front row. This is one of the keepsake recipes Jo prepared for us at the school.*

6	tablespoons unsalted butter
1½	ounces bone marrow, finely chopped
½	medium onion, minced
1	pound Arborio rice
¾	cup dry white wine
½-1	teaspoon saffron threads

About 5 cups simmering beef or chicken broth

6 tablespoons freshly grated Parmesan cheese, plus additional cheese for serving

Freshly ground black pepper

Melt 4 tablespoons of the butter with the marrow in a saucepan large enough to cook the rice, making sure the marrow dissolves. Add the onion and sauté gently until soft and transparent, about 5 minutes. Add the rice and stir until every grain is coated and shiny about 3 or 4 minutes. Add the wine and keep stirring until it evaporates. Add the remaining hot broth to the rice, ½ cup at a time, stirring constantly, waiting until the broth is absorbed before adding more. The risotto should always be moist. After about 15 minutes, taste the rice. It should be al dente. Add the saffron dissolved in 2 tablespoons of the hot broth, stir, and cook for 3 minutes, adding broth as necessary and stirring constantly. Remove from the heat when still moist and stir in the remaining 2 tablespoons butter and the 6 tablespoons Parmesan. Cover tightly and allow the risotto to set for 3 minutes. Turn out onto a heated serving dish and serve with freshly ground black pepper and more Parmesan as needed.

Note: The risotto should be, as we say in Italy, al onda, or wavy. It should be served slightly moist, not dry.

CURRY RICE

My friend and fellow bridge club member, Pat Benton, shared this delicious recipe with me. In her always unassuming manner, Pat wanted me to be sure to know the recipe was actually from Tea Time at the Masters—the Augusta Junior League award-winning cookbook. This recipe goes beautifully with lamb.

3	cups cooked rice	1	(4-ounce) can mushrooms, drained
½	stick butter	¼	cup ripe olives, chopped
1	teaspoon curry powder	½	cup raisins
1½	teaspoons salt	½	cup almonds, slivered

Combine all ingredients and heat on low.

CHARLESTON PARSLEY RICE SQUARES

We were on that crazy road outside Chattanooga where the signs say "Lane for Runaway Trucks" and the sandbags are piled nearby to stop the trucks that are so unlucky as to lose their brakes. It's enough to unnerve even the most stalwart, so I diverted attention by talking about my favorite subject: recipes.

It wasn't hard to get response from the other girls in the car too because I have a notion that the thought of a runaway truck on a mountain road didn't soothe them at all either.

Carolyn Henderson offered us Charleston Parsley Rice Squares, and because it sounded exactly what I wanted to serve Friday night, I pinned her down to be sure she had it all right. "Exactly," she reassured me. "And if you think it sounds like too much parsley, don't worry; it's not."

This is pretty when cut into squares and served as a side dish with almost any meat or seafood. It's terrific with shrimp.

3	cups cooked rice	1½	cups milk
1	cup cut parsley	¾	cup cheese
3	eggs, beaten		Small onion, grated

Mix all ingredients. Put into a 2-quart buttered casserole. Bake at 350 degrees for about 40 minutes.

RED BEANS AND RICE-LY YOURS

I need to check to see it it's still there. There was a place in the French Quarter in New Orleans called Buster Holme's at 721 Burgundy, and it was as much a part of New Orleans as Jackson Square. Louis Armstrong used to drop by regularly to eat Red Beans and Rice and shoot the breeze, and Vincent Price wouldn't go to the city without seeing Buster. I had anticipated my visit with great enthusiasm which quickly dimmed as we approached the entrance.

The place was more or less a shack; there was a screen door full of holes that had been punched through during the years, and on the screen was the fading paint of a sign that advertised Holsum Bread. No, I don't think so. I had more in mind sort of a Commander's Palace or Antiones. It was too late! Someone greeted us at the door, and not wanting to seem aloof, we smiled and entered—with great trepidation.

And now the rest of the story: That famous Red Beans and Rice that Buster started serving in 1944 for 25 cents a plate was about the best meal I'd tasted in all of New Orleans even though the price had gone up to a dollar. It's a classic. It's a must. It's legendary, and I was so glad I had braved the situation and gone on it.

Later, a friend from California, even more fastidious than I, called me to get names of great New Orleans restaurants for their upcoming visit. I carefully explained but nevertheless recommended Buster Holmes. I wish you could have heard Beryl's review of the restaurant. It was priceless. Here's Buster's famous recipe that traditionally was served on Monday in New Orleans because that was "wash day" and folks had to serve something that could cook on the stove without much doing.

2	pounds red beans	1	cup tomato ketchup
2	tablespoons bacon fat	1	tablespoon vinegar
½	pound pickled pork, diced (or a commercial jar of pickled ham hocks, diced)		Salt and pepper to taste
		1	teaspoon Tabasco pepper sauce
2	cloves garlic, minced		Sprig of fresh thyme or pinch of dried thyme
1	medium onion, chopped	1	cup lean ham, diced (or 1 ham bone)

Pick over beans. Wash and soak them overnight in water to cover. When ready to cook, drain off all the water. In a heavy pot, heat the bacon fat and brown the diced pickled pork or pickled ham hock. Add the garlic and onion and cook for about 10 minutes. Add the beans, tomato ketchup, vinegar, salt, and pepper to taste, Tabasco and thyme. Cover with fresh cold water, making sure that there is enough water, as the beans must cook thoroughly. After the water has come to a boil, reduce heat and simmer the beans until they are semicooked–about 1 hour. Mash about a cupful of the beans and return them to the pot. Add the diced ham or the ham bone and cook slowly for 2 or 3 hours or until the beans are thoroughly cooked and the sauce is thick and creamy. As they say in New Orleans, red beans need no thickening because they got it in themselves. Serve with fluffy Louisiana boiled rice and garnish with fried ham, slices of fried country sausage or pork chops. Also serve chopped onions, vinegar and Tabasco pepper sauce on the side, and lots of New Orleans French bread.

SAVANNAH RED RICE

My love for Rose Crockett McRae goes way back to 1945 when she was a sophomore at Wesleyan and I was a green-as-grass, scared stiff, ungainly and naive freshman. It was customary that the sophomores take on witch—like maneuvers on Rat Night and do their best to intimidate and demean the lowly freshmen. I was unsure enough of my 16-year-old-self in this strange new world, among all those older girls, without having mean girls in black calling me a rat. (Actually I could handle it—I just like to sound pitiful.)

I can't remember too many of the "girls in black", but I'll always remember Rose Crockett who quietly reassured us that all was well and we would survive intact.

Rose and I have remained friends, with her hometown being in Dublin where I lived shortly after my marriage in 1950 and where my daughter's family lives. Now Rose lives in Savannah, and once in a great while we make contact, always joyously. At one point Rose sent me a copy of Savannah Style saying that she enjoys it a lot. I enjoy it too and especially want to share a most typical Savannah recipe, Red Rice. I was reared on Red Rice as was almost everybody else in and around Savannah.

This is the recipe that someone always prepared when we had church dinners or family reunions. It travels well and is real good at room temperature.

¼	pound bacon	3	teaspoons salt
½	cup onion, chopped	¼	teaspoon pepper
2	cups rice, uncooked	⅛	teaspoon Tabasco sauce
2	(16-ounce) cans tomatoes, crushed		

In large frying pan, fry bacon until crisp; remove from pan. Crumble and reserve. Sauté onions in bacon grease until tender. Add rice, tomatoes, crumbled bacon and seasonings. Cook on top of stove for 10 minutes. Pour into large, greased casserole dish, cover tightly and bake at 350 degrees for 1 hour.

VEGETABLES AND SIDE DISHES

RUSSIAN PILAU

By a convoluted route, a 1933 cookbook is in my possession, and it is one of my prized possessions. Called The Savannah Cookbook, *my Aunt Marie gave her copy to another niece Dorothy Dious in Tampa. That was long before she knew of my interest in cooking—in fact I was a small child because Dorothy is much older than I.*

In 1989 when Dorothy was "minimizing," she asked if I would like to have the cookbook. "Is a ten pound robin fat?", as my husband used to jokingly reply to a ridiculous question. Of course, of course, of course.

This Pilau recipe is so-o-o good. When I was a child, we referred to pilau as "purlow." And in this cookbook I found this notation: "Many of the old cooks call pilau perlew; and we are apt to smile indulgently and explain with raised eyebrows that they mean "pilau," but we would not feel quite so patronizing about it if we realized their authority." In looking over an old South Carolina cookbook which specializes in rice dishes, I found this spelled "purlow", so perhaps our admiring imitators are not so far afield after all.

Don't be misled by the title of this recipe. It's just as "Savannah" as it gets.

1 cup raw rice	2 cups of cold meat or shrimp or fish or crabs
1 large tablespoon butter	Salt and pepper to taste
1 teaspoon minced onion	1 pint tomatoes (canned or fresh)

Wash rice well and drain. Put butter in large frying pan and when melted cook onion in it until a light brown, then add raw rice and stir constantly in onion and butter until brown, being careful not to burn. Season. Then add tomatoes, one pint of hot water, and when absorbed another pint of boiling water, and cook, covered, until rice is tender–about 30 minutes. Add chopped meat or fish and let simmer slowly a few minutes before serving.

ORANGE RICE

This rice is wonderful to serve with the Rock Cornish Game Hens with Orange Sauce. (See Main Dishes section.) Actually it goes with many kinds of poultry and meats but especially poultry.

⅔   cup celery with leaves, chopped

2   tablespoons onion, finely chopped

¼   cup butter

1½ cups water

2   tablespoons orange rind, grated

1   cup orange juice

1   teaspoon salt

⅛   teaspoon dried thyme

1   cup raw long-grain rice

Sauté celery and onion in butter until tender. Add water, orange rind, juice, salt and thyme. Bring to a boil. Slowly add rice. Reduce heat and cook covered for 25 minutes or until rice is tender.

GRITS WITH CREAM AND CHEESE

At a lovely party at 103 West in Atlanta (one of its finest restaurants), the chefs prepared recipes from Nathalie Dupree's latest cookbook to honor her at the celebration. Everything was good, but the Grits with Cream and Cheese must have been brought in from another planet. It was absolutely fantastic. It is recommended to be served at dinner, rather than breakfast. It's a very special dish you'll always remember. The thing to forget is the calories and fat grams.

½   cup quick grits

2   cups heavy cream

2-3 tablespoons butter

    Salt

    Freshly ground white pepper

½   cup freshly grated Parmesan, Swiss, or Monterey Jack cheese

Place the grits and cream in a heavy saucepan, stirring. Cook the grits according to package directions, substituting cream for water. Stir occasionally, being careful they don't burn. If grits begin to separate and turn lumpy, add water to keep them creamy. Remove from the heat, taste, add the butter and salt and pepper to taste, then stir in the cheese. May be made ahead and reheated over low heat or in a microwave.

BAKED GRITS WITH CAVIAR

This is a favorite from a favorite, Martha Thornton of Macon and Milledgeville. You would never know that Martha is considered one of our state's most astute business women when you see her turned loose in the kitchen.

She served this spectacular dish at a supper for jazz musicians who were in Macon to play at the Grand Opera House for Macon's Cherry Blossom Festival. The musicians who didn't know doodly about grits went away believers and even requested the recipe to take back to New York. Martha says the grits shouldn't be too firm when you mix. And the recipe serves 12 people very generously.

2 cups quick grits

1 cup milk

4 eggs, beaten

1 (3-ounce) package cream cheese

6 tablespoons butter

1 pound bacon, cooked and crumbled

1 (8-ounce) can water chestnuts, chopped and drained

1 (8-ounce) mushroom pieces, drained

½-¾ cup chopped pecans

3 (4-ounce) cans red caviar

Cook grits according to directions. Add milk, eggs, cream cheese, and butter. Blend well. Stir in bacon, mushrooms, water chestnuts and pecans; blend well. Spoon into greased shallow 2-quart pan. Bake at 350 degrees for 20 to 30 minutes. Spread caviar on top and serve hot.

BARLEY CASSEROLE

Nina McCunniff surprised us when the bridge club was vacationing at Hilton Head by having all of us over to her house for dinner. Nina was a former member of the bridge club (before my time). I was the only one who really didn't know her well. I had met her once when she stopped in a bridge meeting to say "hello", and I had heard so many times what a lovely hostess and wonderful cook she is. I was really looking forward to dinner at her house on Barnacle Road where she lived with her retired military husband.

The dinner far exceeded all our wildest dreams, and it was true—she is a lovely hostess—gladly giving us a tour of her beautiful beach home and sharing with us so many interesting facets of her life on the island. We wanted to stay all night and almost did.

Since barley is not an item on most of our grocery lists, I was intrigued with this dish that she served. It was delicious-and just as a lovely hostess would do, she provided all of us with copies to take home.

1	cup barley	½	can water
½	stick butter	1	package (½ pound) sliced mushrooms
1½	cans French onion soup		

Cook barley in butter in frying pan until brown. Add all other ingredients and cook for a minute or so. Pour into a greased casserole dish. Cover and bake at 350 degrees for 30 to 40 minutes.

PEMBROKESHIRE GARLIC POTATOES

One of my life's most moving experiences took place on a yacht cruising the Mediterranean. No. A private jet flying to Monaco. No. A chauffeur-driven limousine on the way to the Kennedy Center. No. We were on a rattling old bus that was coming into a section of road in the Welsh countryside that was completely covered overhead with green trees; the sun was setting and I was a long way from home. Everybody on the bus suddenly started singing How Great Thou Art, *and God spoke to me just as surely as if He had been sharing my seat on the bus. Well, of course, He was sharing it. It was something I'll never forget.*

I'll never forget either the good friend I met, Rosie Holmes from Treetop, Wales, and how we corresponded for years. Rosie and I like to swap recipes, and this is one that she said came from an inn in Pembrokeshire, Wales.

1½ pounds potatoes (about 3 medium) peeled	12 ounces Cheddar cheese, grated
½ teaspoon salt	⅔ cup whipping cream
Freshly ground pepper	4 garlic cloves, crushed

Combine potatoes in large saucepan with enough water to cover and bring to boil over high heat. Reduce heat and simmer until potatoes are tender, about 20 minutes. Drain well; let stand until cool. Preheat oven to 350 degrees. Slice potatoes thinly and arrange in lightly buttered shallow baking dish. Sprinkle with salt and pepper. Top with ⅓ of cheese. Pour over ½ of cream. Top with ⅓ of remaining cheese. Pour over remaining cream and top with remaining cheese. Sprinkle garlic evenly over top. Bake until browned and crisp, about 40 minutes.

SWEET POTATO GRATIN

One of the most elusive recipes I've ever pursued has been the Sweet Potato Gratin as served at the Idle Hour Country Club in Macon. At our garden club's Christmas party there, this sweet potato dish was on the menu, and everybody was sampling and smacking and wondering what on earth could make a simple sweet potato so out-of-this world delicious.

I checked every source, even bribed a waitress later to see if she could talk the chef into sending out the list of ingredients. I knew I could handle it from there, but I knew the minute I saw it, that the recipe was not the one I wanted.

One night while having dinner there with a friend, the manager came to our table and said, "Is there anything I can get for you?"

He shouldn't have asked. I was too quick to ask him for the sweet potato dish served at Hill and Dale Garden Club's Christmas banquet. He agreed and disappeared. In a few minutes I noticed he was having dinner with the assistant manager, and my hope for the recipe waned tremendously.

Well, I had done all I could at the risk of being obnoxious, so I determined not to pursue my quest any further. As the manager started to leave the dining room, he saw us and snapped his finger, indicating he had forgotten. Thus, in just a second, the highly coveted recipe was in my hands, and I never intend to let it go.

Here is the recipe for enough to serve about six people. Of course, I have had to adapt the recipe from the chef's rendition.

1	large sweet potato	⅛	teaspoon granulated garlic
4	ounces brown sugar	4	eggs–(I use 2)
4	ounces honey	1	pint heavy cream (I use much less)

Slice potato very thin and place some slices in bottom of a buttered casserole dish. Sprinkle brown sugar and drizzle honey sparingly over potatoes. Sprinkle on some of the granulated garlic (or garlic salt). Layer again and again until all potatoes are used. Beat eggs lightly, combine with cream and pour all over the potatoes. Put casserole dish in a pan of water and bake at 325 degrees for about an hour or until potatoes test tender-done.

SWEET POTATO SOUFFLÉ

Blanche Flanders Farley has always been one of my most admired people. There's hardly anything Blanche cannot do and do well. She's a poet and writer and has edited the dearest little book called Like a Summer Peach. *I treasure my copy that includes wonderful poetry and old southern recipes to whet your appetite. Blanche has a marvelous poem, simply called "Soufflé", in which she paints a picture of making Sweet Potato Soufflé for her daughter. Then a Sweet Potato Soufflé recipe is included. What fun the book is.*

3	cups sweet potatoes, cooked and mashed	½	cup milk
¾	cup sugar	½	cup margarine, melted
2	eggs		One bag of large marshmallows

Mix all ingredients except marshmallows and place in buttered casserole. Bake at 350 degrees for 40 minutes. Remove from oven and cover with large marshmallows. Bake until marshmallows are a golden brown.

YATES APPLES

Twice I have used Yates Apples in cooking demonstrations—once at Riverside United Methodist Church in 1992 and again at the Courier Herald Cooking School in 1995. Many times I have used them for dishes at home, and always I just stand back and smile because they are so simply beautiful. They are great around the Thanksgiving turkey and gorgeous around a wheel of cheese. They're really well worth the little trouble that you go to, and you, too, will stand back and smile. (You might frown a bit trying to find the Yates apples, but I always find them in the mountains around the first of November, and they keep beautifully in the refrigerator. Sometimes they even appear in the supermarkets around Thanksgiving).

Peel and core apples with apple corer. Put apples in a pot and just cover with water. Add about ½ cup sugar for every dozen apples. (The apples are small.) Add approximately 1 tablespoon of red food coloring and about ½ cup of cinnamon red hots candy. Stew over medium heat only until barely tender. Drain (save liquid if desired for another batch). Drain apples on paper towels. Stuff with a mixture of 3 ounces cream cheese, ½ cup Major Gray's Chutney and ¾ teaspoon curry powder. They are prettier if stuffing is piped with a pastry tube. Use green galax leaves if available with the apples.

MEXICAN FIESTA BISCUIT BAKE

It was my good fortune to have just returned from the Pillsbury Bake-Off® contest with this wonderful recipe in tow when I suddenly remembered I was having 15 people for brunch on Saturday. I knew this recipe was good because I had tasted it in San Francisco at the Bake-Off® contest, so I did not have to do a taste-testing. Combined with link sausage, some fresh fruit and a few other good dishes, this was just super.

2	tablespoons margarine or butter
1	(17.3-ounce) can Pillsbury® Grands!® Refrigerated Buttermilk Biscuits
1	(10.8-ounce) can Pillsbury® Grands!® Refrigerated Buttermilk Biscuits
1	(16-ounce) jar (1¾ cups) medium thick and chunky salsa
12	ounces (3 cups) shredded Monterey Jack cheese
½	cup chopped green bell pepper
½	cup sliced green onions
1	(2¼-ounce) can sliced ripe olives, drained
1	cup salsa, if desired

Heat oven to 375 degrees. Melt margarine in oven in 13x9-inch glass baking dish or non-aluminum baking pan. Tilt evenly to coat dish. Separate dough into 13 biscuits; cut each biscuit into eighths. Place biscuit pieces in large bowl; toss with 1¾ cups salsa. Spoon evenly into margarine-coated dish. Sprinkle with cheese, bell pepper, onions and ripe olives. Bake at 375 degrees for 35 to 45 minutes or until edges are deep golden brown and center is set. Let stand 15 minutes. Cut into squares; serve with 1 cup salsa.

NOODLE RING

Several of my friends were recruited to accompany me to Julie Dannenbaum's Cooking School at the gorgeous Greenbrier Hotel in West Virginia in the '70's. Katherine Porter, Iris Gillis, Dixey Smith and I learned so much it was incredible, and we loved every minute of the adventure.

This is one of Julie's great recipes on which she wrote (if I may brag), "To Louise—a great student!" I was so proud of that because I had the feeling all during the course that she was looking with disdain on my many questions asked in a Southern drawl that the Pennsylvania teacher found hard to fathom.

1	pound noodles, ¼-inch wide	1	pound grated Cheddar cheese
1	tablespoon vegetable oil	6	eggs, beaten lightly
3	cups milk	2	teaspoons salt
2	cups soft bread crumbs	1	teaspoon freshly cracked white pepper
½	cup plus 4 tablespoons softened butter, plus butter for mold		

Cook noodles in 4 quarts of boiling salted water according to package directions, adding a little oil to the water so noodles won't stick together. While noodles cook, prepare cheese sauce. Bring milk to a boil, lower heat, add bread crumbs, and stir with a whisk. Beat in ½ cup softened butter and the cheese, and whisk over low heat until smooth. Pour a little of the hot sauce into the eggs, to warm them; then stir eggs into sauce. Heat through over medium heat, but do not boil. Stir in salt and pepper. When noodles are done (they should be tender, but firm to the bite), drain thoroughly and toss in a large bowl with remaining 4 tablespoons softened butter to keep them from sticking. Stir in cheese sauce and pour mixture into a heavily buttered 12-cup ring mold or soufflé dish. Set in a bain-marie (a water bath-water should be 1-inch deep and hot) and put it in a preheated 375 degree oven. Bake for 45 minutes. Remove from oven and let the mold stand in the hot water for 5 minutes, before turning it out onto a serving platter.

HANGOVER BREAKFAST

Chef Tell (Tell Erhardt) was a bombastic German chef who lured me and a group of my friends to the Pinehurst Hotel and Country Club in North Carolina to attend his fascinating cooking school. At that time (1985) he was the owner of a prestigious restaurant in Philadelphia and was billed as America's most popular short order gourmet cook by Newsweek Magazine. Tell was the former executive chef at the famed Kronen Hotel in the Black Forest in Germany and had intriguing stories of mystery and romance that he interspersed between courses in the cooking school. And if you didn't pay strict attention, he might catch your eye by tossing a chicken or a lobster across the classroom. We loved it—and loved him, too. He was a great teacher and an unappointed comedian. I can see him now, shaking that frying pan back and forth rhythmically as he created what he called Hangover Breakfast. I'm not so sure, but I think he ought to know of what he speaks.

6	tablespoons butter or margarine		½	cup diced ham
½	cup diced onion		6	large eggs, beaten
3	large potatoes, peeled, cooked and sliced			Salt
				Freshly ground black pepper

Melt the butter in a large frying pan. When it is hot, add the onion, potatoes and ham. Sauté, stirring occasionally, for 5 to 6 minutes. Push the mixture to one side of the frying pan. Pour the beaten eggs into the empty side of the pan and let them sit for a few seconds. Then shake the pan back and forth until the eggs are set. The onion mixture will spread itself through the eggs while you are shaking the pan. Turn the eggs over on themselves as you would for an omelet, turn out of the pan, season with salt and pepper to taste, and serve immediately.

EGGS DERBY

Attending the Kentucky Derby (in 1984) has to be a highlight of almost anybody's life. I cannot tell you, however, which horse won the derby that year, but I certainly gleaned this recipe for Eggs Derby which we were served on a riverboat cruise up the Ohio river while in Louisville. Not only was the food delicious, there was a wonderful jazz band aboard to entertain us. Staying at the beautiful old Gault House in Louisville was very special, too.

6	eggs, hard-cooked	1½	cups heavy cream, scalded
¾	cup minced country ham		Salt and pepper
2-3	tablespoons heavy cream	6	large mushrooms, sliced
	Salt and pepper to taste	¼	cup butter
2	tablespoons butter	¼	cup grated Parmesan
2	tablespoons flour	2	tablespoons butter
1½	cups milk, scalded	½	teaspoon paprika

Halve eggs. Mix yolks with ham, cream, salt, and pepper. Return yolks to whites and place in buttered casserole. Melt 2 tablespoons butter; stir in flour until smooth. Remove from heat. Add scalded milk and cream, stirring until smooth. Add salt and pepper. Simmer 10 minutes. Sauté mushrooms in ¼ cup butter. Add to the cream sauce. Pour over eggs. Top with Parmesan, butter, and paprika. Bake at 450 degrees 8 to 10 minutes, until golden.

PINEAPPLE CASSEROLE

Nobody has a better spirit than my friend and fellow bridge club member, Dean Zimmerman. Dean has had more than her share of physical problems, but she smiles through it all and just doesn't complain. It's always fun to be around Dean. She shared a wonderful recipe with me on which she wrote: "You must have this," and she underlined it. You MUST HAVE it, too. And be sure to believe it when she says, "It's delicious with chicken, pork or ham."

1	(20-ounce) can crushed pineapple, drained	1	cup sharp Cheddar cheese, grated
¼	cup sugar	½	cup Ritz cracker crumbs
3	tablespoons flour	½	cup butter, melted

Preheat oven to 350 degrees. In a blender or with a wire whisk, combine pineapple juice, sugar and flour. Add pineapple and cheese, pour into a buttered 9-inch pie plate. Top with cracker crumbs and pour melted butter over the top. Bake at 350 degrees for 25 minutes. This dish is great for a brunch.

MOST DELICIOUS TURKEY DRESSING

When Francis Shurling owned the Exchange Bank of Wrightsville, he always had fabulous Christmas parties at the Johnson County Golf and Country Club. Friends and employees of the bank always anticipated with great glee the holiday season and the wonderful party.

The story goes, and I really think it's true, that some people would withdraw money from other banks and deposit it in the Exchange Bank just to get an invitation to the "party of the year." Jean Joiner of Tennille was the marvelous caterer for the Christmas dinner, and everybody always knew they were in for a big treat. Jean prepared everything to taste perfectly, but her Dressing for the Turkey is what had people going back for seconds. Thirds? Fourths?

Jean was always sweet to share her recipes and gave me this treasured heirloom recipe years ago. I use it every year at turkey time and always think it is the best ever. The amounts depend on how much you want to make. You have to use your own intuition. The secret of the whole thing is to use so much good chicken stock or broth that the mixture almost pours into the casserole dish.

6	buns (hamburger or hot dog)	4	tablespoons butter
1	stack pack saltine crackers	4	eggs
1	pan corn bread (Jiffy is delicious)		Salt and pepper to taste
3-4	stalks celery, chopped		Hot chicken or turkey stock
1	large onion, chopped		

Crumble bread, crackers and cornbread in a large bowl. Sauté onions and celery in butter until tender. Add to crumbs. Beat eggs and add to mixture. Salt and pepper. Pour stock over crumbs until almost pourable. Put into a buttered casserole and bake at 350 degrees until tests done.

BROCCOLI À LA HOLLANDAISE

My friend Martee Wills and her husband Paul, both journalists, were a great source of information to me before they moved off to Florida and left me. There was no subject they couldn't research for me, and recipes were one of Martee's specialties. She mailed me a whole batch of good recipes from Cross Creek Cookery by the delightful writer Marjorie Kinnan Rawlings. She said of broccoli, "Charles Brown, in his Gun Club Cookbook, remarks that broccoli may be spelled with 2 c's, but that does not help its flavor." He shares the sentiments of former president George Bush, but not mine. Broccoli and Hollandaise Sauce is one of my favorite dishes and one that I first learned to cook under my mother's watchful eye. She was an expert at this fickle sauce.

Cut broccoli heads or florets an hour before mealtime. Discard any portion of the stalk with a tendency to toughness. Wash and let stand in cold water. Have ready boiling, slightly salted water that will not more than cover the broccoli. Boil until just tender. Drain well, cover with Hollandaise sauce and serve at once. The Hollandaise can be safely set off the burner while the broccoli is draining in a colander–no longer.

HOLLANDAISE SAUCE

I can remember very well the first time my mother served broccoli and Hollandaise Sauce. I thought I had died and gone to heaven. It is so delicious, and Mother always seemed to get it just right. I have used this recipe over and over again, even bravely serving it to guests in my early days of cooking.

3	egg yolks	2	tablespoons fresh lemon juice
¼	teaspoon salt	½	cup butter, divided into 3 pieces
	Dash of cayenne pepper		

Beat egg yolks, salt and cayenne pepper in top of a double boiler, gradually adding lemon juice and stirring constantly. Add about ⅓ of butter to egg mixture, cooking and stirring until butter melts. Add another ⅓ of butter, stirring constantly. As sauce thickens, stir in remaining butter. Cook until thickened.

BROCCOLI CASSEROLE

My recipes are copied on everything from paper sacks to paper napkins. I would never part with all these "originals" because they tell a story all their own. Here's one that Nanelle Dunlap Frost copied for me on a Western Union Telegram blank because many years ago they had the franchise in Wrightsville. I wouldn't take anything for it because of its history and because it's a super recipe too.

2	large onions, chopped	½	cup milk
1	stick oleo	1	package frozen broccoli, cook, drain and chop
2	cups cooked rice		
1	can mushroom soup	¾	cup grated cheese

Cook onions in oleo until tender but not brown. Add cooked rice, soup, ½ cup milk and cooked broccoli. Pour in greased baking dish and cover top with grated cheese. Cook until cheese is melted at 400 degrees.

ORIGINAL GREEN BEAN CASSEROLE

It was all set. Plans were for a luncheon featuring several of the tried and true classics from several years ago. The Original Green Bean Casserole was to be the green vegetable and one for which I couldn't wait. I love that old casserole! The ingredients were all placed on the counter in readiness for preparation, and then panic overwhelmed me. Where was the recipe? Nowhere! A half day search was all in vain. So, too, were searches through zillions of cookbooks. Why had no one recorded this well-known old standard? All right. Some of my friends were sure to have it. "Sorry."

When all torn up about my futile search, I began to return the ingredients to their cupboard hiding places, and there underneath the green bean cans was the elusive recipe—put there by "you know who." Don't ever let this out of your hands. It's a keeper.

1	can (10¾ ounces) condensed cream of mushroom soup		Dash pepper
½	cup milk	4	cups cooked green beans, drained
1	teaspoon soy sauce (optional)	1	can (2.8 ounces) French fried onions

In 1½-quart casserole, mix soup, milk, soy sauce, pepper, beans and ½ can onions. Bake at 350 degrees 25 minutes or until hot. Stir. Sprinkle remaining onions over bean mixture. Bake 5 minutes or until onions are golden.

FRENCH CUT GREEN BEANS WITH WATER CHESTNUTS

I think I was attending cooking schools long before I realized that I had an intense interest in food preparation. It just seemed like a fun thing to do.

This old, old recipe, along with several others, is printed on fine stationery with a "Truffles" logo on the bottom. I vaguely remember going to this school in Atlanta, and because the recipe suggests using the slicer, I do believe it was a class sponsored by Cuisinart. Anyway, if you don't have a Cuisinart or other food processor, you may slice by hand because this is a good recipe worth using, one that I've chosen many times when looking for that "green vegetable."

To toast the sesame seeds put on baking sheet and put in 250 degree oven for about 5 minutes. Watch carefully to prevent burning.

1½	pounds green beans	½	teaspoon salt
6	tablespoons butter	1-2	tablespoons toasted sesame seeds
1	can water chestnuts (5½-ounces)		

Break the ends off the beans and snap them into 2-inch lengths. Drop them into 4 quarts of boiling water; when the water returns to a boil, cook for 5 minutes. Drain in a colander, and immediately run cold water over the beans to stop the cooking and set the color. When the beans are cool enough to handle, stack them in the food processor feed tube horizontally and slice them using moderate pressure. Heat the butter in a 12-inch sauté pan and sauté beans over moderate heat. Meanwhile, slice the water chestnuts. Add them to the beans with the salt. Sauté the mixture until it is hot throughout. Taste for seasoning and make any necessary adjustments. Arrange the vegetables on a serving plate and sprinkle with sesame seeds.

BEAN BUNDLES

This is one of my favorite recipes—not just because it's from my dear friend, Luella Rowland. Not just because Luella and her doctor husband, J. Roy, have been my friends forever. Not just because Luella and J. Roy served us so well in the House of Representatives in Washington. Not just because they invited me up for a whirlwind of food-related activities in the nation's capital. Not just because Luella took me to the greatest party of my entire career—the First Lady's Luncheon at the fabulous Shoreham Hotel when Nancy Reagan was First Lady. Not just because Luella and J. Roy are hosts with great graciousness. It's because this is, without a doubt, one of my favorite vegetable recipes. I serve it over and over again at parties—always to diners who want more and who need the recipe. If you can possibly locate Le Sueur beans, they are by far the best. Then too, you may do your own whole beans by snipping off the ends and steaming the beans until barely tender.

2	(16-ounce) cans whole green beans, drained	1	(8-ounce) bottle commercial French dressing
12-16	slices bacon, cut in half	4-5	whole pimentos, cut into strips

Arrange green beans in bundles of 8, wrapping a half slice of bacon around each bunch. Place beans in a 13x9x2-inch baking dish. Pour dressing over beans. Cover and chill for 3 hours. Bake uncovered at 350 degrees for 40 minutes, turning beans after the first 20 minutes of cooking. Remove beans from dish with slotted spoon. Garnish bean bundles with strips of pimento before serving.

BLACK BEAN TAMALE PIE

This recipe is one of my favorites from my dear friend Jim Foble, who lives in New York where he has written for several national magazines; served as test kitchen director for Food and Wine *and has written many cookbooks. It was fun to be taken by Jim to a wonderful Indian restaurant in New York. Jim knows the ropes and had the waiters all bowing and scraping when he entered.*

Jim is noted for being a master at infusing flavor into food and this recipe proves it. I have served this many times—always to rave reviews.

3	cans (16-ounces each) black beans, rinsed and drained
½	cup dry sherry
2	tablespoons fresh lemon juice
2	tablespoons olive oil
3	cups fresh or thawed frozen corn kernels
1	fresh jalapeño chili, minced with the seeds
1	large garlic clove, minced or crushed through a press
1	teaspoon ground cumin
1	teaspoon dried oregano, crumbled
2	teaspoons salt

¼	teaspoon black pepper
5¼	cups water
1½	cups peeled, seeded and coarsely chopped tomatoes (fresh or canned)
¾	cup diced whole scallions
½	cup chopped cilantro
2	cups coarse yellow cornmeal
1½	cups low-fat plain yogurt
2	cups coarsely grated sharp Cheddar cheese (8-ounces)
½	cup canned tomato sauce

For serving:

Sour cream	Radishes
Black olives	Cilantro sprigs

In a sealable plastic bag or shallow dish, combine the black beans, sherry, and lemon juice. Marinate in the refrigerator 2 to 12 hours. Drain before using. Spoon the olive oil into a large heavy non stick or well-seasoned skillet over moderately high heat. Add the corn, toss once, then let brown very well, about 5 minutes. Toss again and continue browning for a minute or two. Add the jalapeño, garlic, cumin, oregano, ½ teaspoon of the salt and pepper. Cook a minute or two, then pour in ¼ cup of the water to deglaze the pan. Turn out into a large bowl and toss in the tomatoes, scallions and cilantro. The recipe may be prepared a day ahead to here. Preheat the oven to 350 degrees and prepare the casserole. Bring 3 cups of the water and the remaining 1½ teaspoons salt to a boil in a large, heavy saucepan over high heat. Meanwhile, in a medium bowl, stir together the cornmeal and remaining 2 cups cold water. Add the cornmeal mixture to the boiling water and stir constantly until the mixture returns to a boil. Reduce the heat to low and cook, stirring frequently, until the mixture is as thick as mashed potatoes, about 5 minutes. Stir in 1 cup of the yogurt. Cook over very low heat,

VEGETABLES AND SIDE DISHES

stirring frequently, until again as thick as mashed potatoes, about 8 minutes. Spread about ⅔ of the cornmeal batter in the prepared casserole (keep the remainder covered over hot water to keep warm), making a 1-inch raised edge all around. Spoon the drained black beans on top and press in lightly. Sprinkle 1½ cups of the cheese over the beans. Add all of the corn-tomato mixture and spread in to an even layer. Spoon the remaining cornmeal mixture over the top in dabs and spread to make an even layer that covers the top (it's okay if some of the vegetables show through). Spoon the remaining yogurt and the canned tomato sauce in alternating diagonal lines. Sprinkle with the remaining ½ cup Cheddar. Bake about 1 hour, or until deep golden brown on top. Remove from the oven and let stand for at least 15 minutes before serving. Cut into squares, remove them with a spatula and serve hot with a dollop of sour cream, a couple black olives and radish slices and a sprig of cilantro, if desired. If making ahead, cool to room temperature, cover with foil and refrigerate.

CABBAGE CASSEROLE

Ann Adams Wall, originally from Dublin, is one my favorite bridge partners because we always share Dublin news about mutual friends and because we always share recipes. When Ann describes for us how much her husband Lowe enjoyed a particular recipe, it almost makes you want to desert the bridge table to go home and start cooking. "Almost," I said. There's not much that would make me want to leave the bridge table.

Ann says Lowe really is crazy about this good cabbage dish. The amount of ingredients can be adjusted to your taste and needs.

1	pound ground beef, cooked	1	medium onion, diced fine
1	medium cabbage, shredded	1	can (10¾ ounces) mushroom soup

Layer the ingredients in a greased casserole and bake at 350 degrees for 45 minutes or until cabbage is tender.

MAPLE BAKED BEANS

Bringing me a cookbook is a sure way to my heart. When my son Bill went in 1995 to Iron Mountain, Michigan, on business for the kaolin company for which he worked at the time and thought to bring me a cookbook, it was special indeed. It's called Fresh Market–Wisconsin *and really has some good recipes.*

They say that this is maple syrup country and that although farmers markets are few and far between, motorists don't need to travel far to locate a homestead that sells the sweetest flavor of Wisconsin—maple syrup.

This recipe for Baked Beans with Maple Syrup is so good but so big that you might have to halve the recipe or freeze the extras. It serves 16 or more people.

2	pounds white or navy beans	1	small onion, chopped
½	pound bacon, cut into 1-inch pieces	1	tablespoon salt
1	cup ketchup	¼	teaspoon ground black pepper
1½-2	cups dark maple syrup	1	teaspoon dry mustard

Sort, wash, and soak beans eight hours or longer in cold water. Drain and rinse. Place beans in large, heavy pot, cover with cold water, bring to simmer and cook ½ hour or until a little soft. Meanwhile, cook bacon pieces until crispy. Stir bacon, bacon fat and remaining ingredients into the beans. If necessary, add enough hot water to barely cover the beans. Cover pot and bake 2 to 4 hours until fully tender, stirring once or twice during the first hour. As beans cook, add additional hot water only if necessary. Or, if there's too much liquid, leave the lid off towards the end of cooking. Cooked beans may also be held in a slow oven for several hours. They taste best on the second or third day you serve them. Leftover beans may also be frozen.

URSULA'S CARROTS

Margaret Duckworth Sewell and I go way back to college days when she used to pick up the dropped stitches for me when I was trying to knit argyle socks for my boyfriend. Margaret was the best knitter in the class although we weren't really majoring in knitting. She could talk and look at you, and at the same time be completing intricate patterns in those crazy socks.

We still keep in touch because we are both closely tied to our Alma Mater, Wesleyan, and have even served on a Wesleyan board together. Now Margaret has a precious granddaughter who is a graduate of Wesleyan—doesn't time fly!

At one point in our journey, Margaret brought me a copy of her church's, (Northside Drive Baptist in Atlanta) cookbook called What Can I Bring? *Haven't you said those same word yourself many times?*

Evidently what Margaret would bring is Ursula's Carrots because that's a recipe she has in the book. Ursula is a cooking school instructor in Atlanta and has fantastic recipes. Margaret and I both have attended her classes.

2	pounds carrots, sliced thin		Salt
1	cup orange juice	6	tablespoons Grand Marnier Liqueur
	Grated peel of 1 orange	3	ounces butter

Boil carrots in orange juice and orange peel until juice is absorbed and carrots are crisp tender. Salt and toss with 6 tablespoons of Grand Mariner and butter. Serve hot.

SILVER QUEEN CORN PUDDING

It was in a little gift shop in Cashiers, North Carolina, that I first encountered the beautiful cookbook by the Junior League of Charlotte called Dining by Fireflies. *The title alone was enough to catch me, but after looking through the book I knew I had to be dining by fireflies. It's wonderful.*

You can be sure they know what they're doing when you come to the recipe called Silver Queen Corn Pudding. Any Southerner worth his fireflies knows that Silver Queen Corn is one of the finest products to come out of the South since country ham. It's sweet and delicious, and when combined with butter, eggs, and cream, you just might eat the whole casserole (serves 6) by yourself. Please share no matter how hard it is for you.

8	ears fresh white corn, husks and silks removed
½	cup butter, melted
5	eggs
1	pint half-and-half
½	tablespoon sugar
	Salt to taste
	Pepper to taste

Preheat oven to 300 degrees. Grate corn on corn scraper or cut kernels from cob with sharp knife (but be sure to go over cob several times with knife). Combine corn with melted butter in large bowl. Beat eggs and fold into corn. Add remaining ingredients and pour into 2-quart casserole dish. (Can be made 1 day ahead up to this point and refrigerated.) Place in pan of water and bake 1 hour 15 minutes or until set in center. (Can be baked 1 day ahead and reheated.)

CRANBERRY CHUTNEY

My precious niece, Lisa Futrelle, gave all of us jars of Cranberry Chutney that she made herself one Christmas. When I had served mine atop a block of cream cheese with Wheat Thins, I wanted some more, and Lisa was in Aspen snow skiing. Thus, I improvised and found a truly good recipe that parallels Lisa's. You might want to give this for little hostess gifts for Christmas or birthday presents. Had you thought about your secret pal?

1	pound cranberries	1	medium onion, chopped
	Grated rind of 1 lemon	1	teaspoon salt
	Juice of 1 lemon		Dash of cayenne
1	cup water	1	tablespoon finely chopped crystallized ginger
1	cup packed brown sugar		
½	cup golden raisins	½	cup orange marmalade

Combine all ingredients, except last two. Bring to boil and simmer, uncovered, stirring occasionally 10 or 15 minutes, or until cranberries are tender and liquid begins to thicken. Add remaining ingredients and chill. Serve with meats or curried dishes. Will keep four weeks in refrigerator.

STUFFED EGGPLANT

This is an old, old recipe that my mother served as long as I can remember—and that's a long time. Even though I've shared the recipe many times, I've never really seen anybody else (except family members) serve it quite this way. It is truly delicious and makes a lovely presentation for a dinner party or just a special family meal.

1	large eggplant	1½	cups grated sharp Cheddar cheese
½	stack-pack saltine crackers	2	tablespoons butter
1	medium onion, diced fine	2-3	tablespoons milk
3	eggs, beaten		Salt and pepper

Immerse whole eggplant in boiling water in large stockpot. Turn to low and simmer until eggplant tests tender when pierced with an ice pick. Remove from water and place in a greased casserole dish. Split eggplant in half–longways. Scoop out inside being sure not to damage the skin and place pulp in mixing bowl. Crumble crackers and add: onions, eggs, cheese, and butter, salt and pepper to taste. Combine with eggplant. If mixture seems too stiff add a tablespoon or two of milk. Stir mixture well. Stuff back into the two eggplant skins. Bake at 350 degrees until eggplant looks brown on top and seems to be cooked completely.

CUCUMBERS IN SOUR CREAM

It was 25 cents well spent. Even if I didn't like the cookbook, I had more than a quarter's worth of fun at the Manchester, Tennessee, yard sale that my friend, Nelle Bray, and I just stumbled upon in August of '85.

Our real mission was to see Nelle's daughter, Joanna, in a horse show in Shelbyville. That was wonderful, and we loved every minute of Joanna's spectacular performances, but we veered off the path one day to run over and see the world famous Jack Daniel Distillery in Lynchburg. Going back to Shelbyville, we saw they were having a huge yard sale under some beautiful shade trees on a spacious front lawn in Manchester. Nelle wasn't interested in that "old second hand junk," but I twisted her arm and begged for just 5 minutes. An hour later I was suggesting to Nelle that maybe we should be leaving. She had become a convert under the tutelage of none other than The Yard Sale Queen.

I treasure The Cook in the Parlor *that I bought because it reminds me of pleasant times gone by with my good friend Nelle, and because it's full of good recipes. I can't resist this Cucumbers in Sour Cream—made with those little pickling cucumbers that are so good.*

Chill 2 cups of sliced cucumbers in ice water. Season 1 cup of sour cream with vinegar, salt and pepper. Add 1 teaspoon each of chopped chives and parsley. Drain the cucumbers and mix lightly with the sour cream.

VEGETABLES AND SIDE DISHES

STUFFED MIRLITONS

Because Tony Benedetto was president of the New Orleans Jazz Club, he became a "must know" for my husband who adored Dixieland jazz (me too!) After meeting Tony, we became friends as couples, and on a very special occasion we were guests at their home in Orleans Parrish. Edea Benedetto was a talented artist as well as an excellent cook, and we soon were good friends, swapping recipes back and forth. At her dinner party she introduced us to mirlitons, also called chayote squash, which she grew in her backyard. That was 1980; today I buy mirlitons in the market here and really enjoy making Edea's special dish.

4	large mirlitons (or yellow squash or eggplants)	2	teaspoons N'Awlins Seasoning (or ½ teaspoon each: salt, pepper, thyme, and basil)
4	tablespoons butter		
2	tablespoons vegetable oil	1	cup chopped ham
2	onions, chopped	1	cup chopped shrimp, crawfish or crabmeat
½	cup chopped green pepper		
2	cloves garlic, minced	1	cup bread crumbs
		¾	cup grated Cheddar cheese (optional)

Boil mirlitons in water to cover until fork tender (40 to 60 minutes). Cut in half, remove seeds, and drain cutside down on paper towels. In butter and oil, sauté onions, green pepper, and garlic until soft. Leaving shells intact, scoop out pulp from mirlitons and add to sautéed vegetables. Stir and add seasoning, ham, and seafood. Cook over medium heat about 15 minutes, stirring often. Add bread crumbs last; stir well while cooking an additional 5 minutes. Fill shells, sprinkle with cheese (or bread crumbs and butter dots) and bake in baking dish at 350 degrees about 20 minutes, or until tops are browned.

AMERISWEET ONION ITALIAN TORTE

Amerisweeet Onions are Michigan's answer to Georgia's Vidalias. They come in the fall after the Vidalias are all over, so it's really a good thing. This is a recipe that they mailed me in August of '99 just before their crop came in. I tried it and found the delicious Italian flavors delightful in this unique and simple to prepare torte. If tortillas overlap the pan, just trim them off to fit. Although this calls for a 9-inch pan, I make them in about 5-inch pans and find the individual servings more desirable.

1	tablespoon vegetable oil	¾	cup prepared pesto
2	Amerisweet onions, diced	⅓	cup grated Parmesan cheese
3	medium tomatoes, diced	2¼	cups grated mozzarella cheese
5	large (9-inch) flour tortillas, plain or flavored	¼	cup tomato sauce

In large skillet, heat oil over medium high heat. Sauté onions until tender and transparent. Stir in tomatoes and cook until most of the liquid evaporates; set aside, reserving 2 tablespoons for topping. Lay one tortilla in bottom of a 9-inch springform pan. Spread ¼ of pesto over tortilla, top with ¼ of onion/tomato mixture, ¼ cup of Parmesan cheese and ½ cup mozzarella cheese. Repeat three times. Top with last tortilla, reserved topping, and remaining ¼ cup mozzarella cheese. Bake in a 350 degree oven for 20 minutes. Remove from oven; cool for 5 minutes. Remove rim of springform pan; cut into wedges.

ONION RINGS

My friend Skippy Davis, who is a business writer for the Macon Telegraph, at one time in her career was Skippy Lawson, food editor of the Macon Telegraph. In any role, Skippy is a winner and a delight to know.

I was intrigued recently to find an old yellowed clipping entitled Fry Those Onions! *that Skippy had written. It seems that Mrs. Rupert Webb of Macon had written in wanting the Onion Ring recipe that Betty Jean McCullars of Reynolds had submitted in 1977. Nell Hawkins of Dublin sent it in; Skippy Lawson of Hawkinsville printed it and now I'm involved in the situation. How could you possibly have so many actors and so many towns involved in such a simple recipe? It's worth all the involvement though.*

1	large onion	⅔	cup water
1	egg white (beaten stiff)	1	cup self-rising flour
1	teaspoon salt	2	teaspoons salad oil

Mix into stiffly beaten egg white all other ingredients, except onions. Dip sliced onions (which have been soaked in ice water with a little sugar for about an hour) into mixture. Fry until brown in deep fat.

RUTABAGA TIMBALES

Why is the delicious rutabaga so often shunned in the produce department and not given entrance to many of the finest kitchens? Rutabagas are good. And this recipe is so tasty you'll want to serve it at a dinner party for the most discriminating guests. My sister-in-law and I prepared this one time for company, and we liked that we could do it the day before and just increase the baking time by 5 to 10 minutes.

1	pound rutabagas (about 1 large), cut into 2-inch pieces	¼	teaspoon pepper
2	cloves garlic, cut in half	4	eggs
1	teaspoon salt	½	cup half-and-half

Heat 1-inch water (salt if desired) to boiling. Add rutabagas and garlic. Cover and heat to boiling; reduce heat. Simmer 30 to 40 minutes or until tender; drain. Heat oven to 350 degrees. Grease six 6-ounce custard cups or individual ramekins. Place rutabagas, garlic, salt and pepper in blender or food processor, stopping occasionally to scrape sides, until smooth. Beat eggs in large bowl. Mix in half-and-half and rutabaga mixture. Pour into custard cups. Place cups in a pan 13x9x2-inches, on oven rack. Pour very hot water into pan to within ½-inch of tops of cups. Bake 30 to 35 minutes or until knife inserted halfway between center and edge comes out clean. Remove timbales from cups. Serve warm.

GINNY'S SPECIAL SPINACH

Mary Ann Norris' sister-in-law, Ginny Dilcher from Atlanta, shared a lot of recipes with Mary Ann and me when we were neighbors in Wrightsville. This is one that we particularly liked, especially since we had both just acquired our first microwave ovens and we were anxious to use them to their full potential. It's really good, and if you don't care for spinach, you may substitute broccoli.

2	(10-ounce) packages frozen chopped spinach	⅓	cup grated Parmesan cheese
2	cups small curd cottage cheese	2	beaten eggs
1	teaspoon salt	1½	cups grated Swiss cheese

Cook spinach in packages placed on large paper plate 7 to 9 minutes, rotating ¼ turn halfway through cooking time. Rest 5 minutes. Blend spinach, cottage cheese, salt, Parmesan cheese and eggs. Place 1 small glass in the center of 1½-quart glass casserole and pour ingredients around glass. Bake 12 to 14 minutes, rotating dish every 4 minutes. Sprinkle with cheese. Rest 5 minutes. Invert dish for serving.

LAKE RABUN SPINACH

Let's just call it Lake Rabun Spinach. A group of college friends was enjoying a few days at Beverly Banks' lovely three story home right on the lake, and as always the conversation turned to great recipes recently tried. I promise I do not direct the conversation every time. Sometimes I deliberately avoid talking about food, and invariably someone else always broaches the subject. This time it was about spinach casseroles that had been tried, and it was interesting that three of the girls had tried the same recipe, but all three had done something different. Carolyn adds artichokes and lemon juice; Marty puts sliced tomatoes on top before cooking: and Becky uses basil leaves as a garnish. Do whatever you want to, but be sure to use the three basic ingredients.

2	packages chopped, frozen spinach, cooked and drained	8	ounces cream cheese
		1	stick butter, melted

Mix all ingredients and put into an ungreased casserole. Mix the following topping and spread across the casserole. Bake at 350 degrees until tests done.

Topping:

½	stick butter	2	cups herb crumb seasoned dressing

Water to mix until consistency of raw dressing.

SPINACH

I own a 1938 Mumford Complete Cookbook and in it is written—From Emma Hinton "our cook." It was in Mother's collection but moved to mine in 1999 when she broke up housekeeping at 97 years old.

There are so many intriguing recipes in this little red hardback book but when we think of Emma, we think spinach. After the luncheon guests left one day, Aunt Caddie said to Emma, "Please, Emma, come show me where you picked the spinach. It tasted rather strange." And when Emma led Aunt Caddie to the garden, all the petunias had been trimmed to the ground. Sorry, no petunia recipe,—just this in memory of Emma and her little cookbook.

Spinach	Butter
Water	Hard-cooked eggs, chopped

Pick, wash and drain the required amount of spinach. Put into a kettle or saucepan without any water over medium heat. In a few minutes the spinach will wilt and send out sufficient water to cook it. Boil for 20 to 30 minutes briskly so the water will be reduced. Season with butter and garnish with chopped eggs.

SPINACH TIMBALES

When I first encountered Spinach Timbales at an upscale restaurant in Atlanta, my quest in life was to then learn how to make them at home. It seemed pretty obvious what you should do, and I did it—over and over and over again. But I still didn't have locks on the Spinach Timbales recipe.

Then one day I stumbled across the recipe, and I've had it right ever since. It was the cheese that I was missing.

½	cup onions, finely chopped		Cayenne, to taste
5	tablespoons butter	5	eggs
⅔	cup plus 2 tablespoons bread crumbs	1	cup milk
½	cup Gruyère or Swiss cheese, grated	3	cups spinach, chopped and cooked
½	teaspoon salt	3	eggs, hard-cooked
⅛	teaspoon nutmeg		

Cook onions in 1 tablespoon butter over low heat for 10 minutes. Do not let them color. Combine onions with ⅔ cup bread crumbs, cheese, salt and freshly grated nutmeg and cayenne, to taste. Beat in 5 eggs, one at a time and gradually add milk heated with remaining butter until milk is hot and the butter melted. Fold in spinach and pour mixture into a buttered 1½-quart mold. Sprinkle with 2 tablespoons bread crumbs. Set the mold in a pan of boiling water and bake it in a moderately slow oven at 325 degrees for 35 to 45 minutes, depending on the depth of the mold, or until a knife inserted in the center comes out clean. Remove the mold from the water and let it stand for 5 minutes. Run a small knife around the edge to loosen it and turn out timbale on a serving platter. Cover the top with chopped, hard-cooked eggs and surround timbale with sections of egg. Serve with a sauceboat of melted butter and lemon juice.

VEGETABLES AND SIDE DISHES

MY FAVORITE SQUASH CASSEROLE

There are about as many squash casseroles as there are squash but this one is the best. It so narrowly missed getting in this book that it makes me shiver. Just as the book was going to press, I was in the kitchen cooking for a sick friend and decided to make my squash casserole. I ran to the manuscript to retrieve the recipe and horror or all horrors, I had failed to include it. Here it is— just under the line.

½	package herb seasoned stuffing	1	can cream of chicken soup (undiluted)
2	cups diced, cooked, yellow squash	1	grated raw carrot
1	(8-ounce) carton sour cream	½	cup melted butter

Butter casserole dish. Cover bottom with pulverized stuffing mix. Combine all other ingredients and put into casserole. Add more seasoned stuffing crumbs on top. Pour melted butter over top. Bake at 350 degrees until bubbly.

YELLOW SQUASH ON TOMATO SLICES

So many recipes I call "my favorites." And they are. This one certainly is a favorite—way up near the top of the list. I serve it over and over at luncheons and dinner parties, and every time I try it anew, I think, "Wow! That is so good!" It's good anytime, but if you can manage to have it when tomatoes are homegrown and tender yellow squash are in the produce section, you'll have a dish fit for a king. Don't you dare think for one minute that you can make it without Durkees. That's the secret ingredient. It's delicious, but it's also beautiful if you arrange the tomatoes on a large silver platter or if you serve the individual plates.

8	yellow squash	¾	stick butter
1	large onion	6	thick slices tomato
	Dash salt, pepper, and celery salt		Durkees dressing
	Herbed crumb dressing		

Wash squash, cut into cubes. Peel onion; cut into small pieces. Combine squash and onion; add seasonings. Steam until tender. Drain. Stir in a few crumbs of herbed crumb dressing and butter. Cut thick slices of firm tomatoes; sprinkle with salt, pepper, and cover with Durkees. Heap squash onto tomato slices; sprinkle with finely pulverized herbed crumb dressing crumbs. Bake at 400 degrees for about 20 minutes. So tomatoes will remain firm, don't overcook.

BUTTERNUT SQUASH

The entire cookbook could be devoted to my (much younger than I) friend Nan Souma and her pursuits in the kitchen. Nan is a seasoned cook and a hostess to be envied—although at times her methods drive me crazy. Nan can be having a party for 100 people at seven o'clock, and at six the kitchen looks like the worst terrorist attack has just taken place. Go back at seven and Nan is beautiful, all dressed to the nines, and greeting her guests with a captivating smile and much warmth and graciousness. I need to take lessons.

Nan's obstetrician husband, John, is of Lebanese descent, and Nan has spent untold hours perfecting dishes that are important to John.

Nan has benefits, charity parties, alumnae affairs, Sunday School parties and many other events in her gorgeous home, always shared generously. At one time she turned her carport into a juke joint complete with a juke box (that usually is in her large kitchen) and black and white tile floor for an Elvis party. I love her style. And I love her flair. And I love Nan. She's a joy.

One time she did a demonstration on cooking squash for me at our garden club, and everyone loved it. She let us taste, too. This is one of her good recipes, one that she says easily doubles for a crowd and is easy to freeze. "It's lighter than sweet potatoes," Nan says, "and goes especially well with ham."

2	cups cooked butternut squash, pureed	1	stick margarine, melted
3	eggs, beaten	1	teaspoon coconut extract
¾	cup sugar	½	teaspoon ground ginger

Combine all ingredients and put into a greased casserole. Bake at 300 degrees until almost set.

Topping:

2	cups crushed corn flakes	½	cup pecans
½	cup brown sugar	1	stick margarine

Combine all ingredients and sprinkle on top of soufflé and bake 15 to 20 minutes more.

VEGETABLES AND SIDE DISHES

FIRE AND ICE TOMATOES

In October of 1981 my darling daughter, Carol, was in Tennessee for the Georgia–Vanderbilt game. She spent the weekend with her friend Melanie Lucas, whose mother was a committee member of the James K. Polk Cookbook *from Columbia, Tennessee. Mrs. Lucas very graciously sent me a copy of the cookbook with a notation that* Ladies Home Journal *was doing an upcoming feature on the book and was starring this great-sounding recipe. The name of it causes you to salivate.*

A note on the brown paper bag in which the cookbook arrived said, "Mama, I hope you enjoy the cookbook. Love, Carol" Of course I enjoyed it—as well as this great recipe—so good in the summertime when tomatoes are so delicious.

6	large tomatoes, cut into quarters	½	teaspoon salt
1	onion, cut into slices and separated	4½	teaspoons sugar
1	bell pepper, cut into strips	⅛	teaspoon red pepper
¾	cup vinegar	⅛	teaspoon black pepper
1½	teaspoons mustard seed	¼	cup cold water
1½	teaspoons celery salt		

Combine vinegar, water and seasonings. Boil 1 minute. Pour over vegetables and chill several hours. Will keep 2 to 3 days.

EDISTO TOMATO PIE

When I was a very young inane teenager, I had a great, good time visiting my dear friend, Jan Rountree, who had moved to Edisto Island, S. C. Three of us, the Arden girls and I, went on the train and had more fun than we were entitled to have. We were fascinated with towns along the way like Adams Run and Monck's Corner. Edisto was just as foreign to us, but soon we were exploring the island; crabbing in the creeks; soaking up the sunshine, and having a great vacation.

Although Jan's mother, "Miss Agnes", was a lovely, sweet lady who was well educated, well read, and entertaining, she couldn't cook. At least she didn't cook like I was used to. I thought I'd starve to death. There was no fast food in those days, and every meal was served at home. Recently, when I was mailed a copy of Pon Top Edisto *put out by Trinity Episcopal Church, I just smiled out loud, remembering the "olden days." This pie is wonderful served with shrimp and grits, butter beans and slaw.*

1	(9-inch) deep dish pie shell, prebaked at 375 degrees for 10 minutes	½	teaspoon black pepper
5	large tomatoes, peeled and thickly sliced	3	teaspoons dried basil
			Garlic powder to taste
½	teaspoon salt	¾	cup mayonnaise
		1¼	cups grated Cheddar cheese

Layer tomatoes in pie shell, sprinkling each layer with salt, pepper, basil, and garlic powder which have been combined. Combine mayonnaise and cheese; spread over tomatoes. Bake at 350 degrees for 35 minutes or until golden brown and bubbly. Let stand 5 minutes before serving.

Main Dishes

Jacques Pepin and Louise at Sea Island Cloister

Mark Ballard "Designs" Louise's table for a charity auctioned dinner.

Veal at Harrod's in London

Sara Sanders and Louise at Disney World with Chip of Chip 'n Dale.

Mary Jane Powell, Louise, and Nancy Millard in Jamaica.

JAPANESE AMAZU CHICKEN

As I stood in the large hotel ballroom in Dallas and watched Marie Rizzio compete for the $25,000 grand prize along with 49 other contestants in the National Chicken Cooking Contest, I'll admit I had misgivings. "Who would want chicken and bean sprouts?" I mused as I moved on to the next cooking station. When Marie glowingly accepted the check for first prize, I'll admit I still had misgivings. Not until I had prepared the recipe in my own kitchen did I become a believer. This is, without any doubt, one of the finest recipes to ever come out of a cooking contest. It was sort of ironic that the recipe was of African origin; had been tasted and recreated from a Canadian restaurant; was prepared by a Michigan woman; and in Dallas. For one of my summer sun porch suppers I entertained a chef and his wife from San Diego. Of course I had trepidation. Who wouldn't? I settled on serving Chicken Amazu and glory of all glories, the chef said, "Louise, this is marvelous and so California. My people will adore it—would you consider sharing the recipe?" Yes, and with you too.

4	boneless, skinless chicken breast halves, cut into ½-inch strips	⅓	cup thinly sliced radishes
3	large eggs, lightly beaten	3	tablespoons sliced green onions (tops reserved for garnish)
¾	cup cornstarch		Amazu Sauce (recipe below)
⅓	cup vegetable oil		Toasted sesame seeds
4	cups fresh bean sprouts		Finely chopped red pepper
1	small salad cucumber		

In large bowl, mix together eggs and cornstarch. Dip chicken strips into mixture, coating well. In large non-stick fry pan, place oil over medium high heat. Add chicken (half at a time) and cook about 5 minutes or until browned. Drain on paper towels and keep warm. In large saucepan of boiling water, cook bean sprouts 3 minutes; drain. Using vegetable peeler, cut cucumber into thin strips. Toss together bean sprouts, cucumber, radishes and green onions; place on serving dish and arrange chicken on top. Drizzle with Amazu Sauce. Garnish with toasted sesame seeds, red pepper and green onion tops.

Amazu Sauce:

In a small bowl, mix together ¼ cup soy sauce, ¼ cup sugar, ¼ cup rice vinegar and 1 tablespoon sesame oil; blend well.

SMOTHERED CHICKEN DRUMMETTES

The visit to Gladys Knight's home has been detailed in the Appetizer section with a beautiful recipe for Gazpacho and Guacamole. But the chefs at the Bellagio prepared that and this recipe is one of Gladys' own. She said that she often chooses chicken because of its nutritional value as well as its versatility and taste.

1½	pounds chicken drummettes	3	tablespoons olive oil
¼	cup Worcestershire sauce	1	garlic clove, minced
1	cup orange juice	1	cup mushrooms, sliced
1	package Italian herb mix	1	tablespoon butter
½	teaspoon cayenne pepper	1	onion, sliced
1	teaspoon black pepper	½	yellow pepper, sliced
1	tablespoon salt	½	green pepper, sliced
1	teaspoon curry powder		

With cool water, rinse drummettes; drain. Place chicken in airtight container; add Worcestershire sauce and orange juice. In small bowl, mix together herb mix, cayenne pepper, black pepper, salt, and curry powder. Add to chicken mixture; stir well. Cover chicken in container; refrigerate at least 40 minutes and up to 2 hours. In large saucepan, heat olive oil over medium-low heat. Add garlic, mushrooms and 1 tablespoon butter. Simmer about 1 minute. Add drummettes; cook, turning. Add onion slices and both peppers. Adjust heat to medium; cover and cook about 20 minutes, turning chicken occasionally.

CHICKEN BREASTS WITH BRIE

My good friend, Becky Bowdre, will always have fond memories of having represented the state of Georgia in the National Chicken Cooking Contest in Little Rock, Arkansas, soon before Governor Clinton was to become President Clinton and when Hillary hadn't thought of being a New York Senator and Chelsea was just a little curly haired adolescent. The only thing that marred an otherwise perfect trip was my gift to Becky of a twice life-sized, hand carved wooden chicken to commemorate the occasion. I found the chicken in the hotel gift shop and just knew Becky would adore it. What I didn't think about was that I was going on to Hot Springs for an extended stay and Becky was returning to Macon alone-except for the enormous bird. Although Becky would never curse I know she had horrible thoughts about me as she dragged the chicken from Little Rock to Atlanta to Macon. Once home with it, though, she confessed she warmed up to it pretty well and even grew to appreciate it.

Becky's recipe was wonderful, just like all her recipes. And I'm keeping it forever—or until she gets rid of the chicken.

6	broiler-fryer chicken breast halves, skinned and boned	1	egg white, slightly beaten
¾	teaspoon garlic salt	6	tablespoons margarine
½	teaspoon white pepper	½	cup white wine
6	tablespoons Brie cheese, divided	1	Granny Smith apple, unpeeled and cut into thin slices
3	tablespoons green onions, chopped	2	tablespoons crabapple jelly, divided
1	cup Bremmer wafers, crushed		Parsley sprigs or chopped watercress
½	cup pecans, toasted and chopped		

On hard surface, pound chicken to ¼-inch thickness. Season with garlic salt and white pepper. Put equal amounts of Brie cheese on each chicken breast half. Sprinkle with equal amounts of chopped green onion. Roll up breasts, tucking in ends, and fasten with wooden picks.

Mix cracker crumbs and chopped pecans. Dip chicken breasts in egg white, and then roll in crumb mixture. Melt margarine in large non-stick frying pan, and sauté chicken breasts until golden brown. Add wine, cover, and simmer 30 minutes or until tender. During the last 5 minutes of cooking, add slices of apple. Remove picks and serve chicken on platter, surrounded with apple slices. Put small teaspoon of crabapple jelly on top of each breast. Garnish with sprigs of parsley or chopped watercress.

MAIN DISHES

ICED CHICKEN BREASTS

This recipe is one that makes the rounds quite often and is always mighty welcome when it does. I have served it many, many times—even carried it to Lake Sinclair one time to serve at a birthday luncheon on the screened porch of our cabin. I made a notation that I liked it better with Vidalia onions, fresh chives with the cream cheese, and ½ teaspoon curry. Any way you do it, it is so good and a wonderful summertime specialty.

4	whole chicken breasts, skinned, boned and halved	¼	teaspoon salt
2	(10½-ounce) cans chicken broth	1	finely chopped green onion and top
1	(3-ounce) package cream cheese with chives		Crisp Bibb lettuce leaves
¼	cup mayonnaise	2-3	large tomatoes, peeled and chilled
2	tablespoons lemon juice	2	large avocados
½	teaspoon grated lemon peel	½	cup toasted slivered almonds
			Pitted ripe olives

Cook chicken breasts in broth until tender. Refrigerate in broth to cool. Thoroughly mix cream cheese, mayonnaise, lemon juice, lemon peel, salt and onion. Remove chicken from broth. Completely coat the rounded side of each breast with the cream cheese dressing. Arrange lettuce leaves on 8 dinner plates. Cut tomatoes into 8 thick slices and place on lettuce; sprinkle with salt and pepper. Arrange a chicken breast on each tomato slice. Halve and peel the avocados, cut each into 4 slices and arrange beside chicken. Sprinkle chicken with toasted almonds and garnish with ripe olives. Serve with vinegar and oil dressing.

CHICKEN AVOCADO MELT

I couldn't wait to get home from the National Chicken Cooking Contest in Jackson, Mississippi to serve the winning dish, Chicken Avocado Melt. I knew it was good and a beautiful dish because I had sampled it at the contest. It was my splendid triumph—everything went right and the dish was perfect. Because I was planning to write a column about it, I invited guests and asked them to give me an honest critique of the dish. Oohs and ahs were prevalent with everybody really raving—all but one. One of the men, with a not so sophisticated palate said, "Well, I'll admit it looks pretty and tastes good but why couldn't you have just fried the chicken?" Oh, well, there's one in every crowd.

4	broiler-fryer chicken breast halves, boned, skinned	3	tablespoons cooking oil
2	tablespoons cornstarch	1	firm, ripe avocado, peeled, sliced
1	teaspoon ground cumin	1½	cups shredded Monterey Jack cheese
1	teaspoon garlic salt	½	cup sour cream, divided
1	egg, lightly beaten	¼	cup sliced green onion tops
1	tablespoon water	¼	cup chopped sweet red pepper
⅓	cup cornmeal		Cherry tomatoes
			Parsley sprigs

On hard surface, pound chicken to ¼-inch thickness. In shallow dish, mix together cornstarch, cumin, and garlic salt; add chicken, dredging to coat. In small bowl, mix egg and water. In another small bowl, place cornmeal. Dip chicken, first in egg, then in cornmeal, turning to coat. In large frying pan, place oil and heat to medium temperature. Add chicken and cook 2 minutes on each side. Remove chicken to shallow baking pan; place avocado slices over chicken and sprinkle with cheese. Bake in 350 degree oven for about 15 minutes or until fork can be inserted in chicken with ease and cheese melts. Top chicken with sour cream; sprinkle with onion tops and pepper. Garnish with cherry tomatoes and parsley.

BARBARA BUSH'S LEMON CHICKEN

It was such a thrill to meet Barbara Bush at a lovely luncheon in Washington in 1988. There were many dignitaries there but in her quiet, unassuming way, Mrs. Bush stood out from all the others. If I'm not mistaken it was when Reagan was ready to go out of office and Bush was running for president. I remember wishing the Bushes good luck and Mrs. Bush replied, "Thank you, darling."

Rub 6 chicken breasts (boneless) with lemon juice, salt and pepper and a little flour. Sauté in butter for 7 minutes on each side. Remove from heat and put chicken in baking dish.

Mix together in sauté pan:

2	tablespoons Vermouth	2	tablespoons lemon juice
1	cup heavy cream	1	little lemon, grated

Deglaze the sauté pan from browning the chicken, scraping in all the ingredients. Strain the sauce over the chicken breasts. Sprinkle Parmesan cheese over the top and brown lightly under the broiler for a few minutes.

LEMON DILL CHICKEN

It wasn't because it was prepared by one of our country's most prominent chefs. It truly was a delicious concoction—beyond words. Paul Prudhomme was at the Southeast Hospitality Show in Atlanta in the autumn of '93 and I was there with my mouth hanging open at the way this giant of a man could combine ordinary ingredients to make taste sensations you would never believe. He gave us this wonderful recipe for Lemon Dill Chicken that I treasure. I had my picture taken with Prudhomme and later when I knew he was going to be doing a demonstration for us on a river boat in New Orleans, I took the picture to get him to autograph it. Then someone took a picture of his autographing the picture and if I see him again I think we'll get a picture of his autographing that picture. Have you eaten at his restaurant, K. Pauls in the French Quarter? It's among the greatest of the entire city, state or even country. This recipe is an elegant dish with a combination of unusual and wonderful flavors. Not only does it taste marvelous, it makes a very attractive main dish you'll really be proud to serve.

Seasoning Mix:

1	teaspoon salt	¼	teaspoon black pepper
1	teaspoon dill weed	¼	teaspoon white pepper
1	teaspoon dried sweet basil leaves		

8	(2 to 3 ounces each) boneless, skinless chicken breasts	2	cups julienned onions
		½	cup fresh lemon juice
1	tablespoon plus 2 teaspoons cornstarch	2	(1-gram) packets artificial sweetener, optional
1	cup apple juice		
1½	cups defatted chicken stock		

Combine the seasoning mix ingredients in a small bowl. Sprinkle all surfaces of the chicken evenly with 2 teaspoons of the seasoning mix and rub it in well. Dissolve the cornstarch in ¼ cup of apple juice and set aside. Preheat a heavy 10-inch skillet, preferably nonstick, over high heat to 350 degrees about 4 minutes. Place 4 of the chicken breasts in the skillet, lower the heat to medium, and brown them for at least 1 minute per side. Remove these 4 breasts, brown the other 4, and set all the chicken aside. Return the heat to high and stir in ½ cup of the stock, scraping the bottom of the skillet to clear it of all the browned bits. Add the onions and the remaining seasoning mix, stir and cook until all the liquid evaporates, about 3 to 4 minutes. Stir in ¼ cup of the lemon juice, scrape the bottom of the skillet again to clear it, and cook until liquid evaporates, about 3 to 4 minutes. Add ½ cup of the apple juice, clean the bottom and sides of the skillet, and cook until about half of the liquid evaporates, about 2 or 3 minutes. Stir in the remaining cup of stock, the ¼ cup of lemon juice, and the ¼ cup apple juice. Bring to a boil (will take 2 to 3 minutes), whisk in the cornstarch, apple juice mixture and return it to a boil. Return the chicken to the skillet, lower the heat to medium, and cook until the chicken is done all the way through, about 4 to 5 minutes. Turn off the heat, remove the chicken, and if desired, whisk in the artificial sweetener.

❖ Paul Prudhomme autographs for Louise ❖

WADE BOGGS' BAKED CHICKEN

Can you imagine that the featured speaker at a chicken seminar I attended in Charleston, S.C. was Wade Boggs, the 1983 Major League batting champion. There was a good reason Boggs was the featured speaker: he had compiled a cookbook called "Fowl Tips" and makes it his business to tout chicken whenever possible.

Boggs says: "It may sound strange, but I maintain that chicken has played a major part in the success of my baseball career. It all started back in 1977 when I was coming up in the minors. My wife Debbie and I ate chicken a lot back then—maybe two or three times a week. Chicken was cheaper than other meats and we were trying to save our money. Besides, we just plain liked the way chicken tasted. But during spring training that year, I noticed something peculiar. On those days when I ate chicken before a game, I always got at least two hits. Then one day after a particularly delicious meal of Debbie's Lemon Chicken, I went out and played what I guess was my first perfect game in professional ball. Now it's no secret that I'm a very superstitious person. Before stepping into the batter's box I always make the Hebrew "Chai" sign for good luck. Going out on the field I'm always careful to step over the foul line, and coming back into the dugout I always step on the line. So when I started getting hits after eating chicken, I just naturally began eating more chicken. And I'll be doggoned if my batting average didn't continue to rise. Don't ask me to explain it. I won't even try. All I know is that now I eat chicken before every single game we play."

2-3 pounds chicken (fryer)	Dash salt
1 medium-size onion, (halved, peeled)	

Preheat oven to 400 degrees. Rub chicken with raw onion, inside and out. Rub salt into chicken, again inside and out. Place the onion halves in the body cavity. Place chicken breast side down in shallow baking dish or pan. Do not cover pan. Bake for 45 minutes. Turn chicken breast side up and bake for an additional 15 minutes.

CHICKEN 'N DUMPLINGS

The Pirate's House *is located on one of the most historic spots in Georgia. When Oglethorpe and his little band of colonists arrived from England in 1733, they came ashore in the vicinity of the present City Hall on Bull and Bay Street in Savannah, approximately seven blocks due west of the Pirate's House location. Within one month Oglethorpe established on this spot the first public agricultural experimental garden in America. The Herb House built there in 1734 is the oldest house in Georgia.*

In 1753 an inn for visiting seamen was built. Just a block from the Savannah River, the inn became a rendezvous of blood-thirsty pirates and sailors, who would drink the fiery grog and share adventures from Singapore to Port Said. They also would shanghai unwary seamen to complete their crews. Stories still are told of a tunnel that ran underneath the inn to the river where they dragged the men, often drugged and unconscious, to ships waiting in the harbor. Life-size stuffed figures of these pirates can be viewed down in the tunnel entrance and they captivate the imagination of young visitors to this historic spot. Their Chicken 'N Dumplings will captivate you too.

1	frying chicken, cut up		2	slices lemon
3	cups water			Salt and pepper
½	cup chopped onions			Dumpling batter
½	bay leaf			

Simmer chicken with all ingredients except dumplings for 45 minutes or until tender. Remove bay leaf and lemon. Drop dumpling batter on top of chicken with teaspoon. Cover tightly and simmer 15 minutes without removing cover.

Dumpling Batter:

1	cup sifted flour		1	teaspoon minced onion
1	teaspoon baking powder		2	egg yolks
¾	teaspoon salt		½	cup milk
⅛	teaspoon nutmeg, optional			

Sift dry ingredients. Add onion. Beat egg yolks with milk and add to dry ingredients. Mix lightly until blended.

BASIC FRIED CHICKEN WITH CREAM GRAVY

We were a group of hungry food editors in Madison, Georgia waiting for the big lunch to begin under the huge white tent set up on a vacant lot. As guests of the National Broiler Council we are always entertained lavishly. The day in the gorgeous little town of Madison was certainly no exception, in fact it was superlative. Besides a tour of the town and the marvelous luncheon, there were food demonstrations going on in several of the gorgeous historic homes. We wanted to see them all so we had to hurry but when we got to the kitchen where Damon Fowler, cookbook writer and food authority from Savannah, was cooking we just had to pause and drool while he was showing how to cook good old southern fried chicken. Many of the writers from other parts of the country just couldn't believe it. He even used lard! Since then, my and Damon's paths have crossed several times, once when he was autographing copies of his Classical Southern Cooking at a bookstore in Macon. This recipe is from his book and is southern to the bone.

2 young fryers (2½ to 3 pounds each), cleaned and disjointed Salt and black pepper in a pepper mill	2 cups all-purpose flour, or more About ¾ pound lard (all right, vegetable oil if you must)

Gravy:

2 tablespoons cooking fat from chicken 1 tablespoon all-purpose flour from chicken coating	1½ cups light cream or half-and-half Salt and pepper in a pepper mill.

Put the chicken pieces in a basin of cold water and soak them for a few minutes. Drain well and pat them dry with a clean towel. Season them liberally with salt and black pepper and set aside. This is a modern adaptation, but it works better than the old spread-on-a-dinner-plate-and-dredge method: Put the flour in a medium-size brown paper bag, fold over the top, and give it a quick shake to loosely dust the inside of the bag with the flour. Put the lard in a large, deep, cast-iron skillet that will hold both chickens without crowding. Place the skillet over medium-high heat and heat until the lard is completely melted and hot, but not smoking, around 325 degrees to 350 degrees. A few pieces at a time, drop the chicken parts into the paper bag, fold over the top, and shake until they are thoroughly coated. You may need more than 2 cups of flour, so check before dropping in more pieces. Take the coated pieces out of the bag, shake off the excess flour, and slip them skin side down into the hot fat. Repeat until all the chicken pieces are coated and in the pan. (If you don't have a large enough pan, you can use 2 pans or cook the chicken in batches. But don't flour the pieces until you are ready to cook them.) Reserve the leftover flour. Cook the chickens slowly until the bottom side is a rich golden brown, about 12 to 15 minutes. Carefully turn them and continue cooking until each piece is golden brown on all sides and just cooked through, about another 12 to 15 minutes. The juices of a punctured piece should run clear, but try not to test it this way more than you can help, or you will dry the chicken out. Some recipes direct that the chicken is done when it no longer sizzles as you turn it over, but that will only lead to certain disaster. If it doesn't sizzle, it's because it's dried out and overcooked. Remove the chickens to a pan lined with butcher paper or paper towels. Drain them briefly, but keep them warm.

For the gravy pour off all but 2 tablespoons of the cooking fat into a heat proof bowl. Put the skillet back over the heat and throw in a tablespoon of the flour left over from coating the chickens. Cook the flour in the fat, scraping the pan to keep it from scorching and to loosen any bits of crust that may remain in the skillet, until it begins to brown. When the flour turns a light brown, slowly add the cream, stirring constantly to keep it from lumping, and cook until the gravy is lightly thickened. Let it simmer gently for 3 or 4 minutes, but don't let it get too thick. Season it to taste with salt and a few grindings of black pepper and pour into a sauce boat. Don't strain it: the little bits of crust are an essential part of the flavor. Transfer the chicken to a serving platter and serve at once.

HOT CHICKEN SANDWICH

I really don't know how long ago I acquired this good recipe but the large gas range on the back of the Blue Home Kitchen *recipe was selling for $249.00. The* Blue Home Kitchen *put out a lot of recipes that were worth saving and this is one of them. It's just a quick and delicious little lunch when you're in a hurry and special enough to serve to guests.*

6	slices dry whole-wheat toast	⅓	cup evaporated milk
⅓-½	pound sliced cooked chicken	6	large or 12 small tomato slices
1	(10½-ounce) can condensed cream of chicken soup	4	partly cooked bacon slices, cut in thirds
		6	stuffed olives, sliced

Preheat broiler. Place toast slices on a shallow baking pan. Cover with slices of chicken. Combine soup and evaporated milk in saucepan; heat to simmering. Pour hot soup mixture over sandwiches. Arrange tomato slices on top of sandwiches. Top with bacon slices and olives. Broil until sandwiches are hot and bacon is crisp.

THE COUNTRY CAPTAIN

Haven't times changed so much since the '40s? President Roosevelt (FDR) would call Warm Springs before leaving Washington and ask the cook at the Little White House in Warm Springs to be sure and have ready his favorite dish, Country Captain. Then he would board the train and slowly make his way to his secluded little home in Warm Springs. Now they would e-mail the request and board a jet and be in Warm Springs before Daisy could get the chicken going. Actually they might pick up some chicken at Kentucky Fried on their way in. At one time this recipe was for sale in Warm Springs for 50 cents. This is a spicy kind of chicken dish that I'll have to admit is not my favorite recipe. I made it immediately after securing the recipe and have never made it again. However, since so many people do like Country Captain and since this is Roosevelt's own recipe; and since I think it is worthy of preserving as one of my special recipes, I include it here.

1	hen or 2 fryers	1	large or 2 small cans tomatoes
3	onions, chopped	1	large or 2 small cans mushrooms
1	tablespoon butter	1	teaspoon curry powder
3	green peppers, chopped	1	teaspoon thyme
1	cup raisins or currants	1	small can tomato paste or sauce
1	garlic clove, finely chopped	2	cups boiled rice
	Salt and pepper to taste	1	cup chicken stock
1	cup nuts, pecans or peanuts, chopped		

Boil hen or steam fryers. Sauté onions in butter. Add green peppers, raisins, garlic, salt, pepper, nuts, tomatoes, mushrooms, curry powder, thyme and tomato paste to sautéed onions. Skin and bone chicken. Add to sauce with chicken stock and simmer for 1 hour. Serve over rice and garnish with green pepper, nuts, and raisins.

MOTHER'S CHICKEN TETRAZZINI

Mother introduced us to this outstanding dish after we were all married and living in other places. It soon became a family favorite though and one that we have had on many occasions. Sometimes when I have a little spare time, I make a recipe of this, put it into disposable foil pans about loaf pan size, and freeze it to have for hurried meals or to take to friends and neighbors. I use all the chicken from a whole stewed fryer. It really is one of my favorite recipes.

3	cups chopped cooked chicken		1	(8-ounce) can mushrooms
½	cup butter		2	cans mushroom soup, undiluted
1	cup chopped celery		1	cup grated cheese
3	medium onions, chopped		1	(8-ounce) thin spaghetti
1	bell pepper, chopped			

Sauté raw vegetables in butter. Add mushrooms and soup and cheese. Add spaghetti which has been cooked in chicken stock. Add chicken. Put in buttered casserole. Bake at 375 degrees until bubbly and brown.

CURRIED CHICKEN CRÊPES

This is a delicious recipe that I have found to be the best chicken crêpe recipe I have ever tried. The use of apples makes it so tasty and the curry is just the finishing perfect touch.

1½	tablespoons olive oil			Pinch of sugar
½	medium onion, chopped		½	teaspoon salt
1	apple, chopped		1	carrot, grated
2	tablespoons flour		2	tablespoons lemon juice
1½	tablespoons curry powder		4-6	cups chicken, cooked and shredded
1½	cups chicken stock			Crêpes
2½	cups milk			

Heat olive oil in a large skillet. Add onion and apple and sauté until onion is transparent. Add flour and curry and cook 1 minute. Add chicken stock and milk slowly, stirring constantly. Then add sugar and salt. Bring to a slow boil, add the carrot and lemon juice and simmer covered for 7 to 10 minutes. Sauce should be on the thin side as the chicken will absorb some moisture and some will bake off. Divide the chicken among the crêpes, cover with 2 tablespoons of the sauce and roll up. Place crêpes in a buttered baking dish and spoon over the rest of the sauce. Bake uncovered at 350 degrees for 20 minutes or until bubbling.

CHICKEN AND CORN TORTILLA CASSEROLE

This is a recipe from the Christ Church Cookbook *that was submitted by one of my younger friends, Claire Smith, who is the daughter of my contemporary and friend, Fran McCommon. Claire has the reputation of being one of Macon's finest cooks. When her name is attached to any public serving of food everybody always says in accord, "Oh, yes, it's going to be good if Claire Smith has anything to do with it." Therefore when I see a recipe with Claire's name on it, I always try it. This was actually sent to me by another friend, who is a wonderful cook, who said, "Try this—I did and it's very good." Not only did I try it, I got on a jag with it and couldn't quit. I served it every time I entertained for a month or two and then I made up a batch of it and divided it into about four or five small casseroles and put it in the freezer to take to friends when I need something. You'll really enjoy this recipe.*

½	cup butter	2	pounds Velveeta cheese
1½	cups onions, chopped	2-3	cups cooked chicken, chopped
2	(10-ounce) cans tomato and chili*	2	cups sour cream
1	(28-ounce) canned tomatoes, chopped	15	stale 5-inch corn tortillas, broken into small pieces

*If I can't find this I use a can of stewed tomatoes and small can of chili; (we prefer mild.)

Preheat oven to 325 degrees. In large skillet, sauté onions in butter. Drain all tomatoes; reserve juice. To onions, add the drained tomatoes and chili, tomatoes, cheese, chicken and sour cream. Line the bottom of a greased 9x13-inch baking dish with tortilla pieces. Top with chicken mixture and bake uncovered 45 minutes at 325 degrees. Add small amount of reserved tomato liquid if it seems too dry.

CHICKEN AND ALMOND MOUSSE

Vera Matthews, whose husband at one time owned the Chevrolet dealership in Wrightsville, was the town's authority on entertaining and serving lovely food. Along with all her attributes, she owned a huge old house that lent itself so beautifully to great parties. This is a recipe that Vera served right often at her bridge luncheons. It's good she did because everybody was always disappointed when she didn't.

1	envelope gelatine		Few drops of fresh lemon juice
1	cup cold chicken broth		Dash of cayenne pepper
3	egg yolks, lightly beaten	½	teaspoon dried, crumbled rosemary
1	cup ground cooked white chicken		Salt
½	cup ground blanched almonds	1	cup heavy cream, beaten stiff

Sprinkle the gelatin over the broth, then heat just until the gelatin has dissolved. Pour the hot liquid over the egg yolks in a steady stream, stirring vigorously. Return the mixture to the saucepan, and heat gently, stirring constantly until it thickens slightly. Add the ground chicken and almonds (they may be ground very successfully in a food processor), lemon juice, cayenne pepper, and rosemary. Season liberally with salt, as chilled foods always become more bland. Chill until the mixture thickens to the consistency of an unbeaten egg white, then fold in the whipped cream. Pour into a 4-cup mold and chill.

CHICKEN-DIJON QUICHE

In promoting the Pillsbury Bake-Off® contest, Pillsbury sent little pamphlets of wonderful recipes using Pillsbury® pie crusts. Since I had a little group of ladies coming over for an executive board meeting of the garden club, I surprised them by asking them to stay to sample the new quiche recipe I had discovered. It is truly a good recipe but as for any quiche, I always recommend that it is much superior when you first take it out of the oven. However one of the girls at the luncheon, who is an excellent, award-winning cook, disagreed with me so just use your own discretion about warming it after the initial baking.

Crust:
1 Pillsbury® refrigerated pie crust (from 15-ounce package)

Filling:
2 tablespoons butter or margarine

½ cup sliced fresh mushrooms

¼ cup chopped onion

1 clove garlic, minced

¾ cup cubed chicken

1 teaspoon dried Italian seasoning

¼ cup white wine

1 ounce (¼ cup) shredded fresh Parmesan cheese

1 ounce (¼ cup) shredded Gruyère or Swiss cheese

1 cup whipping cream

1 tablespoon Dijon mustard

3 eggs

Heat oven to 400 degrees. Prepare pie crust as directed on package for 1-crust baked shell using 10-inch tart pan with removable bottom or 9-inch pie pan. Place prepared crust in pan; press in bottom and up sides of pan. Trim edges if necessary. DO NOT PRICK CRUST. Bake at 400 degrees for 9 to 13 minutes or until crust appears dry and is very light golden brown. Meanwhile, in medium skillet, melt margarine over medium-high heat. Add mushrooms, onion and garlic. Cook and stir until tender. Stir in chicken, Italian seasoning and wine; cook over medium heat until liquid evaporates, stirring occasionally. Spread chicken mixture over bottom of partially baked shell. Sprinkle with 2 tablespoons each of the Parmesan and Gruyère cheese. In medium bowl, combine cream, mustard and eggs; beat well. Pour over cheese; sprinkle with remaining Parmesan and Gruyère cheese. Bake at 400 degrees for 23 to 28 minutes or until quiche is golden brown and knife inserted near center comes out clean. Let stand 5 minutes before serving.

CHICK 'N PUFFS

My daughter, Carol, had tasted this recipe of Sandy Ballance's and thought it was out of this world. Therefore the next time I was in The Collection *in Dublin, I asked Sandy if there was any way she'd give me the recipe. If you've ever been in* Dottie Smith's The Collection, *you know she and her daughters Sandy and Wendy will go out their way to be helpful. Thus Sandy gladly gave me this recipe which is truly a good one.*

⅓   cup crushed seasoned croutons
¼   cup finely chopped pecans
1   (3-ounce) package cream cheese
2   tablespoons softened butter
½   teaspoon lemon pepper
1   cup cooked chicken, finely chopped

1   (2-ounce) can mushrooms, drained, finely chopped
1   can Pillsbury® Refrigerated Crescent Rolls
3   tablespoons melted butter

Place croutons and pecans in small bowl. In medium bowl combine cream cheese, 2 tablespoons butter, seasonings. Stir in chicken and mushrooms. Separate rolls into 8 triangles; place 2 heaping tablespoons mixture on each triangle. Roll up, starting on shortest side of triangle-roll to opposite point. Tuck sides, point under to seal completely. Dip rolls in melted butter; coat with crumb mixture. Bake on ungreased cooked sheet at 375 degrees for 15 to 20 minutes until golden brown. (May be prepared up to 2 hours before serving. Cover, refrigerate. Bake at 375 degrees for 20 to 25 minutes.)

KING RANCH CHICKEN CASSEROLE

My friend Linda Cloaninger, has an abiding interest in good food and knows what to do about it. She and I always enjoy sharing recipes and talking about good places we've found to eat. One night at bridge she asked me if I had ever tried the King Ranch Casserole. The answer was "no" but it was "yes" the next time we talked. This is a delicious chicken recipe and one that freezes well. Linda says "Add a platter of chopped tomatoes, lettuce, sweet onions and a bowl of refried beans for a great meal."

10	corn tortillas, cut up		2	cans Ro-Tel tomatoes, diced
3	cups chopped cooked chicken		1	onion, diced
2	cans cream of chicken soup		8	ounces Monterey Jack cheese, grated
1	(8-ounce) carton sour cream		8	ounce Longhorn Cheddar cheese, grated

Line 3-quart baking dish with ½ the tortillas. Top with ½ the chicken. Mix soup, sour cream, tomatoes and onion and spread ½ of mixture on chicken. Top with ½ of the shredded cheese. Repeat layers. Bake at 350 degrees for 1 hour. May be prepared a day ahead and refrigerated. I add ½ to ¾ cup milk to sauce as tortillas soak up liquids when setting. I often prepare in 2 casseroles and freeze one for later.

ROCK CORNISH GAME HENS

I've long forgotten who was coming to dinner but I do remember that it was someone that I wanted to serve a really special meal. After great deliberation about menus and almost deciding on a seafood, I chose instead to do game hens. It's always too much of a surprise when one or some of your guests are allergic to seafood and I wasn't sure about my guests' allergies. This recipe turned out to be really good, served with Orange Rice (in Side Dish section). I mounded the rice in the center of an enormous round platter and placed the hens all around the rice with the little legs sticking up in the same direction. Orange slices and small sprigs of basil and parsley decorated the platter and it was beautiful and delicious. You may use whole hens also.

Cornish game hens	Pepper
Salt	1 small jar orange marmalade

Wash and dry hens. Split each one into half. Salt and pepper each half. Bake according to package directions, basting at intervals with orange marmalade. Serve with Orange Rice in Side Dish section.

SAVORY SAUSAGE RICE

Lynda Colston Turner of Warthen and Sandersville was trained by one of the best cooks in the world, her mother. Lynda has become a wonderful cook too, and since she was at one time my sixth grade pupil, I especially treasure this delicious recipe that she gave me years ago.

2	pounds sausage	2	(1¾-ounce) package chicken noodle soup mix
1	cup green pepper, chopped		
¾	cup chopped onion	1	cup raw rice
2½	cups celery	½	teaspoon salt
4½	cups boiling water		

Brown sausage and drain. Add pepper, celery and onion. Sauté. Combine soup mix and water in large saucepan. Stir in rice. Cover and simmer 20 minutes. Add sausage mixture and salt. Mix well. Pour into greased 13x9x2-inch dish and bake at 350 degrees for 20 minutes. Freezes real well.

RISE AND SHINE SAUSAGE OATMEAL CUPS

When you have overnight guests, you also have breakfast guests. Since I'm not a "morning person" I always look for things to serve for breakfast that can all be ready at the same time. This is a neat way to get the morning sausage and eggs served together. You can make the sausage cups ahead and freeze or refrigerate them. Then when you're ready just reheat them and fill them with the eggs and voila—you have breakfast and no one has to know you're grumpy in the morning.

Cups:

1	pound roll sausage, uncooked	1	egg white
1	tablespoon finely chopped onion	¼	cup milk
⅔	cup rolled oats		

Filling:

8	eggs	2	tablespoons fresh chives, dill or green onion tops, chopped fine
½	cup soft cream cheese		Salt and pepper to taste
¾	cup chopped and seeded tomatoes, drained		

Preheat oven to 350 degrees. In a medium bowl, combine the "cups" ingredients listed above. Divide the mixture evenly into 12 muffin tin cups. Press mixture firmly around the bottom and sides to form hollow cups. Bake 12 to 15 minutes or until done. Remove from oven, drain cups on paper towels and keep warm. In large skillet, begin scrambling the eggs. When almost done, fold in remaining ingredients and finish cooking. Divide the mixture into the sausage cups and serve hot. Makes 12 sausage cups. Refrigerate leftovers. Note: sausage cups can be prepared in advance and refrigerated or frozen. Reheat when ready to fill.

CRANBERRY GLAZED PORK TENDERLOIN

I was provoked that I was having to wait in the doctor's office when I needed to be at home getting ready for a visit from my cousins for the weekend. All of a sudden I found a cookbook and I was immediately transported to the land of no stress at all. It's amazing how you can get lost just reading the delicious recipes. Then I found one that I just knew would be an ideal main course for the first night of the weekend. I borrowed pads of paper with pharmaceutical advertising and quickly copied Cranberry Glazed Pork—a recipe that turned out to be just perfect for a cool autumn evening.

1	cup fresh cranberries		1	teaspoon curry
1	cup coarsely chopped apples		⅛	teaspoon red pepper
⅔	cup packed dark brown sugar		2	(¾-pound) pork tenderloins
½	cup water		1	tablespoon orange zest
¼	cup chopped onion			(or grated orange rind)
1	tablespoon peeled fresh ginger, grated			Salt and pepper
				Cooking spray

Preheat oven to 350 degrees. Combine first 8 ingredients in small saucepan and bring to a boil. Cover and reduce the heat to low and simmer for 20 minutes. Uncover and simmer for 2 minutes until the mixture begins to thicken. Remove from the heat and cool for about 10 minutes. When cool place in the food processor and process until the mixture is smooth. Divide into 2 parts. Salt and pepper the pork and place on a pan coated with vegetable oil spray. Spread half of the cranberry mixture over the pork and bake for about 30 minutes or until the temperature of the pork reaches 160 degrees. Remove to a serving platter and spread the remaining cranberry mixture over the pork loin.

DOUBLED BUTTERFLIED PORK LOIN

This is perhaps one of my masterpieces and deserves saving forever. I did this in a cooking demonstration and loved the response. So, it's complicated. Some things just are. This is worth all the time and trouble. First you have to double butterfly the pork loin and don't depend on your butcher to know how. You must either take him the directions or do it yourself.

1. Butterfly (cut lengthwise almost all the way through) a 3 to 4-pound boneless loin.
2. Lay open loin and pat flat.
3. Starting in the center of open loin, butterfly again on the left side.
4. Butterfly again on the right side; lay open and pat flat.
5. Evenly spread desired stuffing (about 2 cups) over loin.
6. Start with the shorter side and roll.
7. Tie loin securely at 2 to 3-inch intervals with kitchen twine.
8. Place loin in shallow roasting pan and roast at 350 degrees for 1 to 1½ hours or to 155 degrees to 160 degrees on a meat thermometer. Baste at 20 minute intervals with Basting Sauce.
9. Let loin rest 5 to 10 minutes before slicing to serve.

For the Basting Sauce:

Melt 1 cup apple jelly and ½ cup Calvados over low heat.

For the Stuffing:

1	large apple, diced	1	cup herb-seasoned bread crumbs
1	medium onion, chopped	2	tablespoons Calvados
2-3	tablespoons vegetable oil		

Sauté the onions and apples in the oil over medium heat. When tender add the crumbs and Calvados and mix well. Remove from heat. Stuff the loin.

To present the dish:

Remove the string and place the meat on a serving platter and slice it about ⅓-inch thick, leaving a portion unsliced. Place Yates Apples (in Side Dish section) around the roast and intersperse them with green apple leaves, parsley, celery leaves, basil or galax leaves from the mountains.

MAIN DISHES

BRUNSWICK STEW

As the California friends were coming, I decided to really go southern. What better could I do than Brunswick Stew and barbecue for one of the meals? In order to make it truly authentic, I decided to use a hog's head for the stew. The beautiful, part-time actress and her trumpet-playing-husband who played with Skinny Ennis' band on the west coast (Beryl and Skinner Hicks) were lovely guests. They responded to the southern cooking with even more enthusiasm than I had dared to hope for, and upon their return to California, Beryl called back to find out about Brunswick Stew. "I've told all my friends about it, Louise, and I'm even going to make some for them if you'll give me the recipe." Flattery will get you everywhere, Beryl, and I was happy to share. When I explained to her that the first ingredient was a hog's head, maybe a bit difficult to find in Beverly Hills, she quickly nixed the whole idea after picking herself up off the floor. You can use a pork shoulder with great success too. I've made this a zillion times—always putting bags of it in the freezer. It makes a great quick supper if you stop by on the way home and pick up the barbecue to go with it.

Boil until tender and falling off the bone a pork shoulder or a fresh hog's head. Remove the meat from the bone and grind it with the meat grinder–run it through twice. Add the meat back to the strained stock. Add canned tomatoes which have been pulverized in blender, onions, Worcestershire sauce, catsup, vinegar, lots of black pepper, and salt. Add canned corn and either small English peas or butter beans. Cook very slowly for several hours, stirring occasionally to prevent sticking. The amounts are not definite. I cook it to taste and according to the amount of pork I use.

TALMADGE COUNTRY CURED HAM

Nothing pleases me much more than a delicious country ham. It is a lot of trouble to cook one properly but oh, my goodness, it's more than worth the work. The holidays are always more exciting when the prospect of a good country ham is luring you to the kitchen. I like Betty Talmadge's recipe for cooking a ham and have used it over and over and over again. Do yourself a big favor!

1	country cured ham (12 to 15 pounds)	2	bay leaves
6	onions	24	whole cloves plus more for decoration
3	cups light brown sugar	2	teaspoons dry mustard
2	cups white vinegar		

Wash the ham thoroughly, soak it overnight in water, and drain. Place in a roasting pan with 2 cups of water, add the onions, 2 cups of the brown sugar, the vinegar, bay leaves and 24 cloves. Cover the roasting pan and bring it to a simmer on top of the stove. Continue to simmer-do not boil-20 minutes to the pound. The ham is done when the small bone at the hock end can be twisted out. Let the ham cool in the liquid. Pour off liquid. Preheat the oven to 450 degrees. Remove the skin and cut off excess fat, score, and insert whole cloves in a decorative pattern. Mix the remaining 1 cup brown sugar with the mustard to make a glaze; press it onto the ham. Bake 20 minutes to glaze. To serve, slice thinner than you would a commercial ham.

MAIN DISHES

SHRIMP GRAVY

Because it's dated on the bridge score sheet on which it was copied, I know it was in 1991 that our little bridge club, (The McJaals) was enjoying a week at Amelia Island at my college roommate's, Joyce Clay's condo right on the beach. A little publication called Amelia Now *had some great-sounding recipes and I called the editor to ask her about some of them. This is the one that she said her son would kill for. I wouldn't go that far, for sure, but I might nudge you slightly if I thought you were serving yourself more than your share.*

	About 2 ounces white bacon (unsmoked salt pork), cut in cubes	2	pounds raw shrimp, shelled, deveined and floured
½	cup green pepper, chopped fine	1	envelope Lipton's Onion Soup Mix
½	cup celery, chopped fine		Water (about 1 cup)
			Pepper

Fry white bacon until golden brown. Remove. Pour off excess fat. (If not enough fat rendered for sautéing, add little vegetable oil.) Sauté chopped celery and bell pepper. Remove. Add floured shrimp and stir until lightly cooked. Add Lipton's onion soup mix to the sauté and add water to gravy consistency. Return bacon, celery and bell pepper to shrimp. Add a little pepper. (No salt necessary.) Cook over lowest heat about 10 minutes to meld flavors. Serve over cooked rice.

DEVILED SHRIMP

The bright yellow cookbook, The Linley Heflin Cookbook, *was chosen by one of Dublin's best cooks, Camilla Curry, to be sold for the 1984 project of Friends of the Library in Dublin. The organization presented me a preview copy that I treasure dearly. The Deviled Shrimp is one of the book's best—though I haven't found a recipe in it yet that wasn't delicious.*

1½	pounds fresh cooked shrimp	½	teaspoon salt
¼	cup chopped onion		Freshly ground pepper
1	clove garlic, minced	¾	cup milk
2	tablespoons butter	¼	cup cream
1½	tablespoons flour	¼	pound sharp cheese, grated
½	teaspoon dry mustard	1	tablespoon Sherry

Shell and devein shrimp. Simmer onion and garlic in butter in skillet until golden. Blend in flour and seasonings. Add milk and cream gradually, stirring constantly until thickened. Add grated cheese and wine. When cheese melts add shrimp and heat thoroughly. Serve hot over Holland rusk or noodles. You can use lobster or crabmeat instead of, or combined with shrimp.

BLEU CHEESE GRITS WITH SAUTÉED SHRIMP

Elise Griffin was for many years one of Atlanta's premier cooking school instructors. I made several trips to her home where she conducted her classes in a garden house in the backyard. It was always exciting news when Elise came to Macon to teach a course and it was particularly exciting when she introduced us to this spectacular shrimp dish. She told us we could substitute canned creamed corn for the fresh corn and Parmesan cheese for the Bleu cheese—just be sure to grate it yourself.

2	quarts half-and-half		2	cups corn kernels, fresh
2	cups quick grits (don't use instant)		1	tablespoon minced garlic
¾	teaspoon salt			Several dashes Tabasco sauce
1½	cups crumbled bleu cheese		1	tablespoon Worcestershire sauce

Bring half-and-half to a boil in a large pot, slowly add grits and salt, stirring constantly. Bring back to a boil then reduce heat and cook, stirring about 5 more minutes. Add bleu cheese, corn, garlic, Tabasco and Worcestershire and stir until cheese is melted and grits are thick. Serve immediately, topped with sautéed shrimp.

Note: Not a bleu cheese fan? Leave it out or add Parmesan or no cheese at all.

Sautéed Shrimp:

⅓	cup butter		1½	pounds medium shrimp, peeled and deveined
¼	cup chopped shallots			Chopped basil and tomatoes for garnish

Melt butter in skillet and add shallots. Cook until soft 2 to 3 minutes. Add shrimp and cook until shrimp are pink and cooked through. Serve on top of grits. Sprinkle with basil and tomatoes.

SAN ANTONIO GUMBO

If you've ever been to San Antonio, you've known the River Walk and Jim Cullum's famous Reedy Creek Jazz Band. Stroll along the river and you'll be tempted to eat in almost every one of the many good restaurants. And always try to work in at least one order of their famous San Antonio Gumbo. It is delicious.

6	tablespoons flour
5	tablespoons bacon drippings
2	onions, finely chopped
1½	cups finely chopped celery
1	clove garlic, pressed
1	(28-ounce) can tomatoes
1	(15-ounce) can tomato sauce
5	cups water

Salt and pepper to taste
2 pounds raw shrimp, peeled
2 (7½-ounce) cans king crabmeat or 3 (6-ounce) packages frozen crabmeat
1-2 (10-ounce) packages frozen cut okra
3 tablespoons Worcestershire sauce
1 teaspoon chili powder

In a large, heavy kettle, brown flour in bacon drippings until dark brown. This takes a long time. Add onions, celery and garlic and cook until onions are transparent and slightly browned. Add tomatoes, tomato sauce, water, salt, and pepper and boil over medium heat for about 1 hour. Add seafood and okra. Cook about 30 minutes or until desired thickness is obtained. Add Worcestershire sauce and chili powder and continue to cook 5 to 10 minutes. Serve over rice.

NANCY TARBUTTON'S SEAFOOD BAKE

In the '70s, Nancy and Ben Tarbutton were welcoming guests to their stately new home in Sandersville. Always the charming hostess, Nancy would never have ignored my request for her delicious main course recipe that she served at one of her scrumptious dinners. It came in the mail just a day or two later and I have guarded it carefully for all these years.

2	tablespoons flour		1	tablespoon dry sherry
2	tablespoons butter			Cayenne pepper and salt
1	pint half-and-half cream		1	pound crabmeat or 1½ pounds shrimp or half shrimp and half crab
1	tablespoon Worcestershire sauce		1	can artichoke hearts, sliced
1	tablespoon paprika		1	cup grated New York sharp cheese
1	tablespoon lemon juice			
2	tablespoons catsup			

Make a sauce by combining flour and butter in saucepan over medium heat. Add cream and stir until thickened. Add Worcestershire, paprika, lemon juice, catsup, sherry, salt and pepper. Stir well.

Layer seafood, sliced artichoke hearts and sauce until casserole dish is filled. Top with cheese. Bake at 300 degrees.

CRABMEAT LOUIS

Crabmeat Louis is a famous New Orleans dish and one that I like to think is named for the greatest jazz trumpeter of them all, Louis Armstrong, who was from New Orleans. This recipe is from a jazz history and cookbook given to me in 1980 by another great jazz musician, clarinetist Pud Brown and his sweet wife Louise. They came to Dublin to play in the Shamrock Festival and stayed with us.

1	pound crabmeat (cooked)			Juice of ½ lemon
1	large head (or 2 small) romaine lettuce		1	tablespoon capers
1	cup homemade mayonnaise		¼	teaspoon cayenne
½	cup tomato sauce			Salt and freshly ground black pepper

Remove the coarse ribs of the lettuce leaves, and finely shred the green part of the leaves. Mix mayonnaise, tomato sauce, lemon juice, capers, cayenne, salt and pepper. Add shredded lettuce to this mixture. Add the crabmeat and mix it in gently so as not to break it up. Serve in 4 individual salad bowls.

SAVANNAH PIE

When I was growing up in Guyton, a small town near Savannah, it was always a special bonus to stop by Mathews Seafood Company *down by the old marketplace when we were returning home after a day of shopping in the city. There are so many wonderful ways to prepare the crab, shrimp, and fish that we used to buy but this Savannah Pie is a favorite.*

1	recipe (10-inch) pie pastry	2	tablespoons butter
1	cup shredded Swiss cheese	¼	teaspoon dried tarragon, crumbled
1	cup shredded Cheddar cheese	¼	teaspoon Old Bay seasoning
1	pound cooked crabmeat	¼	teaspoon freshly grated nutmeg
1	cup dry-roasted cashews, chopped	⅛	teaspoon freshly ground pepper
8	eggs, beaten	1	large red onion, minced
3	cups whipping cream	1½	(16-ounce) packages frozen chopped spinach, thawed, squeezed dry
	Salt and freshly ground pepper to taste		

Fit the pastry into a 10-inch springform pan and bake using the pastry recipe directions. Layer the Swiss cheese, Cheddar cheese, crabmeat and cashews in the prepared crust. Beat the eggs and cream in a mixing bowl. Season with salt and pepper to taste. Pour half the mixture over the layers, reserving the remaining portion. Place the springform pan on the center rack of an oven preheated 450 degrees and reduce the temperature to 350 degrees. Bake for 35 to 40 minutes or until the custard portion is set but not brown. Melt the butter in a large heavy skillet over medium-low heat. Stir in the tarragon, Old Bay Seasoning, nutmeg and ⅛ teaspoon pepper. Add the onion and cook for 10 minutes or until translucent, stirring occasionally. Add the spinach and sauté for 3 minutes. Set aside ¼ cup of the reserved egg mixture. Stir the remaining egg mixture into the spinach. Spread evenly over the pie. Pour the ¼ cup egg mixture that was set aside over the top. Bake for 25 to 30 minutes longer or until the custard is set and the top is golden brown. Let stand for 30 minutes. Place on a serving plate and remove the side of the pan. Cut into wedges to serve.

OYSTERS À LA RUSSE

It was intriguing and at the same time disturbing to see the Titanic Exhibit when it was in Memphis. Lavish meals were served on the ill-fated ship and one of the passengers, Kate Bass, wrote: "On the night of the wreck our dinner tables were a picture! The huge bunches of grapes which topped the fruit baskets on every table were thrilling. The menus were wonderfully varied and tempting. I stayed at table from soup to nuts."

Oysters à la Russe was one of the dishes served on the Titanic.

2	tablespoons vodka	1	plum tomato, seeded and finely chopped
½	teaspoon lemon juice	1	tablespoon finely chopped chives
¼	teaspoon prepared horseradish	12	large oysters, in the shell
	Dash hot pepper sauce		Coarsely cracked black peppercorns
	Pinch each granulated sugar and salt		

In bowl, stir together vodka, lemon juice, horseradish, hot pepper sauce, sugar, and salt. Gently stir in tomato and chives. Wash oysters under running water to remove any loose barnacles or sand. Insert tip of oyster shucker between shell halves near hinge; twist upward to open shell. Discard top shell. Using blade of shucker, sever connective membrane that holds oyster to bottom shell. Place open oysters on bed of shaved or crushed ice. Spoon vodka relish over each oyster; dust with cracked pepper.

MAIN DISHES

OYSTER CASSEROLE

W. L. and Helen Lake of Dublin have been my admired friends for over 50 years. They excel in elegant dining, beautiful table settings, flowers galore both inside and outside, and gracious entertaining with style. Through the years they have shared their wonderful recipes with me and this is one that Helen wrote on an index card for me—a long, long time ago-maybe before oysters became almost cost prohibitive.

Save up your money and invest in 3 pints of oysters and expect your investment to pay dividends with this scrumptious dish.

3 pints oysters	Tabasco sauce
½ pound saltine crackers, coarsely crumbled	Worcestershire sauce
Salt and pepper	3 cups oyster liquid
1 stick butter, melted	1 pint whipping cream

Butter 3-quart casserole. Layer crackers, oysters, seasonings and butter. Put 1 drop Tabasco sauce and 1 drop Worcestershire sauce on each oyster. Do 2 layers ending with crackers. Pour oyster liquid and cream over all. Bake at 350 degrees 45 minutes to 1 hour.

JIMMY CARTER'S FAVORITE FRIED FISH

My college friends, Louise Gartrell and Margaret Sewell gave me copies of their two church cookbooks, What Can I Bring? *and* What More Can I Bring? *from Northside Baptist in Atlanta. They are two of my favorite "girls" (after 50+ years) and these are two of my favorite books.*

Having just made a trip with my Sunday School Class to Maranantha Baptist in Plains to hear our greatly spiritual former president speak, I just had to try his recipe for fish from What More Can I Bring? *I think it's the peanut oil that does it—don't you, Mr. President?*

Fish	Bisquick or pancake mix
A-1 or Heinz 57 sauce	Peanut oil
Dash Tabasco sauce	

Fillet fish, cut in strips about the size of French fries. Marinate several hours in A-1 or Heinz 57 sauce with a touch of Tabasco sauce. Shake in a bag with Bisquick or pancake mix. Deep fry in peanut oil. Serve hot or cold.

POMPANO EN PAPILLOTE

In the '50s I had this dish at one of the first world-class restaurants I ever visited. I loved Bourbon Street and all the jazz but the food in New Orleans won my heart. Antoine's in the same place on St. Louis Street in the French Quarter since its 1840 foundings, is a special place to dine. It's an enormous property with 3 floors—and so much good food you wouldn't believe it. This is the dish I ate there in the 50's.

Fish Velouté Sauce:

2	tablespoons butter
2	tablespoons flour
1½	cups warm fish or chicken stock

Salt and white pepper to taste
Additional butter

3	tablespoons butter	1	onion, sliced
1	cup chopped green onions	2	teaspoons salt
1	cup raw peeled shrimp	5	whole black peppercorns
1½	cups white wine, divided	2	bay leaves
1	cup lump crabmeat		Juice of 1 lemon
	Salt, white pepper, and cayenne to taste		Water
6	(16-ounce) skinned pompano fillets		Parchment paper

To make Velouté Sauce: Melt the butter and stir in the flour. Stir and cook until the mixture becomes foamy. Add the warm stock and bring to a boil. Turn heat down to simmer while adding salt and pepper to taste. Remove from heat and dot top of sauce with a few pieces of butter to prevent a film from forming. Makes 1½ cups of Velouté Sauce.

Melt the butter and sauté the green onions until they become limp. Add the shrimp, 1 cup of the wine, and bring to a boil. Blend in the velouté sauce and the crabmeat. Season to taste with salt, pepper, and cayenne. Simmer gently for 10 minutes, then let cool. Poach the pompano fillets for 3 minutes in a shallow pan with the sliced onion, 2 teaspoons salt, peppercorns, the remaining ½ cup wine, bay leaves, lemon juice, and enough water to cover. Remove the fillets from the poaching liquid and keep warm. Cut parchment paper into 6 heart-shaped pieces, about 10 inches long and 14 inches wide. Spoon some of the sauce onto the center of one half of the heart-shaped paper and top with a pompano fillet. Fold the other half of the paper over the top and seal the edges by folding edges tightly together. Place these on an oiled baking pan, and bake at 400 degrees for 15 minutes or until the paper begins to brown. Bring to the table and cut the top of the paper open.

MAIN DISHES

CHARTRES STREET TROUT

*While in New Orleans one year for the Sugar Bowl, the friends who were with us knew
Chris Blake who owned a really good restaurant, Christopher Blake's. They were able to get
reservations. The Chartres Street Trout was a memorable dish. "The secret to good fish is,"
Chris said to us in a whisper, "to be on the dock when the boats come in. It has to be FRESH."*

Chris shared his recipe for the delicious fish and it's a simple and simply good way to do trout.

6	fillets of fresh trout	¼	teaspoon Tabasco sauce
1	stick butter	4	tablespoons large capers
	Juice of 2 lemons		Chopped parsley or chervil
	Salt and white pepper to taste		

Place trout in a buttered pan. Dot each trout with small pieces of butter and cover with
buttered white butcher paper or parchment paper. Bake in a moderate oven (350 degrees) for
15 to 20 minutes, depending on the size of the trout. Do not overcook the fish. When fish are
done, immediately add the juice of the lemons to the butter in the pan, along with salt and
pepper to taste and the Tabasco sauce. Add the drained capers. Serve immediately with
chopped parsley or chervil and buttered wedges of toast.

BAKED SHAD

*Near Guyton, my birthplace, flows the dark and wild Ogeechee River that has some of the
finest river fishing anywhere around. (It also has alligators that used to bellow at night when we
were spending the night in our river cabin—kinda scary to a young child.) It was always a good
deal when the early morning fisherman would pull in their boats just loaded with shad. Of course
a special bonus was to find a good shad roe inside one of the fish. This is a good recipe for Baked
Shad if you're so lucky as to get your hands on one.*

1	large shad	1	large onion, thinly sliced
	Salt and pepper		Juice of 2 lemons
2-3	strips bacon	1	quart milk

Salt and pepper fish; place in large roaster. Put bacon and onion slices over top of fish; pour
lemon juice and milk over. Bake, covered, at 250 degrees for 6 hours, without opening oven
door. All bones dissolve.

SHRIMP-STUFFED FLOUNDER

Becky Bowdre, Shirley Butler, Helen Dunwoody, Joann Floyd, Laurie Kay, Edyth Snow, Blanche Westmoreland, Elizabeth Wyche, Gloria Wynn, Mary Jean Yates...these Macon "girls", all friends of mine, have been playing bridge together for over 50 years. They decided that they really cook and serve marvelous meals better than they play bridge so under the guidance of several of the members who qualify as seasoned gourmets, in 1986 they published Table Talk— *one of the finest area cookbooks I know.*

My darling friend, Mary Jean, has this recipe for Shrimp-Stuffed Flounder that is delicious with Hollandaise Sauce over it.

¼	cup butter	2	tablespoons parsley, minced
1	clove garlic, minced	1	teaspoon salt
1	medium onion	¼	teaspoon white pepper
⅓	cup minced green pepper		Cayenne to taste
4	tablespoons chopped green onion	8	fillets of flounder (2½ pounds)
24	large shrimp, cooked	8	strips lean bacon
½	cup bread crumbs		

Melt butter in a skillet. Sauté garlic, onion, and pepper until soft. Dice 16 shrimp and add to sautéed mixture with bread crumbs, parsley, salt, pepper, and cayenne. Remove from heat. Spread 2 tablespoons shrimp mixture onto each fillet, and roll up lengthwise. Partially cook the bacon to remove excess grease, and when cool, but still limp, wrap around each fillet. Refrigerate on a cookie sheet until ready to bake. Arrange the fillets in a lightly greased baking dish and bake at 350 degrees for 25 to 30 minutes, or until fish flakes easily with a fork. Pour Hollandaise sauce over fish, when ready to serve, and garnish with remaining shrimp.

COURT-BOUILLON

Years ago we dined at the Royal Orleans in the French Quarter in New Orleans. We were guests of a couple who were residents of the Crescent City so when Rose and Willard suggested that I try the Snapper Court-Bouillon, of course I followed their plan. This dish was so absolutely fantastic that I couldn't believe it. At that point in my life it might have been the best thing I ever tasted. That was before I started food writing so I had no idea of trying to request the recipe. I thought I'd just come home and search all the cookbooks and find it but not true. I never have seen the recipe duplicated anywhere. Therefore I had to do it myself and if I do say so, I finally worked out a fairly respectable duplication. I'll never forget buying a large red snapper in Savannah years ago and preparing this recipe for some of Mother's friends. They liked it too. The amounts of ingredients are not given. I'm sorry—you'll have to fly on your own with this one but it's certainly worth a try.

Large red snapper, dressed

Onions, chopped

Bell pepper, chopped

Celery, chopped

Fresh tomatoes, cubed (or canned)

Olive oil

White wine

Rice

Hollandaise sauce

Sauté onions, bell pepper, and celery in olive oil. Add tomatoes and simmer for several minutes. Place snapper in a baking dish and pour vegetables over it. Pour wine over fish. Cover with foil and bake at 350 degrees until fish flakes done. Place fish over a bed of fluffy, hot rice with vegetables spooned over it. Top with Hollandaise sauce and serve.

VEAL SCALOPPINE

When I refer to my A Southern Collection *published by the Junior League of Columbus, I always am reminded of good times in Columbus. Not only did we have family there, I attended flower shows; graduated from the Memphis in May barbecue judging classes and went to a lovely party on their beautiful river walk. The most exciting experience of all was going to the Steeplechase and meeting the celebrated author and former jockey for the Queen of England, Dick Francis.*

Although we didn't have this recipe at the Steeplechase, we did have outstanding food and spirits. This is from A Southern Collection *and is a great way to serve veal.*

1½ pounds veal cut very thin from the loin or round	4 tablespoons hot butter
Seasoned flour	1 bouillon cube
Parmesan cheese, grated	½ cup water
	3 tablespoons Madeira or sherry

Pound the meat with a mallet until it is even thinner. Dredge it with seasoned flour and sprinkle with Parmesan cheese. Sauté the slices until a golden brown on both sides, in butter. Remove them to a hot platter. Dissolve bouillon cube in water. Add this to the pan and stir in Madeira or sherry. Scrape the pan well, pour the sauce over the meat.

❖ Mary Jean Yates, Carolyn Ray and Louise at Steeplechase in Columbus ❖

RACK OF LAMB WITH VEGETABLES

My dear friend, Iris Gillis and I did something we'd wanted to do for a long time. We went to Atlanta and spent the night and treated our "deserving selves" to a marvelous meal at The Abbey. The Abbey was an old church converted into a restaurant and we weren't too sure about the sacrilege of the occasion but we were greatly impressed after we overcame our original misgivings. A lovely harpist played heavenly music from the loft as we dined on several courses that really fulfilled our wish for an extravagant indulgence.

This Rack of Lamb was served surrounded with grilled vegetables such as tomatoes, zucchini, yellow squash, and green beans. This is great. Someone commented that they had been served this dish in many restaurants here and abroad but The Abbey's was by far the best.

2½-3	pound racks of lamb, ribs partially split	¼	cup (½ stick) melted butter
2-3	garlic cloves, minced	4	cups beef stock
	Salt and freshly ground pepper	1	tablespoon tomato paste
2	medium carrots, diced	2	bay leaves
2	medium onions, diced	1	garlic clove, minced
2	celery stalks, diced	1	teaspoon rosemary
½	cup dry bread crumbs	1	teaspoon cornstarch
		¼	cup water

Preheat oven to 350 degrees. Rub lamb with garlic and salt and pepper to taste. Cover rib bones individually with aluminum foil to keep them from burning. Place racks in a large roasting pan, fat side up. Distribute carrots, onions and celery around. Roast, uncovered, until meat reaches desired degree of doneness on thermometer, about 25 to 30 minutes for medium. Preheat the broiler. Combine bread crumbs with butter and spread over meat. Place under broiler about 1 to 2 minutes to brown. Remove meat from roasting pan and keep warm. Place pan on burners; cover and simmer for 10 minutes. Stir in stock, tomato paste, bay leaves, garlic, and rosemary. Bring to a boil; cover and simmer 10 more minutes. Dissolve cornstarch in water. Carefully stir into stock mixture, blending until smooth. Bring to a boil, stirring constantly over high heat; reduce heat to low and cook, uncovered, 5 minutes. Place racks on serving platter. Strain sauce into sauceboat and serve separately.

ROAST LAMB WITH PEPPERCORN CRUST

If you think Nathalie Dupree is a whiz at cooking on her television shows, you should be so lucky as to be invited to one of her parties. The greatest assemblage (both in quality and quantity) of guests that you could ever imagine is invited. The food is always superb and the house is always crowded to the extent that no matter in which direction you turn, you bump into someone interesting—chefs, writers, business people, educators.

Sheila Lukins of The Silver Palate *fame was one of her especially intriguing guests. She had just published a new cookbook and everybody was anxious to get a copy. This recipe is one that Sheila pointed out to me as being delicious and it is!*

3	tablespoons crushed dried peppercorns, an equal mix of white, black and green	½	cup raspberry vinegar
		¼	cup Oriental soy sauce
1	tablespoon fresh rosemary leaves, or 1½ teaspoons dried	½	cup dry red wine
		1	boned but untied leg of lamb, about 5 pounds (weighed after boning)
½	cup fresh mint leaves		
5	garlic cloves, crushed	2	tablespoons prepared Dijon-style mustard

Combine 1 tablespoon of the crushed peppercorns, the rosemary, mint, garlic, vinegar, soy sauce and red wine in a shallow bowl. Marinate the lamb in the mixture for 8 hours, turning occasionally. Remove roast from marinade and drain; reserve marinade. Roll the roast, tying it with kitchen twine. Preheat oven to 350 degrees. Spread mustard over meat and pat 2 tablespoons of crushed peppercorns into the mustard. Set the roast in a shallow roasting pan just large enough to hold it comfortably and pour reserved marinade carefully around but not over roast. Bake for 1½ hours, or 18 minutes per pound, basting occasionally. Roast will be medium rare. Bake for another 10 to 15 minutes for well-done meat. Let roast stand 20 minutes before carving. Serve pan juices in gravy boat along with lamb.

LAMB ON SKEWERS WITH MINT SAUCE

Martha Stewart, not too well known at the time, put on a cooking demonstration in Macon in 1988. My darling friend Lou Davis, who now lives in Hilton Head, S.C., invited me to be her guest for the show but unfortunately the bug bit me and I was unable to go. Lou ran by afterward with an autographed copy of Martha's book Entertaining and after thoroughly perusing every facet of it, I put it on the shelf with many, many other cookbooks.

Just recently my friend Mary Ann Norris stopped by to visit and was pulling books off the shelf to look at them and she shouted, "Oh, you have an autographed copy of Martha Stewart!" Well, yes, I did. I had forgotten. It says "To Louise—Be entertaining always!" I think I must have taken it literally.

4	pounds lean lamb, cut into ¾-inch cubes	1	tablespoon salt
			Freshly ground pepper to taste
½	cup olive oil	1	teaspoon thyme
	Juice of 2 lemons	2	tablespoons chopped fresh mint

Mint Sauce:

4	tablespoons water	⅓	cup finely chopped mint leaves
2	tablespoons confectioners' sugar	½	cup white vinegar

Put lamb and marinade ingredients in a glass or stainless steel bowl. Let stand for 3 hours or overnight in the refrigerator. Using 6-inch bamboo skewers, put 3 lamb cubes on each. This can be done the morning of the party. Grill meat over a charcoal fire or in a hot broiler, being careful not to burn the skewers. If they do begin to burn, cover the exposed portion of the skewers with a piece of aluminum foil. To make mint sauce, boil the water and sugar. Cool and then add mint and vinegar. The sauce is best made ½ hour before serving, serve in a small bowl along with the hot skewered lamb.

PINE BARK STEW

When Mother and I would do a recipe with an inordinate number of ingredients, Daddy's sage remark was always the same: "It's good but you could eat pine bark with all this stuff in it." Here's one that Daddy would have sanctioned called Pine Bark Stew and it's a great way to use fish—fresh or frozen.

½	pound chopped streak-o-lean		1	bay leaf
2	large onions, chopped		2	teaspoons sugar (or 1 packet Sweet and Low)
1	quart (14-ounce) can V-8 juice		1-1½	pounds fresh, cleaned fish or 2 (10-ounce) packages of frozen fish fillets
2	(1 pound) cans stewed tomatoes			
1	tablespoon Worcestershire sauce			
	Tabasco sauce to taste			

Sauté streak-o-lean until lightly brown. Remove pieces and reserve. Sauté onions in pork fat until tan. Remove onions to Dutch oven. Add reserved meat bits and all other ingredients except fish. Simmer 30 minutes. Add fish and simmer until fish flakes, about 20 minutes, but is not falling apart. Serve over a large hunk of toasted homemade bread in a soup bowl. Accompany with a tart coleslaw.

MAIN DISHES

PEPPER STEAK

This is an old recipe from my cousin (in-law) Nony McMichael. Nony is really more than a cousin—she's a friend and I have always loved the too–brief times I've spent with her and her doctor husband, Robert. Such gentle, sweet people I've never seen. Nony has always enjoyed swapping recipes and I have many of hers, usually written on pretty, flowery stationery. This good recipe, Nony says, is from Mrs. Williams who used to teach cooking classes down at the old Vocational-Tech School in Macon. It's a great dish to serve over hot, fluffy rice and will satisfy at least four appetites.

1	pound beef chuck, cut in very thin strips (about 1-inch long and diameter of your little finger.) (Also may use round steak.)	¼	cup water	
		1	cup green pepper, cut in fairly small pieces	
¼	cup cooking (salad) oil	1	cup chopped onion	
1	clove garlic, minced	½	cup chopped celery	
1	tablespoon soy sauce	1	tablespoon cornstarch	
1	teaspoon salt	1	cup water	
		2	tomatoes, cut in eighths	

Brown beef in hot oil; add garlic and cook until garlic is yellow. Add soy sauce, salt and ¼ cup water; cook 45 minutes. Add vegetables (except tomatoes) and cook 10 minutes. Stir in cornstarch blended with 1 cup water. Add tomatoes and cook 5 minutes. Serve over hot fluffy rice.

STEAK SANTA FE

You would have thought Syb and I were world's most intrepid travelers as we motored our way from Albuquerque to Santa Fe in a big white rented Lincoln Town Car.

As we sat in our hotel room, pondering the plane trip home the next morning, we had the wild idea that we could stay over a day, rent a car and make that greatly dreamed about trip to Santa Fe. The walk from the hotel to the car rental spot was worth the whole idea. Albuquerque has marvelous bronze statues all along its city sidewalks and we felt that we were visiting a wonderful art museum.

I drove the big, fine car while Syb spent half the trip with her head buried in the map. The natural sights along the way were absolutely breathtaking with land configurations we'd never seen anywhere. The colors of the soil were amazing. Soon we became brave enough in our venture that we veered off the main road and visited an Indian reservation right down on the Rio Grande.

We found Santa Fe to be an intriguing town with more Indian jewelry than we could ever hope to see. There were many outstanding restaurants too and we had a fine meal of Steak Santa Fe— neither of us remembers where.

4	tablespoons butter	⅓	cup sliced mushrooms
2	tablespoons lemon juice	1	pound bay scallops
1	clove garlic, crushed	¼	cup dry white wine
¼	cup onion, chopped	4	(8-ounce) filet mignons
¼	cup celery, chopped		

Mix vegetables and sauté in lemon juice and butter. Do not brown. Add scallops and simmer 2 minutes. Add wine and simmer 2 minutes. Drain vegetables and scallop mixture. Cut pocket in filets and fill with vegetables and scallops. Broil meat to taste.

BEEF TENDERLOIN DELUXE

Let's just face it. You can serve all the Lobster Thermidor and Roast Pheasant you want, but if you really want to serve the ultimate, just resort to a Beef Tenderloin. Expensive, yes! Easy to prepare, yes! (And doesn't saving time mean a lot these days?) I've tried Beef Tenderloin everywhere from Seattle to Miami and from Augusta (Maine) to Phoenix and I've gathered recipes all along the way. This is my favorite—gleaned somewhere along the Miracle Mile in the Windy City, Chicago.

1	(3 to 4-pound) beef tenderloin	3	tablespoons soy sauce
½	cup chopped onion	2	teaspoons dry mustard
1½	tablespoons butter or margarine, melted	⅛	teaspoon salt
1	cup dry sherry	⅛	teaspoon pepper

Trim excess fat from beef tenderloin. Place beef tenderloin in a large shallow baking pan; bake, uncovered, at 400 degrees for 10 minutes. Sauté onion in butter until tender; add remaining ingredients. Bring to a boil; pour over tenderloin. Reduce heat to 325 degrees; bake 35 minutes or until a meat thermometer reaches 140 degrees to 170 degrees. Baste often with drippings. Slice tenderloin; serve with remaining drippings.

MAIN DISHES

FILET MIGNON IN WINE SAUCE

This recipe is wonderful to serve for company because it can be done ahead and because it is so elegant. We spent a lovely weekend years ago at the beautiful old Gault House right on the Ohio River in Louisville, Kentucky. We were fortunate to get reservations on the steam boat that chugged up and down the river for dinner cruises and I was particularly lucky to get this delicious recipe.

2	tablespoons butter		½	cup water
6	beef filets		2	tablespoons parsley, snipped
½	cup chopped mushroom stems		1	teaspoon salt
¼	cup chopped green onions			Dash of pepper
2	teaspoons cornstarch		12	large mushroom caps
1	cup red wine			

Melt butter in heavy skillet. Brown filets on both sides over moderate heat. Place on squares of heavy aluminum foil on baking sheet. Cook mushroom stems and onions in fat remaining in skillet until they are tender. Blend in cornstarch, add red wine, water, parsley, salt and pepper. Cook and stir until sauce thickens. Spoon 2 tablespoons wine sauce over each filet. Top with 2 mushroom crowns. Bring sides of foil up and pinch corners. Refrigerate until 30 minutes before serving. Bake at 500 degrees, 20 minutes for rare, 25 to 30 for medium or well done. Reheat any remaining sauce and serve with filets.

JAILHOUSE STEW

My bragging rights allow me to say I've eaten everywhere from the House of Lords in London to the House of the Lord in rural Appling County, Georgia; and from the White House to the Jail House. When our able leader Ray Wilkes was Bibb County Sheriff, I was invited to tour the jail and have lunch in preparation for a story I was doing. My heart was torn out when I saw some of the inmates and I pondered long about what course of events had caused them to come to such a sad situation. Especially emotional was seeing a very dignified looking little old lady with white hair who immediately reminded me of my own mother. She was in for murder! "Ray's food" was plain and wholesome and prepared in a kitchen so clean you would have eaten off the floor. Beef Stew, simple and nutritious, yet delicious, was one of the menu items the day of my visit.

1	tablespoon vegetable oil	2	cups cubed potatoes
1	pound ground chuck	1	cup sliced carrots
1	cup chopped onion	1	(10-ounce) package frozen mixed vegetables
1	cup chopped celery		
1	(16-ounce) can whole tomatoes, undrained and chopped	1	teaspoon salt
		1	teaspoon black pepper
2	cups water		

Combine oil, ground chuck, onion, and celery in a large Dutch oven. Cook over high heat until beef is browned, stirring to crumble beef. Cover, reduce heat to low, and cook 15 minutes, stirring occasionally. Drain well. Add remaining ingredients. Bring to a boil; cover, reduce heat, and simmer 20 minutes or until vegetables are tender.

CONFEDERATE BEEF STEW

Since I am the granddaughter of a War Between the States veteran, I always perk up and pay attention to anything labeled "confederate." Thus when I found this recipe I clipped it to try and I am glad. This makes you proud to be a "confederate". It has a more interesting flavor than your standard beef stew. Maybe it's the apple—or maybe the red wine.

2	pounds stew beef	1	small bay leaf
2	tablespoons salad oil	⅛	teaspoon thyme
1	large apple, pared and shredded	4	teaspoons cornstarch
1	medium carrot, shredded	¼	cup cold water
½	onion, sliced	¼	teaspoon Kitchen Bouquet
½	cup water	2½	cups medium noodles, cooked and drained
⅓	cup dry red wine		
1	clove garlic, minced	¼	teaspoon poppy seed
2	beef bouillon cubes		

Cut meat into 1-inch cubes and brown in hot oil. Add apple, carrot, onion, water, wine, garlic, bouillon cubes, bay leaf and thyme. Cover and cook over low heat for 2 hours or until beef is tender. Remove bay leaf. Combine cornstarch and cold water; add to beef mixture. Cook and stir until thickened. Stir in Kitchen Bouquet. Serve over noodles and sprinkle with poppy seed.

CHINESE MEAT BALL SAUCE

Dixey Smith is a cook of extraordinary talent and knowledge. Years ago she and I were roommates at the gorgeous Greenbrier Hotel where we studied culinary arts under the great Julie Dannenbaum. I've forgotten a lot we learned but I'll never forget the ultrasuede suits that Dixie had. They were new at the time and terribly expensive and frankly, I didn't have one, much less several like Dixey. Honest, I didn't maneuver this but my luggage was lost on the plane and for two days Dixey dressed me in her gorgeous suits. Unfortunately my luggage was finally delivered straight to our hotel room.

This is a great recipe of Dixey's that you'll like a lot. Just make your meatballs and cover with this oriental sauce.

1	cup vinegar
2	cups pineapple juice
¾	cup sugar
2	cups canned consommé
2	tablespoons soy sauce
3	tablespoons grated fresh ginger or 5 tablespoons chopped crystallized ginger
½	cup cornstarch
1	cup cold water

Heat together vinegar, pineapple juice, sugar, consommé, soy sauce and ginger. Gradually stir in cornstarch mixed with cold water. Cook, stirring until clear and thickened. Keep meat balls hot in chafing dish with just enough sauce to form a slight glaze.

RATTLESNAKE CAKES

The wildest chefs I've ever met are Jeff Black and Jay Moore who run Hudson's on the Bend outside Austin, Texas. One sight of their picture on front of their Cooking Fearlessly *and you'll see. They are standing side by side laughing uproariously, while their tall white toques are being consumed with flames.*

I almost missed the exciting cooking class they put on in an amphitheater near their restaurant and the scrumptious dinner that followed. My roommate at the hotel back in Austin and I missed the bus that was taking all our group and we were bewildered as to what we should do. Finally I said, "We'll get a cab to take us out there," but we didn't know where the restaurant was— neither did our cab driver. After several frantic calls to headquarters, the driver learned where to go and we were on our way. And we weren't too terribly late—just missed a little of the happy hour that preceded the cooking class.

These seemingly light hearted chefs have a good portion of humor as the main ingredient in all that they do. But their cooking tastes serious and has been experienced by celebrities such as Dan Rather, Willie Nelson, Jimmy Buffet, Bill Gates and George W. Bush.

One of the exciting dishes we were served at Hudson's on The Bend was Rattlesnake Cakes in a Pistachio Nut Crust. Don't say you don't have any rattlesnake handy. Just order from Native Game 12556WCR1/2, Brighton Colorado 80601. Call 800-952-6321 if you just cannot wait.

Rattlesnake was just the beginning. We had a wonderful 5 course meal including Backstrap stuffed with Lobster, Wild Boar and Chicken Nogales served with Blue Grits and Chambord Mousse also known as Tina Turner Mousse.

Rattlesnake Cakes:

1	pound rattlesnake, poached and pulled off bones	2	tablespoons Creole/spicy mustard
¾	cup celery, diced	2	tablespoons cilantro leaves, chopped
1	tablespoon garlic, minced	1	tablespoon basil, chopped
½	cup mayonnaise	2	jalapeños, seeded and minced
2	egg yolks, beaten	¼	cup bread crumbs
		1	tablespoon salt

Combine all above ingredients in a large mixing bowl and blend well.

Nut Crust Mix:

1	cup pistachio nuts	⅓	cup olive oil
½	cup bread crumbs		Chipotle Sauce (recipe below)
	Salt and pepper		

Chop pistachio nuts, bread crumbs, and salt and pepper to a coarse grind in a food processor. With a #70 scoop or your hand, form a ball of the rattlesnake mix about the size of a golf ball or a little larger and drop into the nut crust mix. This should flatten into a 2-inch diameter patty. Make sure you press nut crust all around the cake. Heat oil in a large sauté pan over medium-high heat to about 325 to 350 degrees. At 325 degrees, oil should shimmer like the heat coming off a hot asphalt road in summertime. Sauté about 2 minutes each side until golden brown. Remove from pan. Pat off excess oil and serve atop Chipotle Sauce.

Chipotle Sauce:

2	cups good, rich chicken stock	1	tablespoon Worcestershire sauce
3	cloves shallots, minced	¼	cup brown sugar, packed
2	large chipotle peppers	2	teaspoons salt
4	dashes Tabasco sauce	½	cup cream
3	cloves garlic, minced	1	bunch cilantro (leaves only)
¼	cup sun-dried tomatoes		

Put stock in large saucepan. Add shallots, peppers, Tabasco sauce, garlic, tomatoes, Worcestershire sauce, and brown sugar and simmer for 15 minutes. Puree in a food processor. Add salt. Add cream and cilantro. Mix well. Return to the pot to heat through. When reheating, bring the sauce up to a simmer and serve.

WILD DUCKS WITH ORANGE SAUCE

Don't ever promise to dress the ducks! As my son-in-law, DuBose Porter, came down the squeaking stairs at 4:30 a.m. to go duck hunting, I called to him from my bedroom, "If you shoot 'em, I'll clean 'em." Well, he did, and I did. Not only that I cooked 'em, but it was all worthwhile because they were so-o-o delicious. Try to allow one half duck per person. Salt the ducks and let stand about 10 minutes before proceeding.

1	gallon water	1	teaspoon black pepper
2	onions, peeled and sliced		Accent
2	teaspoons sage	4	tablespoons butter per duck
2	teaspoons celery salt		

Place ducks, sage, onions and celery salt in water and cook gently for 4 to 5 hours. Test often for doneness, since age of ducks will determine cooking time. As ducks become tender remove from water and place in roasting pan. Reserve stock. Put 1 tablespoon butter inside each duck. Sprinkle inside and out with Accent and black pepper. Baste pan of ducks with 2 cups of stock. Add 4 tablespoons of butter per duck. Brown slowly for 20 to 30 minutes in 250 degree oven, basting often. Serve with Orange Sauce. (See Orange Sauce accompanying Cornish Game Hen recipe)

DOVES

Now if I'm totally honest, I'll have to say that for me I'll take my doves fried like chicken any day of the week. If I had to select my last supper, I'm sure it would be fried doves; long-cooked, slow-cooked, grits with milk and butter; and sliced home grown tomatoes. A big glass of ice cold milk. Just in case, though, that you would prefer a more sophisticated recipe for doves, try this.

For 16 doves:

Wash doves and pat dry. Salt and pepper each bird and wrap each in a half slice of bacon. Brown in a heavy skillet in ½ stick butter. It may take more. Add 1⅓ cups wine (white or red or vermouth) and ⅔ cup canned beef bouillon. Liquid should almost cover birds. Cut rind from 1 lemon and add plus the juice squeezed over the birds. Add ½ teaspoon thyme, 1 stalk of celery, cut in several pieces, plus a few celery leaves, 1 tablespoon Worcestershire sauce, 1 bay leaf, ½ teaspoon oregano. Cover and simmer slowly about 1 to 1½ hours. Gravy should be strained. It may be thickened if desired. Allow at least 2 doves per person.

DOVE PILAU

This is a good recipe for cooking dove that is used often in South Georgia. Dove is such a delicious treat, and really so rare for some, that I would not recommend using only the breasts. Use the whole dove and gnaw the bones until they are dry as a sun-baked cow-skull in the desert.

It seems only yesterday that my first grandson, Stephen was a darling little toddler with big blue eyes and blonde curly hair. One of life's greatest thrills was to open my back door and see him standing there ready to come in and take over. Now he's all grown up and in college. He's quite a good dove hunter and takes great pride in sharing his birds for family suppers.

6 doves or 12 dove breasts	1 bay leaf
¼ pound bacon, cubed or ¼ cup bacon drippings	½ teaspoon salt
1 medium onion, chopped	4 drops Tabasco sauce
5 cups chicken broth	1 tablespoon parsley
Pinch of thyme	1½ cups rice, uncooked and washed
	¼ pound button mushrooms

Fry bacon over low heat in a heavy Dutch oven with a tight fitting top until lightly browned. Add doves or dove breasts and brown. Add onion and sauté until limp. Add the chicken broth and all the seasonings. Bring to a boil and add the washed rice. Cover and cook over very low heat about 25 minutes until the rice is tender and the broth absorbed. Stir once with a fork. Add the mushrooms and cook 5 minutes longer.

❖ My grandsons, the Porter boys, Guyton, Asa, Stephen and Inman with their daddy Dubose, returning from the big hunt. ❖

BROILED QUAIL WITH PERSIMMON RELISH

✧ Wolfgang Puck at Spago in Las Vegas ✧

If being in Las Vegas at the world famous Bellagio were not enough, we (food editors) were entertained in the finest restaurants there—all by the National Chicken Council. Wolfgang Puck, world famous California chef had just taken his restaurant to Vegas (May 2000) and we had the privilege of meeting him, dining in his outstanding restaurant, and asking him a zillion questions.

As I was darting out afterward to claim the last seat on the bus, I stopped long enough to buy Puck's Adventures in the Kitchen *which had this wonderful recipe for quail.*

6	boned quail, about 3 ounces each		Pinch of ground cumin
1	very ripe persimmon* (about 4 ounces), pulp pureed		Salt
	Juice of 1 lemon		Freshly ground white pepper

Persimmon Relish:

1	cup diced (about 2 medium) very ripe persimmons*	3	teaspoons chopped cilantro
½	cup diced onion		Pinch of cayenne pepper
½	jalapeño pepper, cored, seeded, and diced		Salt
2	tablespoons lime juice	1	tablespoon cooking oil
			Cilantro leaves

*Persimmons must be very ripe for the best flavor. If not in season, mango or papaya can be substituted.

Split each quail down the back, flatten and skewer the legs into the body with toothpicks or small skewers. In a dish large enough to hold the quail in 1 layer, combine the pureed persimmon, lemon juice, cumin, and salt and pepper to taste. Marinate the quails, turning to coat all sides, for about 2 hours, refrigerated. Prepare the relish: In a small bowl, combine all the ingredients and season with salt to taste. Preheat oven to broil. Heat the oil in an oven proof skillet large enough to hold the quails in 1 layer. Remove the quail from the marinade and arrange in the pan, opened side down. Sauté for 2 minutes and then transfer to the broiler for 2 to 3 minutes, until nicely browned. Presentation: Spoon some of the relish on each of 6 plates. Set 1 quail in the center of the relish, open side down, and garnish with a few cilantro leaves. Serve immediately. To prepare ahead: Through step 3, refrigerating, covered, until needed.

MAIN DISHES

HUNGARIAN SAUCE

This is one of my old, old recipes that represents my early venture into something a little more exciting than meat and potatoes every day (what my husband always wanted). This pleased him though and we had it often until I turned the page onto something else new and different. It is delicious served over chicken breasts that have been boned and skinned and cut into pieces, battered and fried.

2	tablespoons lard or bacon fat	1	cup dry white or red wine
1	medium onion, finely chopped	1	cup chicken stock
1	tablespoon flour		Herb bouquet (parsley, thyme, bay leaf, tied in cheesecloth)
1	tablespoon Hungarian paprika	1	cup sour cream
	Coarse salt		(Use with fish, veal or chicken)
	Pepper		

Heat the fat in a saucepan and fry the onion until golden. Stir in the flour and cook for 2 to 3 minutes. Add paprika, salt and pepper. Add the wine, stock, and herb bouquet, and cook until thick. Add the sour cream, bring to a boil, and serve hot.

LAKE PLACID MEAT SAUCE

I guess you would expect us to be at the Winter Olympics or something at Lake Placid, New York. Actually we were picking up the most gorgeous autumn leaves you've ever seen. The grounds near the Lake were just blanketed with rich-colored leaves that needed to be transported to Georgia for future references. And they have been referred to over and over again between resting between sheets of waxed paper in a kitchen drawer. It's amazing how beautifully they've kept with no special treatment. I refer, also, to this good sauce recipe that we were served there. It's great over grilled fish or meat or even fried fish.

¼	cup soft butter	1	tablespoon minced chives
1	tablespoon lemon juice	½	teaspoon salt
1	tablespoon chopped parsley	¼	teaspoon pepper

Blend all ingredients thoroughly with a wooden spoon. Serve over meat or fish.

SONNY'S BASIC BAR-B-Q SAUCE

Since becoming a Memphis in May accredited barbecue judge I've had lots of fun judging contests all over everywhere. The Big Pig Jig in Vienna, Georgia and the Memphis in May contest in Memphis are among the favorites. For one mile along the Mississippi River in Memphis, barbecue huts are set up where the barbecue cooks just have a ball cooking, tasting and fiercely competing. I've tasted so many sauces, barbecues and Brunswick stews that it's mind boggling. Never have I tasted a barbecue sauce any better than that of my friend Sonny Oxley who is a wonderful cook in his own right. He doesn't compete in the contests and they better be glad. He'd win them all.

2	cups vinegar		2	teaspoons pepper
3	tablespoons soy sauce		1	tablespoon salt
3	tablespoons Worcestershire sauce		¾	cup brown sugar
½	cup lemon juice (Real Lemon o.k.)		1	teaspoon garlic powder
½	cup ketchup		2	tablespoons dry mustard
1	(6-ounce) can tomato paste		¾	teaspoon cayenne pepper
1	cup prepared mustard			

Combine all ingredients in a large saucepan. Bring to a boil and simmer a few minutes. Pour into bottles or jars.

MAIN DISHES

DESSERTS

Louise and President Jimmy Carter ~
two Georgians grinning because it's
dessert time at the White House.

TARTE AUX CERISES ET AU FROMAGE BLANC

I'm nothing if not lucky. Can you imagine going to Paris without restaurant reservations and ending up dining in one of their finest. I took my list of Paris' top ten restaurants and knew where I wanted to go—any of them. I gave the list to the concierge at the Intercontinental where we were staying and asked him to please make reservations for four for dinner. "What year?, Madame," he asked with European coolness probably reserved for naive Americans.

"Wednesday night," I said and promptly made my exit while he picked himself up from the floor.

When we wearily entered our rooms late that afternoon there was a telephone message: "Reservations for four at Tour 'd 'Argent on Wednesday." Thrill of all thrills we were in, I couldn't believe it.

The restaurant is one of Paris' finest and is the oldest, having opened in 1582. From the 4th floor vantage, you see the beautiful Seine River and the rooftops of the city. Duck is their specialty and consequently they have a station set up right in the dining area where they cook the ducks. The dining experience shared by such notables as Henry IV, MMe, de Sevigne, George Sand, and Elizabeth Taylor was indescribably lovely. And this French dessert is too—though not theirs.

12	ounces cherries, pitted–about 2½ cups		7	ounces fromage blanc or cream cheese, at room temperature
2	tablespoons Calvados or kirsch		5	tablespoons whipping cream
2	eggs		½	teaspoon vanilla
¼	cup sugar			

Put the cherries in a bowl with the Calvados or kirsch and allow to stand for at least 30 minutes.

Preheat the oven to 375 degrees. Lightly butter a 9-inch ceramic tart mold.

Using an electric mixer, beat together the eggs and sugar until thick and lighter in color. Add the cheese, cream and vanilla, and continue beating until smooth and well blended.

Drain the cherries and add the liquid to the cheese mixture, stirring to combine. Arrange the cherries in the mold and pour over the cheese mixture.

Bake for 30 to 35 minutes or until golden and set. Serve warm or at room temperature.

❖ Tour D'Argent Restaurant in Paris ❖

MACADAMIA FUDGE TORTE

Excitement was at a high pitch as Alex Trebek lifted the dome off a huge silver server and revealed the name of the world's first-ever winner of $1,000,000 in a culinary contest. It was Dallas in 1996 and Kurt Wait, a single father from Redwood City, California who had created a decadent chocolate dessert was the thrilled-to-death winner.

Kurt said he really was not a seasoned cook but did piddle around in the kitchen because he had to . He said he took this torte to the office "just on a lark" and they jokingly said "Man, you oughta enter the Pillsbury Bake-Off® contest." So he showed 'em. He did. And the rest is history.

Filling:

⅓   cup low-fat sweetened condensed milk (not evaporated)

½   cup semi-sweet chocolate chips

Cake:

1   package Pillsbury® Moist Supreme Devil's Food Cake Mix

1½   teaspoons cinnamon

⅓   cup oil

1   (16-ounce) can sliced pears in light syrup, drained

2   eggs

⅓   cup chopped macadamia nuts or pecans

2   teaspoons water

Sauce:

1   (17-ounce) jar butterscotch caramel fudge ice cream topping

⅓   cup milk

Heat oven to 350 degrees. Spray 9- or 10-inch springform pan with non stick cooking spray. In small saucepan, combine filling ingredients. Cook over medium-low heat until chocolate is melted, stirring occasionally.

In a large bowl, combine cake mix, cinnamon and oil; blend at low speed for 20 to 30 seconds or until crumbly. (Mixture will be dry.) Place pears in blender container or food processor bowl with metal blade; cover and blend until smooth.

In large bowl, combine 2½ cups of the cake mix mixture, pureed pears and eggs; beat at low speed until moistened. Beat 2 minutes at medium speed.

Spread batter evenly in spray-coated pan. Drop filling by spoonfuls over batter. Stir nuts and water into remaining cake mix mixture. Sprinkle over filling.

Bake at 350 degrees for 45 to 50 minutes or until top springs back when touched lightly in center. Cool 10 minutes. Remove sides of pan. Cool ½ hour until completely cooled.

In small saucepan, combine sauce ingredients. Cook over medium-low heat for 3 to 4 minutes or until well blended, stirring occasionally. To serve, spoon 2 tablespoons warm sauce onto each serving plate; top with wedge of torte. If desired, serve with vanilla ice cream or frozen yogurt and garnish with chocolate curls. Refrigerate until serving time.

LEMON PUDDINGS

Way back in 1977 Marian Davis (Mrs. Gordon) and I were killing a few minutes in a gift shop at Sea Island while our husbands were attending a medical meeting. Marian managed to gravitate to the cookbook section even before I, and in a few minutes I heard her holler out loud, "Oh, I can't believe it! Come back here, quick, Louise."

And when I reached the bookrack where Marian was grasping a bright yellow cookbook to her chest she said, "I have at last found the long lost recipe that I've been on a search for ten years." And she pointed out to me Lemon Puddings.

The writer of the recipe says; "Here is the surprise: When done each cup will contain a layer of custard at the bottom and a layer of sponge cake on the top. May be served hot in custard cups with whipped cream. I serve mine cold from the refrigerator and when ready to serve, turn them on serving plates upside down so custard is on top. Top with fluff of whipped cream. Do not grease custard cups."

2	tablespoons butter	5	tablespoons lemon juice
1	cup sugar		Grated rind of 1 lemon
4	tablespoons flour	3	eggs, separated
¼	teaspoon salt	1½	cups milk (sweet or evaporated)

Cream butter, add sugar, flour, salt, then lemon juice and rind. Stir in beaten egg yolks which have been mixed with milk. Fold in stiffly beaten egg whites. Pour into custard cups. Set cups in pan of cold water and bake in moderate oven (350 degrees) about 45 minutes.

BANANA PUDDING

My darling friend Ann Oxley is a wonderful cook who has a grand array of good recipes and yet still likes to try new things quite often.

One day one of Ann's friends called and said she was bringing over a Banana Pudding she wanted her to taste test. Ann said the friend didn't come and didn't come. I think two or three days had passed when she finally arrived with the pudding. Although Ann says she's crazy about Banana Pudding, she just knew the bananas would be black and not good at all. Not true. This pudding, that is delicious, won't weep or turn dark after two or three days. Instead it really might taste better. This makes a large Pyrex dish full—but it won't be full for long.

5	cups milk	1	(12-ounce) carton Cool Whip
3	boxes (regular size) vanilla (instant) pudding	6	large bananas
1	small sour cream	1	large box vanilla wafers (12 ounces)

Mix milk in large bowl with pudding mix. Beat at low speed for 2 minutes. Add sour cream and mix on low speed until well blended. Add half cool whip and mix on low until blended. Save other half of Cool Whip to spread on top.

Layer bananas and wafers with pudding mixture as you would any banana pudding. Refrigerate overnight. Will be better if kept in refrigerator for 3 days. Will keep 8 days or more without bananas turning dark.

GERMAN BREAD PUDDING

Big, funny, and entertaining Chef Tell Erhardt grew up in post World War II Germany when there wasn't a whole lot of excess food. He said in a cooking school that he taught in Pinehurst, N.C. that he and his mother often created their meals out of CARE packages.

This is one of their recipes made of stale bread and fruit. Later he added the Vanilla Sauce which really makes it delicious.

Over my desk still hangs a huge colored poster of Tell that hung in the hotel during the cooking school. Tell signed it—"To Louise—Best wishes, good luck, I see you, Tell." I treasure it and this wonderful German recipe.

2	cups milk	1	pound baking apples, peeled, cored, and sliced
2	eggs	½	cup raisins
3	tablespoons sugar	4	tablespoons butter, cut into small pieces
6	stale seedless rolls, sliced		Vanilla Sauce (see recipe below)

Preheat the oven to 375 degrees, Butter a 1½-quart soufflé dish very well.

Put the milk, eggs, and sugar in a saucepan. Beat to combine well and cook over medium heat until slightly thickened. Set aside.

Make layers in the soufflé dish of first the rolls, then the apple slices, sprinkling each layer with some raisins. End the layers with apples. Dot the apples with the butter pieces and pour on the custard. Bake for 1 hour, or until firm. Serve with Vanilla Sauce.

Vanilla Sauce:

2	cups milk
½	vanilla bean
½	cup sugar
2	teaspoons cornstarch dissolved in 4 teaspoons water
2	egg yolks, beaten

Bring the milk, vanilla bean, and sugar to a boil. Add the dissolved cornstarch and bring to a boil again. Cook for 3 to 4 minutes and add the egg yolks, stirring to combine well. Serve.

❖ Iris Gillis, Louise, Chef Tell Erhardt, Sybil and Mae Brewer at Pinehurst Cooking School. ❖

THOMAS JEFFERSON'S BREAD AND BUTTER PUDDING

In May of '93 my fellow food editor and good friend, Clara Echmann and I found ourselves standing in Thomas Jefferson's kitchen at Monticello. The entire house, the grounds, the gardens were all just unbelievable.

Jefferson designed and built his beautiful Monticello in the late 18th and early 19th centuries on a hilltop in Albemarle County, Virginia. He said, "All of my wishes end where I hope my days will end, at Monticello."

Thomas Jefferson was one of the most versatile and brilliant men to ever lead our country. His interest in food and in growing new varieties of fruits and vegetables and recording all his findings have given us great insight into life at Monticello in the 18th century. Much of the equipment in the house was invented by Jefferson including a calendar clock found in the front foyer, a revolving desk, and a dumb-waiter.

Jefferson was a real genius. In 1993, President John F. Kennedy, speaking to a dinner program of Nobel Prize winners said, "This is the greatest assemblage of brains since Thomas Jefferson dined alone at Monticello."

There were Thomas Jefferson cookbooks on sale at Monticello and you may bet your bottom dollar I was first in line to get one. This recipe for Bread and Butter Pudding was served at Monticello.

Cut a stale, square loaf of bread in slices and spread each slice with a thick layer of butter. Take a deep baking dish, cover the bottom with bread, strew in a few currants or stoned raisins, then another layer of bread, and so until the dish is ⅔ full. Beat 6 eggs, add 1 cupful of sugar, 4 cups of milk, and any kind of seasoning that is preferred. Pour this into the dish and let stand 2 hours. Bake 1½ hours in a slow oven.

PEACH COBBLER

On an old manual typewriter on loose leaf notebook paper, I meticulously typed all of Mother's recipes that I thought would be absolutely necessary for starting married life in 1950. The Peach Cobbler was one that we had a lot in Mother's kitchen and one that I've certainly used and hung onto through the years. I never could quite figure out how the crust comes to the top and leaves the peaches on the bottom but it does. Don't question it. It just does.

4	tablespoons butter	1	cup sugar
1	cup flour	½	cup milk
1	teaspoon baking powder	4	cups peeled and sliced peaches

In the oven melt the butter in the bottom of a Pyrex dish. Sift the flour and baking powder together and mix with the sugar. Slowly add the milk to the flour mixture. Pour this into the dish with the butter and on top of this put the peaches. Bake at 350 degrees for 40 to 45 minutes until brown on top.

PEACH CRISP

Apple Crisp is a nationwide, standard sort of dessert. But you have to live in Georgia and pick the peaches off the trees to achieve the ultimate dessert, Peach Crisp. My friend, Clare Dodd in Marshallville has a wonderful friend and cook in her kitchen named Essie who can create some of the most mouth-watering down south cooking you've ever tasted. Her fried chicken is out of this world as are all her "home cooked" vegetables and breads. Essie likes to make Peach Crisp for us but not half as much as we like her to. We even have the nerve to request it when we're heading toward Marshaville for lunch.

4	cups peaches, peeled and sliced	1	egg, slightly beaten
2-3	tablespoons lemon juice		Dash of salt
1	cup flour	½	stick butter
1	cup sugar		

Slice firm, ripe peaches and fill a 9-inch baking dish and add lemon juice. Mix together the flour, sugar, egg and salt. Spread mixture over top of peaches. Dot with butter and bake in oven at 400 degrees until golden brown on top. Good served with ice cream or whipped cream.

CRANBERRY PEAR CRISP

During Joe Frank Harris' term of Governor of Georgia it was my privilege to visit the mansion to do an article about their young female chef. The First Lady, Elizabeth Harris, was more than gracious to give me a tour, not only of the kitchen, but of the entire mansion. The only common ground I could find between her house and mine was that we are both proud owners of The Transylvania Club's (Sandersville) Georgia plates. Mine were a wedding gift in 1950 from Mr. William Murphy who was president of the C & S Bank in Savannah and our neighbor in the country near Guyton. The plates are the official plates of the State of Georgia and I treasure mine dearly.

The Harris' chef shared with me a special recipe she was cooking at the time for the Governor's supper. And it is good—quite befitting one of such prestige as our Governor and his first Lady.

2 cups fresh cranberries	¼ cup firmly packed brown sugar
3 medium pears, peeled, cored and coarsely chopped	3 tablespoons flour
1 cup sugar	1 teaspoon grated orange rind
¼ cup orange juice	¼ cup butter
2 tablespoons flour	¾ cup regular oatmeal, uncooked
½ teaspoon ground cinnamon	¾ cup chopped walnuts
½ teaspoon ground mace	Whipped cream or ice cream

Combine first 7 ingredients; spoon into a greased 1½ quart casserole.

Combine brown sugar, 3 tablespoons flour and orange rind; cut in butter with a pastry blender until mixture resembles coarse meal. Stir in oatmeal and walnuts; sprinkle over fruit. Bake at 350 degrees for 50 minutes or until golden brown. Serve with whipped cream or ice cream.

RASPBERRY COBBLER

Valentine's Day, 1995. Charleston. Louis's Charleston Grill, owned by the dynamic chef Louis Osteen. It was a perfect setting for a beautiful meal with my sister, Libby, and sister-in-law, Sybil. If the lovely ambience of the restaurant set in one of the most beautiful cities in the United States were not enough, Osteen presented all of us long stemmed red roses and miniature boxes of Godiva chocolates.

The meal is a memory now—a beautiful one. But the raspberry cobbler lives on in reality because I was able to secure the recipe and make it whenever the urge comes—or whenever the price of raspberries dips enough to make 6 cups of them affordable. This can also be made with less expensive blackberries, blueberries or strawberries.

Cobbler Binder:

3	tablespoons sugar	¼	cup all-purpose flour

Cobbler Filling:

¼	cup Cobbler Binder	1	tablespoon unsalted butter, diced and kept chilled
6	cups juicy ripe raspberries		
1	tablespoon lemon zest (be careful not to use the white layer, as it is bitter)	2	tablespoons heavy whipping cream

Topping:

2	cups White Lily self-rising flour	¾	cup heavy whipping cream
2	tablespoons sugar	2	tablespoons heavy cream for brushing tops
½	cup (1 stick) unsalted butter, cut in to ½-inch cubes and kept chilled	2	tablespoons sugar for brushing tops

To make the cobbler binder: In a small mixing bowl combine the sugar and flour. Set aside.

To make the cobbler filling: In a large mixing bowl combine ¼ cup of the cobbler binder, the berries, and lemon zest and let the berries macerate for an hour or more at room temperature. Sprinkle the butter over the filling, then spoon the cream over the butter. When ready to cook, pour the filling into a 9-inch round baking dish or individual oven-proof bowls.

To make the topping: Preheat the oven to 350 degrees. In a medium mixing bowl combine the flour and sugar and mix well. Add the cold diced butter and work into the flour with a pastry cutter, fork, or fingertips until the butter pieces are a little larger than an English pea but not larger than a lima bean. If you are using your fingers, work quickly so your body heat won't melt the butter.

Pour in all of the cream. Using a plastic spatula and light pressure, fold the mixture a few times until it becomes cohesive. Do not overmix. In order to make a light cobbler topping, it is important to work the dough as little as possible.

When the dough is mixed, turn it onto a floured surface and quickly and gently knead it 6 to 10 times or until it just begins to be nearly homogenized. There will be large pieces of butter throughout. Keep a little flour under the dough to make sure that the dough doesn't stick on the bottom and lightly dust the top of the dough so that the rolling pin doesn't stick on the top. Roll the dough to about ⅝-inch thickness.

Cut the dough into 4-inch rounds. Place the rounds on top of the cobbler filling. Use as much as needed of the cream to brush the tops. Then sprinkle the tops with the sugar. Bake the cobbler in the preheated oven for about 40 to 50 minutes or until the top is cooked through completely and the cobbler is thick and bubbly. Gently lift a part of the top and make sure that it is cooked and still not liquid and raw. Remove and serve while warm.

PEPPERMINT ICE CREAM

One bright sunny morning I drove over to Sandersville and out into the country for a luncheon for my former pupil, Lynda Colston, the daughter of one of my best friends in Wrightsville, Lizzie Lee Colston.

It's been so long ago that I sadly cannot remember who made this most delicious of all delicious ice creams. I do remember it was a beautiful home and she was a lovely hostess who graciously shared her recipe with me.

I have made this gorgeous light pink ice cream more than almost any dessert and every time I really cannot believe that it tastes even better than I thought it did. And I thought It was superb in the first place.

1	quart milk	1	pint half-and-half
1	pound peppermint candy	1	pint whipping cream, whipped

Combine milk and candy; cover and refrigerator 12 hours. (Candy will dissolve.) Combine candy mixture, half-and-half and whipped cream. Pour into freezer can of a 1 gallon churn. Churn.

ICE CREAM FILLED ORANGES

We had rented a car and toured the pineapple fields outside Honolulu. For me it was an exciting adventure to see the gorgeous Hawaiian beaches along the way and then the sharp contrast of thousands of pineapples protruding on heavy thick stems from the center of the pineapple bushes. It was perhaps my first time to see pineapples growing. Of course we just had to buy a case to bring home. What an ordeal that turned out to be.

Back at the gorgeous pink stucco hotel where we were staying we were served a lovely citrus dessert that was cool and pleasing and mighty good.

6	navel oranges	3	ounces Cointreau
1	quart orange sherbet		Small amount of pulp and juice of orange
¾	quart vanilla ice cream		Mint, for garnish

Cut off tops of oranges, scoop out pulp with grapefruit spoon and reserve small amount of pulp and juice. Mix sherbet with softened ice cream; add Cointreau, pulp and juice. Stuff into orange shells and freeze 2 hours. Garnish with sprig of mint.

SAVANNAH TRIFLE

Probably everyone who has ever spent more than several hours in Savannah has eaten at the beautiful old Pink House. When I was a young child I looked forward to getting all dressed up and going with Mother to the Pink House to eat when we were on one of our shopping excursions.

Built in 1789, the Pink House has aged so beautifully because the old bricks have turned the covering stucco a unique color. Once used as a Federal headquarters during union occupation, the building now has a tavern, a gift shop, and the restaurant where specialties include this wonderful Savannah Trifle.

1½	quarts milk	½	cup sherry
1½	cups sugar	1	pint whipping cream
2	tablespoons cornstarch	1½	pounds sliced pound cake
6	eggs		Maraschino cherries (optional)

Heat milk in the top of a double boiler, but do not boil. Beat together sugar, cornstarch, and eggs in mixing bowl until smooth. Add this to warm milk and stir until mixture thickens and coats a metal spoon. Set aside until cool. When cool, add sherry to custard. Whip cream. In a 13x9¼x2-inch baking pan, put a layer of cake, a layer of custard, and a layer of whipped cream. Repeat until all ingredients are used. Top each serving with a cherry if desired.

ORANGES SARONNO

As Iris Gillis' niece in New York was hurrying off to the Catskills, she said to her husband Kirk Kakorian, as she kissed him goodbye, "Now, please be nice to Aunt Iris and her little friends from Dublin."

Be nice? Kirk gave us New York on a silver platter studded with rubies and diamonds. Our first surprise was an enormous and quite elegant arrangement of tropical flowers awaiting our arrival at the off Fifth brownstone where we were spending the week at Daphne Roberts' sister's home. Her sister had also taken to the Catskills.

Kirk sent a limousine to take us to Wall Street for a personal guided tour; he took us to several private clubs, all quite elegant, where we were wined and dined graciously. He took us to a splendid new Mexican restaurant, was it Rosalie's, right in the heart of Manhattan. As we were having our marvelous upscale Mexican lunch, I commented to Kirk that I had been advised by an Athens chef to be sure to run over to Jersey to the horse races but none of the girls was interested. "Oh, by all means, come to Belmont. I didn't know you were interested in horses." And then he set in motion plans for us to go to Belmont on Wednesday to see his horse race.

We were whisked to the fourth level (I think it was fourth) to a private club with a great expanse of glass overlooking the tracks. And there was more elaborate food there than you can imagine, all set up for continuous nibbling all day. Particularly memorable were the Oranges Saronno that we enjoyed for dessert. Most memorable of everything, though, was Kirk and our introduction to true Northern hospitality.

Clean out oranges. Save slice off top. Chill. Brush outside of orange shell and top of orange with slightly beaten egg white. Dip into sugar. Let dry until crusty. Fill with sherbet and add a touch of mint.

❖ Katherine Porter, Iris Gillis and Louise
on the sidewalks of New York. ❖

PEACH ICE CREAM

For years I debated whether or not I thought I could afford to buy a free-standing ice maker, one of the real desires of my entire life. I am an ice person from the word go. I love ice. But I do not like ice like the refrigerator makes. I like ice like McDonald's or Wendy's serve. It is clear as a bell, much colder than refrigerator ice and so pure and good.

Finally the ice maker in my refrigerator died. Never have I been so elated over a death. And when I found out that it would cost $300 to replace it, I was especially delighted. It had finally come: my perfect excuse to add a good many dollars and get the free-standing ice machine of my dreams. Do I like it? I am so crazy about it that every time I open the door and extract a scoop full of those clear as a crystal little cubes I thank the Lord one more time for letting me have such a wonderful addition to my kitchen. May it last forever.

Imagine what a joy it is when you're all ready to make a delicious churn of ice cream to just dip in and get all the ice you need without having to run to the convenience store.

Here's one of the ice creams that I like to make.

8	eggs beaten separately		½	pint whipped cream (optional)
6	tablespoons flour		2	teaspoons vanilla (less if you like)
2½	cups sugar			Pinch of salt
½	gallon milk		3-4	cups peaches
1	can evaporated milk			

Beat egg yolks well. Sift flour and sugar together, stir into well beaten egg yolks. Scald milk, pour slowly over mixture, cook until it coats spoon, cool slightly, add beaten whites. After thoroughly cool, add 1 tall can chilled evaporated milk, whipped. Add ½ pint whipped cream, if you want really rich cream. Stir in vanilla and salt. Add 3 to 4 cups mashed peaches (fresh). Churn according to directions with churn.

GRAND MARNIER SOUFFLÉ

This recipe is from The White House where I spent one of the most memorable days of my long, happy life. It was August 1980, and the farmers and businessmen of Laurens County were planning a big barbecue on the South Lawn of the White House. The editor of the newspaper and my dear friend, Doug Hall, asked me to go along to cover the food aspect of the excitement filled day. Never in my wildest dreams did I ever dream I'd spend the day (and half of the night) in that most famous of all buildings in this country.

As the Laurens Countians began to dig pits in the South Lawn to prepare the barbecue, (can you believe it?) others of the group were in the kitchen to make the slaw, potato salad and Brunswick stew. To be perfectly honest, the three tall White House chefs with even taller white toques atop their heads, were slightly more than horrified. They were European trained chefs and had little intercourse with Georgians before the Carters took over the White House.

I managed to stay almost the entire day in the kitchen with short trips out to see the florist, the press rooms, the Rose Garden and to have lunch in a staff dining room right there at the White House.

As a self-appointed psychologist, I was deeply immersed in the psychological aspect of the rapport between the chefs and the untrained Laurens County cooks who had taken over their private domain. Slowly I saw a pattern of change. The cool, aloof Swedes were relaxing their waxen countenances just slightly around the lip-line. After two hours, one of them smiled when I asked a question about something of great interest to him.

As the Brunswick Stew began to bubble (nothing could be taken to the White House already cooked) the chefs began to relax around the nostril area-who wouldn't? Then when one of the hometown men told a funny joke all three of the chefs actually laughed out loud. And from there on-we were allowed free reign in the kitchen and they just stood around and looked.

The barbecue on the South Lawn that evening with all of us sitting on blankets and listening to the music of Bill Monroe was a night to forever remember. And yes, they did get the barbecue pit holes all covered before we left.

10	eggs, separated	¼	teaspoon cream of tartar
⅔	cup sugar	1	tablespoon butter
½	cup Grand Marnier		

Beat 8 egg yolks with sugar in double boiler over hot water until mixture makes a ribbon when spoon is held up. Add the Grand Marnier. Transfer to a bowl and place over cracked ice in a dish, continue beating until mixture has cooled. Beat 10 egg whites until firm, but not dry. Add cream of tartar. Fold into mixture and blend thoroughly. Pour into buttered and sugared soufflé dish. Bake at 400 degrees for 12 to 15 minutes (might take longer) or until risen and browned. Serve at once.

SNOWY EGGS

My precious little Nancy, Nancy Futelle Fletcher, my niece, spent untold hours on Second Time Around, *their Augusta Junior League Cookbook, complement to the award winning* Tea Time at the Masters. *Not only have I benefited greatly from Nan's expertise about the recipe selections, I have had constant recommendations from her about dishes in the book that are good. Rarely do we have a family get together that I don't get a new "recipe review."*

This Snowy Eggs is one of Nancy's recommendations and is also recommended by Nan's mother, Sybil, who is one of the greatest sources of good, new recipes. This is a lovely dessert and is an adaptation of a classic French dessert. The recipe says it serves four which is generous but then when you taste it, you'll want "generous."

2	cups milk	⅛	teaspoon salt
3	eggs separated	1	teaspoon vanilla or ½ teaspoon grated lemon rind
½	cup sugar, divided		

Scald milk in double boiler over simmering water. Remove milk from heat. Slowly stir in slightly beaten egg yolks, ¼ cup sugar and salt. Place over water. Stir constantly until mixture begins to thicken. Remove from water. Beat mixture as it cools to release steam. Add vanilla or lemon rind. Pour into a 9x9-inch square baking dish. Chill. Beat egg whites until stiff. Gradually add remaining ¼ cup sugar. Drop generous tablespoons of meringue onto cooled custard. Preheat oven to broil. Place custard filled dish in pan of ice water. Put in hot oven. Heat until tips of meringue are browned. (Watch carefully during browning process. Custard must not get warm.) Serve chilled.

RUM TRIFLE

"If this doesn't fire you up, your wood's wet." Those words came from the pulpit of my church, Riverside Methodist, and I liked them so much I vowed to one day find the proper place to use them. This is it.

This Rum Trifle was served to a group of food editors by the Junior Auxiliary of Vicksburg, Mississippi and all of us were greatly impressed. It's a wonderful dessert and one that you can make ahead. Most desserts can be made ahead but most of them are not this delicious.

½	cup light rum	1	cup chilled heavy cream
¾	cup golden raisins	8	cups angel food cake cut into ½-inch cubes
¾	cup slivered almonds		
1	(3-ounce) package vanilla pudding (not instant)	8	maraschino cherries
			Sliced almonds, toasted
2½	cups milk		

Pour rum over raisins and slivered almonds in a small bowl. Let soak 1 hour. In a medium saucepan, mix pudding with 2½ cups milk. Cook over medium heat until it boils. When pudding has cooled, whip the chilled cream and fold ½ whipped cream into pudding. In trifle bowl or other pretty, clear crystal bowl, layer ⅓ cake cubes. Sprinkle with ⅓ rum mixture, then ⅓ pudding. Repeat each layer twice, ending with pudding. Cover and refrigerate a minimum of 3 hours and a maximum of 24 hours before serving. Garnish with remaining whipped cream, maraschino cherries, and toasted sliced almonds.

SPANISH CREAM

Although I certainly do not advocate using recipes that call for uncooked egg whites, there are certain recipes that are so memorable that they have to be saved for posterity. Maybe some day soon they'll give us the go-ahead with raw egg whites and then we'll be ready.

Some of my friends say "Bah!" to not using raw egg whites anyway. I say "Travel at your own risk."

This recipe is one that Mrs. McCrary used to always send when the children were sick. It's really soothing to a hurting tummy ache and will "cure" almost any illness. The children called Mrs. McCrary, "Man-gee" and I can see their little faces now when she'd show up with Spanish Cream, cooked especially for them.

1	envelope gelatine	3	cups milk
¼	cup sugar	1	teaspoon vanilla
¼	teaspoon salt	¼	cup sugar
3	eggs, separated		

In top of double boiler mix gelatine, sugar and salt. Stir in egg yolks and slowly add milk, stirring. Cook until mixture coats spoon. Refrigerate until slightly thicker than egg whites. Stir in vanilla. Beat egg whites, gradually adding ¼ cup sugar, until stiff. Fold in the gelatine mixture. Pour into custard cups or ramekins. Chill.

HELEN SMITH'S APPLE WHATEVER

Helen Smith served this at bridge to a greatly receptive group. Everyone was impressed and as usual Helen was downplaying the whole deal like it was nothing. She's really a great cook and has wonderful ideas about what's good and what goes with what. Through the years she has served us numerous winners—and this one is certainly no exception.

1	can crescent rolls	¾	cup orange juice
2	Granny Smith apples	½	stick margarine or butter
1	cup sugar		

Cut rolls in triangles. Cut apples into quarter. Peel and core. Put one-quarter in middle of dough triangles. Wrap apple in dough and pinch dough together. Make sauce out of last 3 ingredients (melt butter but sauce does not need to be cooked). Pour sauce over and bake at 350 degrees for 35 minutes. Serve with ice cream.

Orange juice should be room temperature (not cold) when you mix with melted butter and sugar.

DESSERTS

BETTY'S BOILED CUSTARD

One of my best friends, Betty Ballard, is the Boiled Custard Queen of the Universe. When anyones temperature goes above 100 degrees, Betty is there with the great panacea of all panaceas, her Boiled Custard. It is the best in the universe—not the world—the universe.

Betty spends a lot of time at Saint Simons where she has amassed a group of friends almost equal to those she leaves behind in Macon. Actually, she doesn't totally leave us because if we're lucky and behave ourselves we get invited down to visit.

On a quick shopping trip to the island with Betty one weekend we were staying overnight at the Saint Simons Inn just so we could get going early the next morning looking for that elusive outfit she needed to wear to her niece's, Logan's, wedding.

While we had time to spare in the inn, I grabbed the proverbial note pad from the bedside table and said, "All right. While I'm thinking about it, give me detailed instructions for making the universe's best boiled custard."

4	eggs	1	quart milk
1½	tablespoons cornstarch	1	teaspoon vanilla
1	cup sugar		

Beat eggs with a whisk in top of a double boiler. Mix together cornstarch and sugar and add to eggs. Stir well. Slowly add and stir in milk. While mixing, heat water in bottom of double boiler to a boil. Put the pot with the egg mixture into the pot of water and cook mixture, stirring with a wooden spoon until custard coats spoon well. Remove from heat and add vanilla. Strain while hot into a bowl. Put plastic wrap over custard and put a lid on bowl. Let cool and refrigerate until serving time.

BETTY ANN CARSWELL'S COLD LEMON SOUFFLÉ

With all the delicious desserts to choose from, this is the one that I serve most often when I'm having a dinner party. It's the thing to have because you can make it ahead of time and pull it out of the freezer just minutes before serving. I always put it on a pedestal cake server and put twists of lemon on top and around the base—sometimes with a sprig or two or mint. I like to take it to the table whole and have the dessert plates stacked by my place and slice and serve the beautiful masterpiece from the table.

This recipe was given to me by my longtime good friend, Betty Ann Carswell, in Dublin who served it at a Garden Club Tasters Tour. Everybody was raving over it.

10	eggs, separated		2	tablespoons plain gelatin
1	cup sugar		½	cup cold water or rum
1	cup lemon juice		1	cup sugar
	Grated rinds of 4 lemons		2	cups heavy cream
	Pinch salt			

Beat egg yolks until light and fluffy, add sugar gradually and beat until smooth and light in color. Add lemon juice and rind and salt. Mix thoroughly and cook, stirring constantly until thickened.

Soak gelatin in water or rum and stir into hot custard until dissolved. Cool. Beat egg whites until stiff, gradually add cup sugar, beat until not grainy. Fold egg whites into cooled lemon mixture and fold in whipped cream. Chill.

Spray and line a 10-inch springform pan with halved ladyfingers. Put lemon mixture into pan. Freeze. Take out above 20 minutes ahead of time.

MERINGUES WITH FRUIT

This is one of the most fabulous desserts of all time. It's a bit of trouble to make but can all be done ahead. I have served it at luncheons and dinner parties so many times that I kind of had to let up for fear my guests would recognize the redundancy. Canned Mandarin oranges are good instead of the fresh oranges and more convenient for sure.

4	egg whites	¾	cup pineapple
1	cup sugar	¾	cup green grapes
	Few drops vanilla	1	large banana
½	cup chopped pecans	2	cups whipped cream
2	fresh oranges, sliced	½	cup 4X sugar

Beat egg whites until very stiff. Beat in sugar gradually and add vanilla and nuts. Draw 3 sizes of circles with cookie or biscuit cutters on brown paper or as many as you can get. Spread meringue into circles and bake at 225 degrees for 1 hour. Cool in oven. Chop fruit and add to cream that has been beaten with sugar and vanilla. Stack 3 tiers of meringues with fruit mixture between first 2–then meringue on top. Garnish with mint leaves and bunches of green grapes on side of plate.

Lovely and delicious.

AMBROSIA

What's Christmas without the great southern tradition—a big cut glass bowl of Ambrosia? There are many ways to make Ambrosia: some put coconut—some do not. Some put grapefruit—some do not. Now they're even suggesting kiwis and strawberries. My way is the simplest and for me and my family—the best!

1	dozen juicy oranges	½	cup maraschino cherries, cut into pieces
1	large can crushed pineapple		

Peel and section oranges, squeeze juice from each by hand onto oranges. Add pineapple and cherries. Chill overnight.

STRAWBERRY TOWERS

Years ago I met Babs Wilkinson at a Seafood Seminar in Charleston. She's with the marketing division of the N. C. Department of Agriculture and through the years has kept me on her list of people to receive Tarheel Kitchen, a little pamphlet that she does with N. C. produce news and recipes. I'm afraid I haven't kept up my end of the correspondence but I do look forward to Bab's recipes. This one is simpler than simple but makes an attractive presentation that also tastes good.

1	box of prepared and folded pastry for a 9-inch double crusted pie	⅓	cup sugar
1	quart strawberries	1-2	cups non dairy whipped topping

With a 3-inch round scalloped cookie cutter, cut out 18 pastry rounds from the pie pastry. Place on ungreased baking sheet and prick with a fork. Bake the rounds in a 425 degree oven for 15 minutes (or until lightly browned.) Remove from baking sheet and cool.

Wash strawberries. Reserve 6 berries for garnish. Hull remaining berries and slice. Place in a mixing bowl and sprinkle with ⅓ cup sugar. Let berries stand for 20 minutes. About an hour before serving time, make strawberry towers by alternating pastry rounds and sweetened sliced strawberries to make 6 towers with 3 pastry rounds each, finishing with strawberries on top. Refrigerate for about 1 hour. Just before serving, top strawberry towers with whipped topping and garnish with reserved whole berries.

GRANDS!® STRAWBERRY SHORTCAKE

Needing a super dessert in record-setting time? Here it is and it's so delicious. You don't have to tell anybody you didn't make the biscuits yourself—they'll never know. This runs circles around the sponge cake holders for strawberries that you buy in the supermarket. I serve it all the time.

1	(17.3-ounce) can Pillsbury® Grands!® Refrigerated Biscuits	4-5	tablespoons sugar
2	tablespoons margarine, melted	1	quart sliced strawberries
		1	cup whipped cream

Heat oven to 375 degrees. Dip top and sides only of each biscuit in margarine, then in sugar.

Bake at 375 degrees for 13 to 17 minutes or until golden brown.

To serve, split warm biscuits. Layer biscuits with strawberries and whipped cream.

ANGEL CAKES WITH STRAWBERRIES AND CREAM

It was Cherry Blossom time and I was having some friends over for a luncheon. There's an enormous cherry tree right outside my dining room windows and it lends itself beautifully to Cherry Blossom luncheons. Pink place mats and napkins, pink flowered china and pink stemmed crystal make a pretty table setting with pink roses and cherry blossoms in a lovely old silver bowl for the center piece. Easier than pie but so beautiful for dessert are my Angel Cakes with Cream and Strawberries—the cakes made in individual angel cake pans. If you don't have those you could just make one big cake.

Although I never use cake mix, I do when it's Angel Cake. Angel Food Cake Mix is so good you can't tell it from homemade and then you're not left with 10 or 12 egg yolks.

1	package Angel Food Cake Mix	1	quart strawberries
1	pint whipping cream	½	teaspoon vanilla
	Few drops red food coloring	6	tablespoons 4X sugar

Make cake (or cakes) according to package directions. When cool, beat cream until stiff peaks form. Add food coloring, vanilla and sugar. Frost cakes. Hull strawberries and arrange around edge of cake.

BANANAS FOSTER

Twice in my long food career I have been served perfect Bananas Foster. At Johnson and Wales Culinary School in Charleston a group of food writers sat enthralled as the marvelous chef prepared before our eyes a delicious Bananas Foster.

The second time I had perfect Bananas Foster was at Brennan's in the French Quarter in New Orleans (417 Royal Street). Bananas Foster is one of Brennans most famous and popular desserts. It's really quite simple to make. Be sure to wait until the rum gets hot so that there is a good flame made when it is ignited. This can also be prepared over a stove burner then brought to the dinner table and flamed.

4	tablespoons butter	4	bananas, cut in half lengthwise, then halved
1	cup brown sugar		
½	teaspoon cinnamon	¼	cup rum
4	tablespoons banana liqueur	4	scoops vanilla ice cream

Melt the butter over an alcohol burner in a flambé pan or attractive skillet. Add the sugar, cinnamon and banana liqueur and stir to mix. Heat for a few minutes, then place the halved bananas in the sauce and sauté until soft.

Add the rum and allow it to heat well; then tip the pan so that the flame from the burner causes the sauce to ignite. Allow the sauce to flame until it dies out, tipping the pan with a circular motion to prolong the flaming.

Lift the bananas carefully out of the pan and place 4 pieces over each portion of ice cream, then spoon the hot sauce from the pan over the bananas and ice cream.

MARY BRINSON'S CHOCOLATE DESSERT

My dear friend Latha Tyson, a talented artist with so many other interests too that she's never still a minute, gave me this delicious and easy recipe that she had at her friend's (Mary Brinson's) house in Twin City. I've done this several times and it's always a hit.

Place 8 ice cream sandwiches in the bottom of a pan. Stick fork holes in sandwiches. Saturate with Kahlúa. Spread with Cool Whip. Add a second layer of sandwiches, add Kahlúa. Spread with Cool Whip. Sprinkle with toasted almonds for topping. Freeze. Slice when ready to serve.

WHITE CHOCOLATE ROLL

James Beard called Julie Dannenbaum a most dynamic teacher and writer on food. When I learned she was teaching at the world famous Greenbrier Hotel in West Virginia, I assembled a group; caught a plane and enrolled in her school. It was a fun filled week—moving so fast that we were dizzy trying to take it all in.

This is Julies recipe for White Chocolate Roll that is absolutely delicious. The use of white chocolate in this recipe produces a beautiful cake—the pale yellow color contrasting with the satiny brown filling.

½	pound white chocolate		1	cup sugar
5	tablespoons strong coffee		2	tablespoons dark crème de cacao or Kahlúa
7	eggs, separated			

Filling:

1½	cups heavy cream		¼	cup confectioners' sugar, more if desired
½	cup sweetened cocoa, less if desired		2	tablespoons dark crème de cacao or Kahlúa

Melt white chocolate over low heat; add coffee. Set aside to cool. Oil an 11x17-inch jelly-roll pan, line with waxed paper, and oil the waxed paper. Set aside. Beat egg yolks in electric mixer bowl; gradually add sugar and beat until mixture is very light and creamy. Add chocolate mixture and blend well. Flavor with crème de cacao. In another bowl, beat egg whites until stiff. Fold into egg mixture and spread into prepared jelly-roll pan. Place in a preheated 350 degree oven and bake for 15 minutes. Turn oven off and leave pan in oven 5 minutes longer. Remove from oven and turn cake out onto 2 overlapping strips of waxed paper; carefully remove lining paper and cover cake with a double thickness of paper towels wrung out in cold water. Let cool.

Prepare filling: whip the heavy cream, flavoring it with ¾ cup of the cocoa, the confectioners' sugar, and crème de cacao. Spread on cake and roll up. Just before serving, dust cake with cocoa, or with equivalent confectioners' sugar. May be made earlier the same day.

CINNAMON BLINTZES

While as a guest at a garden club in Dublin, I was intrigued with an especially good little confection that one of the young members had brought. She said that the recipe was from a friend in Charlotte, N.C. who always had a monthly coffee for the young mothers. She said it freezes well and she keeps it always on hand to bring it out for the children.

2	loaves thin white bread	1	cup margarine
2	(8-ounce) packages cream cheese	1	cup brown sugar
2	egg yolks	2½	teaspoons cinnamon
½	cup sugar		

Trim bread and roll thin. Cream together cream cheese, egg yolks, and sugar. Spread thinly on bread slices. Roll up. Melt margarine. Combine brown sugar and cinnamon. Dip rolls in margarine, then in cinnamon mixture. Place close together on cookie sheet. Freeze 5 minutes. Remove and slice each roll in half. Bake desired amount at this point or freeze rest in bags. When ready to use, put in oven straight from freezer on greased cookie sheet (or ungreased if "no stick coating"). Bake 350 degrees for 15 to 20 minutes.

PIES, CAKES AND ICINGS

KITTY'S FAMOUS LEMON PIE

My mother has made enough lemon pies in her life to affect the citrus industry. She is known all over town as the Lemon Pie Queen and her children, grandchildren, and great grandchildren have always been excited when Kitty Kat would serve lemon pie at home or bring a couple of them when she came to visit.

2	cups water	4	egg yolks, slightly beaten
1	cup sugar	1	tablespoon butter
	Juice of 2 lemons	1	(8-inch) baked pie shell
4	tablespoons cornstarch	4	egg whites
	Rind of 1 lemon, grated	4	tablespoons sugar

Combine water and sugar in a medium saucepan and bring to a boil. Mix together lemon juice and cornstarch. Add rind. Combine egg yolks, and lemon mixture. Add boiling water and sugar. Then return to saucepan. Cook slowly, stirring until thick. Add butter. Remove from heat; cover with foil and cool. Pour lemon custard into pie shell. Beat egg whites until stiff and gradually add 4 tablespoons of sugar. Put meringue atop lemon custard being sure meringue touches pie plate all the way around. Bake in a 300 degree oven until golden brown.

MILE-HIGH RASPBERRY PIE

Even though food authorities have run up a warning flag about the use of raw eggs in our recipes, there are a few such dishes that deserve remembering and preserving. My hope is that a way will be found to make it acceptable to use raw eggs, especially the whites that do such a splendid job of making so many desserts light and fluffy. In the meantime, I am holding on tenaciously to a few recipes that I have used and enjoyed so much through the years. This wonderful pie has been the star of many luncheons and dinners at my house and everybody has always seemed to like it a whole lot.

1	(9-inch) pie shell, unbaked	1	tablespoon lemon juice
½	cup slivered almonds	1	cup sugar
1	(10-ounce) package frozen raspberries, thawed	1	teaspoon almond extract
3	egg whites	1	cup whipping cream, whipped

Prepare unbaked pie shell and press almonds into it. Bake until golden brown at 450 degrees, about 10 to 12 minutes. Mix raspberries, egg whites, lemon juice, sugar and almond extract and beat until very stiff. Fold in whipped cream. Spoon into pie shell and freeze at least 5 hours. Remove from freezer 15 minutes before serving.

PIES, CAKES AND ICINGS

LAZY DAY LEMON CHIFFON PIE

Years ago someone was ridding herself of potted plants before winter set in, and she gave my son Bill (to bring to me) a perfectly beautiful lemon tree just covered with gorgeous, beautiful white flowers. I gave the large, hearty plant a good home on my sun porch and nurtured it carefully. Every day I would watch its development because I was totally intrigued with the possibility of growing my own lemons. Finally one day there was a tiny, green lemon—then another and then another. Soon the tree was covered with tiny lemons and the fun began in earnest. I could not believe that it was possible to grow lemons in Middle Georgia in the middle of winter and I was enjoying it immensely. Although a few of the lemons dropped off, it wasn't too long before my tree, about 3 or 4 feet tall, was hanging heavy with huge yellow lemons. It was almost like a miracle. The real miracle, though, was finding the old, old recipe for Lemon Pie that uses condensed milk. They no longer were putting it on the milk can and it wasn't in a single cookbook that I owned. Finally, before the lemon crop was over, someone gave me the recipe and I was delighted. I was so excited that I was finally going to make a pie with all the lemons. Then I realized the recipe called for reconstituted lemon juice. It's delicious anyway and I did garnish with my real lemons.

1	(8- or 9-inch) graham cracker crumb crust, chilled	2-3	teaspoons grated lemon peel, optional
1	(14-ounce) can sweetened condensed milk (not evaporated milk)	3	egg whites
⅓	cup reconstituted lemon juice	¼	teaspoon cream of tartar
	Few drops yellow food coloring		Whipped topping and lemon slices, optional

In medium bowl, combine sweetened condensed milk, lemon juice, food coloring and 1 teaspoon grated lemon peel (optional); mix well. In small bowl, beat egg whites with cream of tartar until stiff but not dry. Gently fold into lemon mixture. Pour into prepared crust. Chill 3 hours. If desired, at serving time, garnish with topping, lemon slices and grated peel.

BEST-EVER LEMON PIE

Ann Landers was always known for her advice column—much of it directed to the lovelorn. When she advised us, one day, to try this lemon pie recipe I decided to follow her advice. She said this is the world's best and easiest to make lemon pie. She said that she got it from a New York taxi cab driver years ago. I have always pelleted cab drivers with a thousand questions when I'm in a strange city but I've never thought to ask them if they have any good recipes. Next time I'll know.

1	baked 9-inch pie shell	3	egg yolks
1¼	cups sugar	1½	teaspoons lemon extract
6	tablespoons cornstarch	2	tablespoons vinegar
2	cups water	3	tablespoons butter
⅓	cup lemon juice		

Mix sugar and cornstarch together in the top of a double broiler. Add the 2 cups of water. Combine egg yolks with lemon juice and beat until well mixed. Add to the rest of the sugar mixture. Cook over boiling water until thick-about 25 minutes. This does away with the starchy taste. Now add the lemon extract, butter and vinegar, and stir thoroughly. Pour mixture into deep 9-inch pie shell, and let cool. Cover with meringue, and brown in oven.

Never Fail Meringue:

1	tablespoon cornstarch	6	tablespoons sugar
2	tablespoons cold water	1	teaspoon vanilla
½	cup boiling water	1	pinch salt
3	egg whites		

Blend cornstarch and cold water in a saucepan. Add boiling water and cook stirring until clear and thickened. Let stand until completely cooled. With electric beater at high speed, beat egg whites until foamy. Gradually add sugar and beat until stiff but not dry. Turn mixer to low speed; add salt and vanilla. Gradually beat in cold cornstarch mixture. Turn mixer again to high, and beat well. Spread meringue over cooled pie filling. Bake at 350 degrees for 10 minutes or until top is lightly browned.

PIES, CAKES AND ICINGS

MISS DAISY BOYKINS COCONUT CREAM PIE

Many years ago I embarked on a very rewarding (not financially) career writing food articles for the Courier Herald in Dublin, Georgia. I shall never forget how I agonized over that very first column and then finally decided to feature Miss Daisy Boykin's Coconut Pie. Miss Daisy was a little-old-lady, never married, retired school teacher who lived next door to my mother in Guyton, and this was her delicious recipe. Mother and I thought Miss Daisy was going to be thrilled to be featured in my very first column but evidently she wasn't. Although Mother supplied her with several copies of the article, she never commented. We were disappointed—but had a lot of good laughs about it.

1	cup sugar	1	teaspoon vanilla
3	tablespoons flour	1	package coconut or 2 cups fresh coconut
3	eggs, separated	1	baked 8-inch pie shell
2	cups milk		

Mix together sugar and flour. Stir in egg yolks and beat well. Heat milk to scalding stage. Add slowly to egg mixture and then back to pot in which milk was heated. Cook over low to medium heat until thick. Remove from heat. Add vanilla and coconut. Pour into baked pie shell. Top with meringue and bake at 300 degrees until light brown.

Meringue:

Beat egg whites until stiff and gradually add 4 tablespoons sugar and a few drops of vanilla.

LEN BERG'S MACAROON PIE

When we were young college girls, one of our greatest treats was to go to Len Berg's in the alley to eat. Macaroon Pie was their and our specialty. Now, over 50 years later, the "girls" still want to go to Len Berg's for Macaroon Pie. It's a wonderful classic.

12	saltine crackers	1	cup sugar
12	dates chopped	1	teaspoon almond extract
½	cup pecans chopped	3	egg whites, beaten dry

Mix first 5 ingredients; to this mixture add egg whites which have been beaten dry. Pour into greased aluminum pie pan. Bake at 350 degrees for 30 minutes. Serve with whipped cream.

NEW PEACH PIE

My friends, Debra and Mark Ballard, are not only hosts to be emulated because of their great creativity but also because of their warmth and graciousness. But that's not the best part: they are hysterically funny when they get the proper time slot.

They are wonderful guests to have too. Once I was hosting a party that included three Frenchmen who were in Macon on business and were the guests of one of my guests. When I told my friend to just bring them on I didn't realize that only one of them spoke any English and the other two didn't have a clue as to what we were saying.

Mark, known far and wide as The Artist, appears regularly on t.v. and in the newspaper and does shows and demonstrations throughout the state, all pertaining to "creating something beautiful" as he says. Not everyone knew at the time of my party that Mark is also a stand up comedian who puts his audience in stitches. After our dinner when we adjourned to the living room, I was worried sick about entertaining our French guests who had no idea what we were saying. In his usual style, Mark arose and went center front to stand in front of the fireplace. Pretty soon we were all doubling over with laughter and the French guests were leading the pack, just having a ball.

Mark and Debra have a wonderful collection of prize recipes and the food that comes out of their kitchen is always marvelous. Mark did a cookbook that included most of his recipes including that wonderful caramel cake for which he is famous. It's the best.

His New Peach Pie is delicious too. I wish Mark and Debra were at my house right now and that we were enjoying a piece of this great pie.

1	(9-inch) unbaked deep dish pie shell	⅓	cup plain flour
4	peaches (depending on the size, it may take fewer)	2	eggs, well beaten
		½	stick butter or margarine, melted
1	cup sugar	¼	teaspoon almond flavoring (or your own choice of flavors)

Peel and slice peaches. Layer them neatly into the pie shell. You want them to cover the bottom of the crust. I usually place my peach slices in a circular design, starting at the outer edge and working my way to the middle.

In a separate bowl, mix the sugar and flour. Add beaten eggs, melted butter and flavoring. I will just go ahead and tell you right now that I put in a whole teaspoon of almond flavoring. I just love it.

Combine well and pour over the peaches. Bake at 350 degrees until the crust is brown and the custard is thick. The pie will serve better if you allow it to completely cool.

PIES, CAKES AND ICINGS

GRANDMOTHER EVA SHEAROUSE'S PEACH AND PRUNE PIE, AS RECREATED BY LOUISE DODD

My maternal grandmother, Eva Shearouse, was a good old-fashioned cook who grew her own chickens and vegetables and cooked everything on a wood stove. I can see her now dipping hot water from the tank that was on the stove. She had feather beds and a fireplace in the bedroom where I slept when I spent the night with her. So many memories I still enjoy from those long ago days. A very special memory was the Peach and Prune Pie she used to make and put in the wire—screened safe near the back door. When we would visit her after school, we'd always head straight to the safe where there was always something good like fritters, cakes or pies. Very unfortunately none of the children nor grandchildren had a copy of Grandmother's Peach and Prune Pie but not to be outdone, I experimented until I think I have it down pat. It is so good! Put a little dob of sour cream or whipped cream on top if you wish. That makes it even better.

2	prepared pie crusts unbaked	1	cup sugar
½	package (about 4 ounces) dried peaches	1	tablespoon lemon juice
½	package (about 6 ounces) dried prunes	½	stick butter

Set oven to 375 degrees. Stew fruits in small amount of water together with sugar until tender. Add lemon juice and butter. Pulverize in food processor. Put into uncooked pie crust. Make lattice strips of pie dough to cover. Turn edges of crust over strips. Bake until lightly browned.

CHERRY CHEESE PIE

Remember when this delicious recipe made the circuit? Everybody was serving it and everybody loved it. It was Cherry-o Cream Cheese Pie. Now it's been resurrected and called just Cherry Cheese Pie. The "o" is missing but the "oh" will never be missing. It is so-o-o- good. A great Valentine or Washington Birthday dessert.

1	(9-inch) graham cracker crumb crust or baked pastry shell	1	(14-ounce) can Eagle Brand Sweetened Condensed Milk (not evaporated milk)
1	(8-ounce) package cream cheese, softened	⅓	cup ReaLemon juice from concentrate
		1	teaspoon vanilla extract
		1	(21-ounce) can cherry pie filling, chilled

In large mixer bowl, beat cheese until fluffy. Gradually beat in Eagle Brand milk until smooth. Stir in ReaLemon and vanilla. Pour into prepared crust. Chill 3 hours or until set. Top with pie filling before serving. Refrigerate leftovers.

PUMPKIN CHIFFON PIE

Years ago my cousin/friend, Mary Cook, served this delicious pie at her lovely new home on Elm Street in Wrightsville. Mary was quick to say that the recipe was Mamie Eisenhower's, clipped from a copy of Army Times while she and Jimmy were doing a tour of duty in Japan. It came a long way but is well worth every step of the way. Pumpkin Pie is good any way you make it, but this chiffon rendition wins the prize.

3	beaten egg yolks		3	egg whites
¾	cup brown sugar		½	teaspoon nutmeg
1½	cups cooked pumpkin		1	envelope gelatin
½	cup milk		¼	cup cold water
½	teaspoon salt		¼	cup sugar
1	teaspoon cinnamon			

Combine egg yolks, brown sugar, pumpkin, milk, salt and spice. Cook in double boiler until thick, stirring constantly. Soak gelatin in cold water, stir into hot mixture. Chill until partially set. Beat egg whites and sugar until stiff. Fold into gelatin mixture. Pour into pie shell and chill until set. Garnish with whipped cream. Makes one big pie or 8 individual ones.

THE BEST PECAN PIE

When one of my very favorite cookbooks labels a recipe "The Best", I have to try it. Cotton Country Collection from Monroe, Louisiana says this is the best pecan pie and I agree. I would say Cotton Country Collection is one of the best too. It's the cookbook that I usually reach for first when I'm trying to cook something and don't know how. Be sure to use the lemon juice even though such a small amount. It is key.

1	stick butter		1	teaspoon vanilla
1	cup light Karo syrup		1	dash of salt
1	cup sugar		1	cup chopped pecans
3	large eggs, beaten		1	(8 or 9-inch) unbaked pie shell
½	teaspoon lemon juice			

Brown butter in saucepan until is golden brown, do not burn; let cool. In separate bowl add ingredients in order listed; stir. Blend in browned butter well. Pour into unbaked pie shell and bake at 425 degrees for 10 minutes, then lower to 325 degrees for 40 minutes.

PIES, CAKES AND ICINGS

PECAN CHIFFON PIE

Friends of mine at one time owned an inn where they served some of the best home cooking you ever tasted. This Pecan Chiffon Pie is the only pecan chiffon pie I've ever tasted and it is delicious. The use of raw egg whites raises the red flag so travel at your own risk. It couldn't be any riskier than a visit into the Okefenokee Swamp, located only seven miles from the pecan pie source.

4	eggs, separated	1	teaspoon vanilla extract
¼	teaspoon salt	1	cup pecans, chopped and toasted
1	cup sugar	1	(9-inch) baked pie shell
1	cup milk		Whipped cream with sugar and vanilla
1	envelope plain gelatin		to taste for topping
¼	cup cold water		

Beat egg yolks; place in saucepan with salt and half sugar. In separate saucepan heat milk and then pour over egg mixture, bring to boil over low heat and cook until thickened. Remove from stove and while still hot stir in gelatin dissolved in water. (Do not let gelatin stand.) Add vanilla, and then cool custard completely. Beat egg whites until stiff, adding remaining sugar. Fold into cool custard mixture. Gradually add pecans. Put into baked pie shell and refrigerate. After pie sets, add whipped cream topping and refrigerate until serving time.

PEANUT BUTTER PIE

Sadie Brantley was my friend for so many years that we both about forgot how many. There were so many facets of Sadie that I loved. She had a dry sense of humor that would just pulverize you when you were least expecting it. She was cordial always and if you wanted to stop by without having to do the courtesy of calling ahead, Sadie always acted like she was glad to have you. She didn't stand on formality. She was an excellent cook and planner and had some mighty pretty parties in her home on West College in Wrightsville. I remember Sadie's serving this delicious pie before most of us had ever heard of peanut pie. We were greatly impressed.

1	baked (8-inch) pie crust	2	eggs
½	cup brown sugar	2	tablespoons flour
½	cup granulated sugar	1½	cups milk
½	cup peanut butter	½	teaspoon vanilla

Combine sugars, peanut butter, eggs and flour. Gradually stir in milk. Cook over moderate heat, stirring constantly until thick. Do not boil. Remove from heat, stir in vanilla. Pour into pie shell. Cool, slice and serve with 1 teaspoon whipped topping for each slice.

RITZ CRACKER PIE

This pie is so good that you won't believe it has no key ingredient except Ritz crackers. You'll declare it has apples in it. You can whip one of these up between the time they call and tell you they're dipping off the interstate to see you (supper time!) and the time they walk in the back door—hungry as wolves.

3	egg whites, beaten to soft peaks	½	cup chopped pecans
1	cup sugar	20	crushed Ritz crackers
1	teaspoon vanilla		

Butter pie plate. Mix all above ingredients. Pour into pie plate and bake at 350 degrees until light brown. Remove; cool and serve with ice cream, whipped cream, Kahlúa or brandied fruit.

SUMMERTIME PIE

This Summertime Pie knows no season at my house. One of my friends recommended it and I've been a believer ever since.

½	cup chopped pecans	1	(8-ounce) package cream cheese, softened
1	(9-inch) unbaked pie crust		
1	cup whipping cream	1	cup sugar
		1	teaspoon vanilla

Press pecans into the bottom of the pie crust. Bake pie crust in a preheated 375 degree oven for 12 minutes or until done. Set aside to cool. Whip cream and set aside. Beat cream cheese, sugar and vanilla. Fold in whipped cream. Pour into completely cooled pie crust and refrigerate until set. Garnish with sweetened fruit, such as strawberries, peaches or cherries.

PIES, CAKES AND ICINGS

OPEN SESAME PIE

When I was at the Pillsbury Bake-Off® contest at Disney World, several of the food editors with whom I was sharing lunch were talking about some of their favorite Bake-Off® winners from years past. It was the Open Sesame Pie that seemed to garner the most unanimous accolades and I could relate because I remember having served the pie at a luncheon in the '50s and subsequently thinking of it as one of my favorite recipes.

1 (15-ounce) package refrigerated pie crust	2 tablespoons sesame seed, toasted*

Filling:

1 envelope unflavored gelatin	1 cup milk
¼ cup cold water	2 egg yolks
1 (8-ounce) package (1¾ cups) chopped dates	1 teaspoon vanilla
¼ cup sugar	1½ cups whipping cream
¼ teaspoon salt	2 tablespoons sugar
	⅛-¼ teaspoon nutmeg

Heat oven to 450 degrees. Prepare pie crust according to package directions for one-crust baked shell using 9-inch pie pan. Press toasted seeds into bottom of crust-lined pan. Bake at 450 degrees for 9 to 11 minutes or until lightly browned. Cool completely. In small bowl, sprinkle gelatin over ¼ cup cold water, set aside to soften. In medium saucepan, combine dates, ¼ cup sugar, salt, milk and egg yolks. Cook over medium heat 10 to 12 minutes or until mixture is slightly thickened, stirring constantly. Remove from heat. Add softened gelatin and vanilla; stir until gelatin is dissolved. Refrigerate until date mixture is thickened and partially set, stirring occasionally. In small bowl, combine whipping cream and 2 tablespoons sugar; beat until stiff peaks form. Fold in date mixture. Spoon filling into cooled baked pie shell; sprinkle with nutmeg. Refrigerate at least 2 hours before serving. Store in refrigerator.

*Tip: to toast sesame seed, spread on cookie sheet; bake at 375 degrees for 3 to 5 minutes or until light golden brown, stirring occasionally. Or spread in small skillet; stir over medium heat for about 5 minutes or until light golden brown.

❖ Louise with Gary Collins at Pillsbury Bake-Off® contest in Orlando. ❖

THE $1 MILLION CREAM CHEESE BROWNIE PIE

It was fun to see a fellow Southerner walk to the stage and receive $1,000,000 for her winning recipe at the Pillsbury Bake-Off® contest in San Francisco. Bobby Sonefeld of Hopkins, S.C. was right well pleased with her Cream Cheese Brownie Pie that the judges said looked and tasted like $1,000,000.

1	(15-ounce) package Pillsbury® Refrigerated Pie Crust, softened as directed on package	3	eggs	
1	(8-ounce) package cream cheese, softened	1	(15.1-ounce) package Pillsbury® Thick n' Fudgy Hot Fudge Swirl Deluxe Brownie Mix	
3	tablespoons sugar	¼	cup oil	
1	teaspoon vanilla	2	tablespoons water	
		½	cup chopped pecans	

Heat oven to 350 degrees. Prepare pie crust as directed on package for one-crust filled pie using 9-inch pan. In medium bowl, combine cream cheese, sugar, vanilla and 1 of the eggs; beat until smooth. Set aside. Reserve hot fudge packet from brownie mix for topping. In large bowl, combine brownie mix, oil, 1 tablespoon of the water and remaining 2 eggs; beat 50 strokes with spoon. Spread ½ cup brownie mixture in bottom of crust-lined pan. Spoon and carefully spread cream cheese mixture over brownie layer. Top with remaining brownie mixture; spread evenly. Sprinkle with pecans. Bake at 350 degrees for 40 to 50 minutes or until center is puffed and crust is golden brown. If necessary, cover edge of crust with strips of foil, after 15 to 20 minutes of baking to prevent excessive browning. (Pie may have cracks on surface.) Place hot fudge from packet in small microwave-safe bowl. Microwave on HIGH for 30 seconds. Stir in remaining tablespoon water. Drizzle fudge over top of pie. Cool 3 hours or until completely cooled. Store in refrigerator.

JOANNE HILBURN'S CHOCOLATE FRENCH SILK PIE

On a beautiful sunny day I was invited to Joanne Hilburn's for a special tasting session of recipes the girls were trying out for Service League. Go no further. When we tasted this sublime French Silk Pie, we knew. It was one of the all-time greats. In fact it was selected as the Recipe of the Year for the Courier Herald *that same year. The pecans in the meringue crust are simply wonderful.*

Meringue:

2	egg whites	½	cup sugar
⅛	teaspoon salt	½	cup broken pecan pieces
⅛	teaspoon cream of tartar	½	teaspoon vanilla

Filling:

1	square unsweetened chocolate	2	eggs
1	stick butter	1	teaspoon vanilla
⅔	cup sugar	½	pint whipping cream, whipped

For meringue: Beat egg whites until foamy. Add salt and cream of tartar. Add sugar gradually and beat until very stiff. Fold in pecans and vanilla. Grease 8-inch pie pan with butter. Arrange meringue as crust. Bake in 300 degree oven for 55 minutes or until golden brown. You might lower temperature to 250 or 275 if your oven gets too hot.

For filling: Melt chocolate. Cool. Cream butter and sugar gradually. Add eggs one at a time, beating 5 minutes after each. Add chocolate and vanilla blending until color is uniform. Put into pie shell. Chill overnight. When served, top with whipped cream and grate chocolate over top.

DOWN IN DIXIE BOURBON PIE

This delicious pie (and many others just as good) was served to us at the Governor's Mansion in Jackson, Mississippi by the Junior Auxiliary in Vicksburg who wanted all of us food writers to taste the offerings from their new cookbook, Vintage Vicksburg. *For this southern girl, it didn't get much better than to be eating Down in Dixie Bourbon Pie in historic and beautiful Jackson, Mississippi.*

1	box chocolate wafers, crushed	1	cup evaporated milk
¼	cup butter or margarine, melted	1	cup heavy cream
21	marshmallows	3	tablespoons bourbon

Mix chocolate wafer crumbs and melted butter. Pat into bottom and sides of a 9-inch pie pan. Bake at 350 degrees until set about 15 minutes. In saucepan, heat marshmallows and milk until marshmallows melt and mixture is smooth. Do not boil. Remove from heat. Whip cream until stiff. Fold into marshmallow mixture. Add bourbon and pour into cooled chocolate crumb crust. Refrigerate 4 hours or until set. Additional whipped cream and chocolate crumbs or chocolate curls make an attractive garnish.

FOURTEEN-LAYER CHOCOLATE CAKE

Several times I have tried those imagination–defying fourteen-layer cakes. Take one to a party and you're immediately recognized as the marvel cook. I really don't plan to make them on a regular basis but when I do, I want to use Carolyn Powell's recipe from the Mount Olive Church of the Nazarene Cookbook *from Wrightsville. I suggest that you grease well and maybe put waxed paper in 8-inch cake pans. You have to work quickly.*

1	cup shortening (part margarine and part shortening)	2	teaspoons vanilla
6	eggs	2	cups sugar
1	cup milk	3	cups sifted self-rising flour

Mix all ingredients; beat until smooth. Batter will be thinner than usual. Put 4 tablespoons in each layer. Bake at 350 degrees until layers are done. Check often.

Filling:

2	cups sugar		Warm water, to make paste with cocoa
1½	sticks margarine	1½	cups evaporated milk
6	tablespoons cocoa		

Mix all and cook until it begins to thicken. Stack cake with filling as cake comes out of oven while hot.

PIES, CAKES AND ICINGS

CHOCOLATE POUND CAKE

I really like this Chocolate Pound Cake. I really like it. Not only is it easy to make and big, it is moist and good. When Herschel Walker was the football star of the world I interviewed his mother for an article for our Courier Herald. She and I both lived in Wrightsville. I learned from Mrs. Walker that Herschel's favorite cake was chocolate and the next time he came home I took him one of these cakes. It and he were both winners.

❖ Herschel Walker (Heisman Trophy is on stage at right) in Wrightsville, his home town. ❖

2	sticks butter		¼	teaspoon salt
½	cup shortening		3	cups flour
3	cups sugar		½	teaspoon baking powder
6	eggs		1¼	cups milk
½	cup cocoa		2	teaspoons vanilla

Cream butter and shortening with sugar. Add one egg at a time, beating well after each one. Sift all dry ingredients and add alternately with milk to butter mixture. Add vanilla. Cook in greased floured tube pan at 325 degrees for 1½ hours or until cake tests done.

Frosting:

½	cup Crisco			
2	cups sugar			
¼	cup cocoa		¼	teaspoon salt
⅔	cup milk		2	teaspoons vanilla

Combine all ingredients, except vanilla, in large saucepan. Bring to boil. Cook 2 minutes stirring. Cool. Add vanilla. Beat. If too thick, add 1 tablespoon cream.

SCRUMPTIOUS TEXAS CHOCOLATE SHEET CAKE

We do listen to the sermon but I'll have to admit we occasionally miss the scripture reading and announcements. Anne Burnham and I always sit together in church and sometimes we have a recipe that just won't keep. One Sunday she suggested that I look in Georgia Land, published by the Auxiliary to the Medical Association of Georgia (of which she's a member) for the recipe for Chocolate Sheet Cake. She said "it's out-of-this world" and she wasn't wrong.

2	cups unsifted flour	1	teaspoon baking soda
2	cups sugar	½	cup buttermilk
1	cup margarine	2	eggs, lightly beaten
5	tablespoons unsweetened cocoa	1	teaspoon vanilla
1	cup water		

Icing:

½	cup margarine	1	pound box powdered sugar
3	tablespoons unsweetened cocoa	1	cup chopped pecans
6	tablespoons milk		

Mix together flour and sugar. Bring to boil the margarine, cocoa and water. Pour over flour and sugar mixture, blending well. Stir soda into buttermilk. Add eggs and vanilla. Mix well. Pour buttermilk over flour mixture and stir until well blended. Pour batter into greased and lightly floured 10x15-inch jelly-roll pan. Bake at 400 degrees for 20 to 25 minutes.

Icing:

While cake is cooking, heat to boiling margarine, cocoa and milk. Add sugar and pecans. Mix well. Pour hot frosting over hot cake. Cool and cut into squares.

DEVIL'S FOOD CAKE

When my late brother, Franklin, was a little boy, he always wanted Devil's Food Cake. My grandmother and my mother could make the best ones you ever tasted—always iced with white icing—never chocolate like some people do today. Now my grandchildren are requesting Devil's Food Cake for their birthday cakes. On several recipes I have made a note of whose birthday and when. This recipe is probably the favorite of them all. It was for Stephen's 16th birthday on March 16, 2001.

¾	cup butter, softened		1	teaspoon salt
2	cups sugar		2	teaspoons baking soda
2	eggs		2	cups buttermilk
2¼	cups cake flour		1	tablespoon vanilla
¾	cup cocoa			

Cream butter and sugar together. Add eggs one at a time. Sift together flour, cocoa, salt and soda. Add alternately with buttermilk to creamed mixture. Add vanilla and beat at medium speed for 2½ minutes. Bake in 3 (8-inch) cake pans lined with greased wax paper at 350 degrees for about 30 minutes or until done. Frost, if desired with Seven-Minute White Icing.

MILKY WAY CAKE

It's funny how my four grandsons have different tastes and different favorites. I can always count on the number two grandson, Guyton, to thoroughly enjoy the sweets and desserts. This is one of his favorite recipes from one of Laurens County's best cooks who declines identification because she doesn't want to be identified with a cake mix recipe. I do share her sentiments but at the same time the both of us know this is one great recipe.

1   box Duncan Hines German's Chocolate Cake Mix

Bake according to directions in a 13x9-inch Pyrex baking dish. Be sure not to overcook.

Frosting:

2	cups sugar	⅔	cup evaporated milk
2	tablespoons cocoa	3	(5.2 ounces) Milky Way candy bars, cut
1	stick butter		into several pieces each

Combine sugar, cocoa, butter and milk in large saucepan and bring to a boil on medium heat. Turn to low heat and cook for 5 minutes. Stir in candy bars and beat. (The candy will not look completely melted.) Cool slightly and ice cake.

DRIED APPLE FRUIT CAKE

From Kitchen Kapers, an Effingham County cookbook, comes this really good recipe for Dried Apple Fruit Cake by our former neighbor in Guyton, Mary Douglas. This is a bit different for an apple cake but really good. Of course I've always thought anything from Effingham County is good. It's home.

1	box dried apples	¼	teaspoon cloves
2	cups dark syrup	¼	teaspoon nutmeg
1	cup sugar	3	cups plain flour
1	cup (½ pound) butter or oleo	1	cup nuts (chopped)
3	eggs	½	teaspoon cinnamon
1	teaspoon soda	1	box dark raisins

Soak apples overnight. Drain. Add syrup and cook slowly until very tender. Cool. Cream sugar and butter. Add eggs. Combine all the dry ingredients, and raisins, and add. Stir in apples last. Bake in slow oven, about 300 degrees.

PIES, CAKES AND ICINGS

HUMMINGBIRD CAKE

Meeting at Mary Douglas' house in Dublin to taste-test recipes for the Service League's Antique Fair Tea Room, *we were all overwhelmed with our introduction to Hummingbird Cake. We thought it was stupendous! We were overwhelmed!*

The recipe is one of Southern Living Magazine's *most requested and is in their* Hall of Fame Dessert Classics.

3	cups all-purpose flour
1	teaspoon baking soda
½	teaspoon salt
2	cups sugar
1	teaspoon ground cinnamon
3	eggs, beaten
¾	cup vegetable oil

1½	teaspoons vanilla extract
1	(8-ounce) can crushed pineapple, undrained
1	cup chopped pecans
1¾	cups mashed bananas
	Cream Cheese Frosting (recipe below)
½	cup chopped pecans, toasted

Combine first 5 ingredients in a large bowl; add eggs and oil; stirring until dry ingredients are moistened. Do not beat. Stir in vanilla, pineapple, 1 cup pecans, and bananas. Pour batter into 3 greased and floured 9-inch round cake pans. Bake at 350 degrees for 23 to 28 minutes or until a wooden pick inserted in center comes out clean. Cool in pans 10 minutes; remove from pans, and let cool completely on wire racks. Spread Cream Cheese Frosting between layers and on top and sides of cake. Sprinkle pecans over top.

Cream Cheese Frosting:

½	cup butter or margarine, softened
1	(8-ounce) package cream cheese, softened

1	(16-ounce) package powdered sugar, sifted
1	teaspoon vanilla extract

Cream butter and cream cheese. Gradually add powdered sugar, beat until mixture is light and fluffy. Add vanilla.

ITALIAN CREAM CAKE

Italian Cream Cake might never have seen Italy but it certainly has seen the inside of many kitchens in this country. This cake is what I call a "standard." No matter where you take it, everybody knows and loves it. The frosting helps to make it perfect.

½	cup butter or margarine, softened	2	cups all-purpose flour
½	cup shortening	1	teaspoon soda
2	cups sugar	1	cup buttermilk
5	large eggs, separated	1	cup coconut
1	tablespoon vanilla extract		

Beat butter and shortening at medium speed with an electric mixer until fluffy; gradually add sugar, beating well. Add egg yolks, one at a time, beating until blended after each addition. Add vanilla; beat until blended. Combine flour and soda; add to butter mixture alternately with buttermilk, beginning and ending with flour mixture. Beat at low speed until blended after each addition. Stir in coconut. Beat egg whites until stiff peaks form; fold into batter. Pour batter into 3 greased and floured 9-inch round cake pans. Bake at 350 degrees for 25 minutes or until a wooden pick inserted in center comes out clean. Cool in pans on wire racks 10 minutes; remove from pans, and cool on wire racks. Spread Nutty Cream Cheese Frosting between layers and on top and sides of cake. Garnish, if desired.

Nutty Cream Cheese Frosting:

1	cup chopped pecans	1	tablespoon vanilla extract
1	(8-ounce) package cream cheese, softened	1	(16-ounce) package powdered sugar, sifted
½	cup butter or margarine, softened		

Place pecans in a shallow pan; bake at 350 degrees for 5 to 10 minutes or until toasted, stirring occasionally. Cool. Beat cream cheese, butter and vanilla at medium speed with an electric mixer until creamy. Add sugar, beating at low speed until blended. Beat at high speed until smooth; stir in pecans.

BANANA CAKE

Agnes Hatcher was my precious little neighbor at one time in Wrightsville. I can see Agnes now standing at the foot of my back steps with something wonderful to eat held up in her hands and a sweet smile on her face. At one point I was searching for a good cake recipe to bake in the Mrs. Macon contest that I had surreptitiously been roped into entering for the garden club. I thought of Agnes'es delicious recipe for Banana Cake and she let me use it. The cake did it—I won the title. The year was 1967.

3	sticks butter	1½	cups buttermilk
3	cups sugar	2	teaspoons soda
3	eggs	2¼	cups bananas
4½	cups flour		

Cream butter and sugar. Add eggs, one at a time, beating well after each one. Mix soda into buttermilk and add alternately with flour to creamed mixture, reserving enough flour to add with mashed bananas. Stir in bananas. Bake in 3 paper-lined 8-inch round pans about 25 minutes at 325 degrees.

Filling:

1	package 10X sugar	Almond flavoring
1	stick butter	Small amount of milk or orange juice

Cream butter and sugar. Add milk or orange juice and almond until proper consistency to spread between layers and on top and sides of cake.

ORANGE CHIFFON CAKE

Years ago Mother rode the train to Atlanta with some friends to attend a flower show. She and a lady from Sandersville sat together and along the way Mother managed to copy her delicious recipe for Orange Chiffon Cake. (Wonder where I got my ability to ease recipes from all my friends and acquaintances?) Frost this lovely, light citrusy cake with an icing of 1 stick butter, softened, 1 (3-ounce) cream cheese, softened, a box of 4X sugar, grated rind of orange, and enough orange juice to make the mixture spreadable.

2¼	cups sifted cake flour	2	teaspoons grated orange rind
1	tablespoon baking powder	¾	cup orange juice
½	teaspoon salt	1	teaspoon vanilla extract
1½	cups sugar	8	egg whites
½	cup vegetable oil	½	teaspoon cream or tartar
5	egg yolks		

Combine first 4 ingredients in a mixing bowl. Make a well in center; add oil, egg yolks, orange rind, orange juice, and vanilla. Beat at medium speed of an electric mixer until smooth. Beat egg whites and cream of tartar in a large mixing bowl at high speed of electric mixer until soft peaks form. Pour egg yolk mixture in a thin, steady stream over egg whites; gently fold yolks into whites. Pour batter into an ungreased 10-inch tube pan, spreading evenly. Bake at 325 degrees for 1 hour or until cake springs back when lightly touched. Invert pan; cool 40 minutes. Loosen cake from sides of pan, using a narrow metal spatula; remove from pan.

LUSCIOUS LEMON CAKE

In 1998 my friends asked me to join them on a trip to Martha's Vineyard and there was no way I could refuse to go to a place I had always envisioned but never seen. It always seemed so glamorous to me that another one of my friends has a home on Martha's Vineyard but I never really dreamed I'd get to this place that the Kennedys helped to make famous.

Our hotel had a large front porch with rocking chairs all in a row and I'll never forget the spectacular view from the porch of a full orange moon coming up over the bay that separated Martha's Vineyard from the well known Chappaquidick Island.

Our visit was shortly after John John's fatal plane crash and our cab driver, a retired WWII officer, gave us all the low down on the high ups. He had driven many of the celebrities of the island and seemed to revel in our interest in his tales.

This is a recipe I gleaned from the hotel and certainly is an exceptional one. It's so soft and delicate, luscious and really beautiful.

3	eggs, separated	¼	teaspoon salt
1	cup sugar		Grated rind of 1 lemon
6	tablespoons hot water		Lemon filling
1	cup flour		Powdered sugar
1	teaspoon baking powder		

Preheat oven to 375 degrees. Beat egg yolks, add sugar and beat until thick and lemon-colored. Stir in water and dry ingredients. Fold in stiffly beaten egg whites. Add grated rind. Grease a cookie sheet that has a rim (jelly-roll pan), line it with waxed paper and grease it again. Pour batter into pan, spreading evenly. Bake 12 to 15 minutes. Immediately cut off crisp edges and turn onto large cloth lightly covered with powdered sugar. Remove waxed paper. Using the cloth, roll up the cake and set aside while you make the filling. When ready, unroll cake, spread on filling and roll back up. Cool completely; transfer to serving dish. Cut with serrated knife.

❖ Mary Jean Yates, Joann Floyd, Betty Ballard and Louise in Martha's Vineyard restaurant. ❖

Lemon Filling:

1	cup sugar
2	eggs
2	tablespoons butter, melted
	Juice and grated rind of 2 lemons

Put all ingredients in double boiler, beat well and stir until thick, 15 to 20 minutes. Cool slightly.

LEMON-COCONUT PARTY CAKE

This is a delicious cake to make ahead and serve the next day—10 or 12 people. It's pretty, too, all covered with whipped cream and coconut.

1   angel food cake

Filling:

2	tablespoons grated lemon peel	1	cup sugar
½	cup lemon juice	1	cup heavy cream, whipped
3	eggs, beaten	1	cup flaked coconut
¾	cup soft butter or margarine		

Make filling: In top of double boiler, combine lemon peel and juice, eggs, butter and sugar. Place over simmering water (water should not touch top of double boiler). Cook, stirring constantly, about 10 to 12 minutes, until mixture coats a metal spoon. Let cool completely. Fold in whipped cream and coconut. With serrated knife, cut cake crosswise into 3 layers. Invert top layer on cake plate; spread with half of filling. Top with middle layer; spread with rest of filling. Place last layer on top. Frost cake completely with the 2 cups whipped cream. Sprinkle all over with coconut. Refrigerate cake overnight before serving.

Frosting:

2	cups heavy cream, whipped	½	cup flaked coconut

PINEAPPLE CAKE

Sally Pullen came over to me at Bob Newsome's fish fry (his lake house being the site of many hours of recruiting Herschel Walker for UGA) and said, "I want you to be sure and try the cake I brought." I almost forgot but just before I started to leave I pinched off a piece. Oh, my goodness! Sally was lucky I didn't get into it at first. This is without a doubt one of the most delicious cakes I know. It's moist and good and pretty too. I have a note on the recipe that says: "Made six for Christmas 1989." I've made many more since then too. It's terrific. Just use a 1-2-3-4 cake. Put the pineapple filling on top of first layer; put second layer on top and frost it; add third layer and frost entire cake with white icing.

Make 3 layers 1-2-3-4 cake

Frost 2 layers with:

3	egg yolks	1	stick butter
2	cups sugar	1	large can crushed pineapple, drained
½	cup evaporated milk	1	tablespoon cornstarch, mixed with small amount of water

Combine all ingredients in a saucepan and cook over medium heat until thick.

1-2-3-4 CAKE

Perhaps everybody knows how to make a 1-2-3-4 Cake. I've made so many through the years that I can whip one up without referring to the recipe. This recipe needs to be preserved for posterity, though because it's the basic of all basic recipes. It can be iced so many different ways: chocolate, lemon, caramel, whatever. I always spray my cake pans and line each one with a single sheet of waxed paper. Through the years I've learned to fold a long sheet of paper vertically 3 times; lay the cake pan on it; run around the pan lightly with the points of the scissors to mark the size; and cut the circle about an inch wider than the scissor marks, making 3 rounds at one time.

2	sticks butter	3	teaspoons baking powder
2	cups sugar	½	teaspoon salt
4	eggs	1	cup milk
3	cups all-purpose flour	1	teaspoon vanilla

Preheat oven to 325 degrees. Cream butter and sugar together until light and fluffy. Break each egg into a saucer and add-one at a time. Beat well-several minutes. Sift together flour and baking powder and add alternately with milk, beginning and ending with flour. Do not beat, just fold in lightly. Fold in vanilla. Divide evenly into 3 pans that have been sprayed and lined with waxed paper. Bake at 325 degrees until cake tests done.

SAVANNAH CREAM CAKE

At a perfectly lovely Mercer University Press Authors Luncheon at the Ritz Carlton Buckhead in Atlanta, we were served this elegant dessert. Elizabeth Terry, owner/chef of Savannah's prestigious Elizabeth on 37th, was one of the authors chosen to speak that day and to honor her, the Ritz chefs lifted a recipe from her cookbook for our dessert. I came straight home and tried it— and tried it—and tried it. It is so delicious and such a truly elegant dessert.

One angel food cake, broken into small pieces.

The Sherry Custard:
1½   teaspoons unflavored gelatin

¼   cup warm water, plus 2 tablespoons tap water

2   egg yolks

¼   cup good dry sherry

¼   cup plus 2 tablespoons sugar

1   cup heavy cream

2   teaspoons vanilla extract

Frosting and Berries:
1   cup heavy cream, whipped

1   pint fresh berries

To make the custard: In a small bowl, sprinkle the gelatin over the warm water and set aside. In a mixer, beat the egg yolks until pale, then stir in the sherry, ¼ cup of the sugar, and the 2 tablespoons of water, and pour into a medium saucepan. Stir constantly over medium heat until large bubbles appear on the surface and the custard is thick, about 4 minutes. Remove from the heat. Whisk in the gelatin mixture and continue to whisk vigorously until the gelatin is completely dissolved. Place the pan over a bowl filled with ice and stir until the mixture is cool but the gelatin has not set. In a separate bowl, whip the cream, the remaining sugar, and the vanilla. Fold into the cooled custard.

In a large bowl, fold the custard into the cake pieces. Spoon the cake into an 8-inch springform pan and refrigerate for at least 2 hours to set.

To top the cake: Remove the sides of the springform and invert the cake onto a serving plate. "Frost" with the whipped cream and serve with the berries.

EIGHTEEN-CARAT CAKE

One of my duplicate bridge partners, Tommy Griffith, brought me an Alaskan Cookbook from her visit there. To prove my sincere appreciation, I baked a carrot cake from the book and took it to her at Christmas time. Certainly it was a nice recipe that I intended to keep forever but somehow I have misplaced the book—not lost it—just misplaced it.

Not to worry—Tommy copied the recipe for me from her book. In accordance with Murphy's Law, my book will be found tomorrow.

1½	cups small diced carrots (3 medium, 8 to 10-ounces)		4	eggs
2½	cups unbleached white flour		1	tablespoon vanilla
1½-2½ cups sugar			1	cup chopped walnuts
2	teaspoons cinnamon		1	cup unsweetened finely flaked dried coconut (available in health food stores "desiccated")
2	teaspoons baking soda		¾	cup drained, canned, crushed, unsweetened pineapple (drink the juice)
1	teaspoon salt			
1¼	cups safflower oil			

Generously coat 2 (9-inch) cake pans with oil and dust with flour. Preheat oven to 350 degrees and arrange racks so they are evenly spaced in center of oven. Place carrots in small glass bowl with 1 tablespoon water. Cover tightly with plastic and microwave on high for 6 to 7 minutes, until tender. Puree carrots-you should have 1 cup puree-set aside. Sift together flour, sugar, cinnamon, baking soda and salt in large mixing bowl.

In a smaller bowl, whisk together oil, eggs and vanilla. Gently stir egg mix into sifted ingredients. Just before batter is fully combined, add walnuts, coconut, pineapple, and carrot puree. Fold together until evenly mixed, but avoid over beating. Divide batter between cake pans and bake 30 to 35 minutes-until a probe inserted in cake comes out clean. Remove from oven-cool briefly in pans. Turn out onto racks to cool completely.

Icing: Cream together 1 (8-ounce) cream cheese and (1 stick) butter until smooth. Gently stir in 1 cup confectioners' sugar and 1 teaspoon vanilla until smooth. The icing should be creamy and somewhat firm. Add a little more sugar if necessary.

To assemble cake: Place 1 layer of cake, top side down, on back side of cookie sheet. Spread top with ⅔ to ¾ cup icing. Set next layer on cake, also top side down. Ice cake filling in between the 2 layers. Optional (Spread orange marmalade over top of cake.) Using a pastry bag, pipe any remaining icing around top or decorate as you like. Carefully put chopped nuts around bottom inch of cake. Chill cake briefly to set icing, then, using a large spatula, transfer to a cake plate. Serve at once, or store refrigerated for several days. (Carrot cake freezes well, iced or not.)

RED VELVET CAKE

I'm traveling down Highway 57 with a station wagon load of lumber hanging out the tailgate with a red bandanna tied tightly on the piece extended farthest. All of a sudden the car started weaving and being uncontrollable and I realized I had a flat tire. Way out in the uninhabited area of Twiggs County and I'm by myself. Several cars passed me. With each one I grew more hysterical. Finally one stopped and it was none other than Munchy Roberts from Wrightsville who would give you the shirt off his back if he thought you needed it. I've always liked Munchy and Hazel a whole lot but more than ever when I saw his car coming to a stop to help me. He unloaded the entire station wagon of heavy lumber, changed the tire, loaded the lumber back, and didn't leave me to shake and shiver all the way home but followed to be sure I was all right. What a good deed never forgotten.

I always knew Hazel was interested in cooking and recipes but I was ever so surprised to see a recipe in the Mt. Olive Church of the Nazarene Cookbook *from Hazel and Munchy. Red Velvet is a real favorite with some of my family and I like making it by Hazel and Munchy's recipe because it always reminds me of them—two cute people.*

1½	cups sugar		2½	cups Swans Down cake flour
2	eggs		1	teaspoon baking soda
1½	cups Wesson oil		1	tablespoon vinegar
1	cup buttermilk		1	bottle red food coloring
1	teaspoon vanilla flavoring			

For Frosting:

1	box 4x sugar		1	stick butter or margarine, softened
1	(8-ounce) package cream cheese, softened		1	cup chopped pecans (optional)

Mix together sugar and eggs. Add oil, buttermilk and flavoring. Sift cake flour and soda together; add to mixture. Add vinegar and food coloring; mix together well. Grease and flour 3 (8-inch) cake pans. Pour batter into pans and bake at 300 degrees for approximately 30 minutes. Cool. Blend together frosting ingredients and put between layers and on top and sides of cake.

PIES, CAKES AND ICINGS

CREAM CHEESE POUND CAKE

Of all the pound cakes, this is my favorite. I was invited down to Chester, Georgia years ago to judge some kind of contest they were having at the church. The group of ladies was called the Sunshine Club and rightly so because they were just as bright and cheerful as the gorgeous morning sun that shone on the trees and fields as I drove down there. They served a delicious lunch and I'll never forget this still warm pound cake made by Myrna Dykes. She gave me the recipe and I have made it at least hundreds of times since then. Sometimes I make it in a long, narrow cake pan and sometimes in a Bundt pan. Either way, it's always a winner.

3	sticks butter, softened		Dash of salt
1	(8-ounce) package cream cheese, softened	1½	teaspoons vanilla flavoring
		6	large eggs
3	cups sugar	3	cups plain flour, sifted

Cream butter and cream cheese, add sugar; cream until smooth, add vanilla and salt; add eggs one at a time, cream until smooth; add flour by cupfuls and mix well. Grease and flour large tube pan. Pour mixture into pan and bake in preheated 325 degree oven for approximately 1 hour 30 minutes.

STRAWBERRY SHORTCAKES

This is one of my favorite desserts to serve for one of my sun porch suppers. It is equally good with fresh sliced peaches instead of strawberries. I make the biscuits about 3 inches in diameter and not too thick because by the time I get it all stacked up it's tall enough.

2⅓	cups Original Bisquick®	½	cup milk
3	tablespoons sugar		Sweetened sliced strawberries
3	tablespoons margarine or butter, melted		Whipped cream

Heat oven to 425 degrees. Stir together Bisquick, sugar, margarine and milk until soft dough forms. Drop by 6 spoonfuls onto ungreased cookie sheet. Bake 10 to 12 minutes or until golden brown. Split shortcakes; fill and top with strawberries and whipped cream.

AMALGAMATION CAKE

My source for this once very popular recipe called it "Malgramation" Cake. Never satisfied to not know the meaning of a word I searched every reference book I had and there was no such word. I even consulted a fellow cook who is a college professor and he too was in the dark. I asked everybody I saw and no one knew. Then when playing bridge with Mary Ann Hamrick from Haddock I happened to mention it again. She was quick to explain that she had been reading recently in Ferrol Sam's book, A Christmas Gift and he devoted two or three pages to the old family recipe—Amalgamation Cake. Now that makes sense—and is in the dictionary too. I'm officially changing the name of my cake to Amalgamation.

At the same card game, Mary Ann regaled us by saying that her 100 year old mother said to her, "They say you are what you eat. If that's the case we must be fast and cheap and easy."

1	cup butter		4	cups all-purpose flour
2	cups sugar		1	cup milk
8	egg whites		1	teaspoon baking powder

Icing:

8	egg yolks		2	cups pecans
2	cups sugar		1	cup raisins
1	cup butter, softened		1	cup coconut
1½	cups milk			

Preheat oven to 350 degrees. Cream butter and sugar. Beat egg whites and fold in. Add flour and milk, a little at a time. Add baking powder. Pour into 7 greased and floured 8-inch cake pans. Bake at 350 degrees 15 minutes or until layers test done. Make icing by beating egg yolks and sugar. Cream in butter. Add milk. Cook slowly until thick. Add other ingredients. Spread between layers and on top and sides of cake.

BLACKBERRY JAM CAKE WITH BUTTERMILK ICING

I have made this cake so many times that I almost don't need a recipe and I have never had a failure with it. It takes a while to make but is certainly worth every minute. I never cease to be amazed at the icing. It starts off white as snow and ends up being a lovely caramel color and taste. I have, on a couple of occasions, used strawberry jam when I didn't have any blackberry jam but I think the blackberry is better.

1¾	cups flour	1	cup sugar
1	teaspoon baking powder	1	cup oil
½	teaspoon salt	3	eggs, beaten
1	teaspoon baking soda	¾	cup buttermilk
1	teaspoon cinnamon	1	teaspoon vanilla
½	teaspoon nutmeg	1	cup blackberry jam
½	teaspoon allspice	1	cup finely chopped pecans
¼	teaspoon ground cloves		

Preheat oven to 325 degrees.

Buttermilk Icing:

3	cups sugar	1	teaspoon baking soda
1	cup butter	1	cup chopped pecans
1	cup buttermilk	1	teaspoon vanilla
2	tablespoons light corn syrup		

For cake: Preheat oven to 325 degrees. Sift and measure all dry ingredients except sugar, mix all together, sift 3 times, add sugar to oil, mix well, add eggs, mix well, add dry ingredients alternately with buttermilk. Stir in vanilla and blackberry jam, stir in nuts well. Bake in 2 greased and floured 9-inch pans about 30 to 35 minutes.

Buttermilk icing: In 4-quart pot over medium heat (be sure to use a 4-quart pot, this icing will boil over) add all icing ingredients except nuts and vanilla. Boil, stirring constantly. Cook until small amount dropped into cold water forms ball. Pour into large bowl and beat with mixer at high speed for a few minutes. Beat with spoon until it cools; add nuts, vanilla, spread on layers.

HOLIDAY COCONUT CAKE

A lovely, fluffy white coconut cake is truly a work of art. And if you like coconut, it is one of the most delicious, moistest cakes you will ever taste. This old recipe that makes a beautiful 3-layer cake is perhaps the ultimate in coconut cakes. Make it for Christmas and Santa will surely come early.

⅓ cup butter or margarine, softened	¾ teaspoon salt
⅓ cup shortening	1⅓ cups milk or fresh coconut juice plus milk to equal 1⅓ cups
1¾ cups sugar	2 teaspoons vanilla extract
3 cups cake flour	4 egg whites, stiffly beaten
3½ teaspoons baking powder	

Filling:

1 cup + 2 tablespoons sugar	2 tablespoons butter
¼ cup cornstarch	3 tablespoons lemon juice
1 cup + 2 tablespoons water	1 tablespoon grated lemon rind
2 egg yolks, slightly beaten	1 cup shredded coconut

Seven Minute White Icing:

1½ cups sugar	¼ teaspoon cream of tartar
2 egg whites	1 teaspoon vanilla extract
5 tablespoons cold water	1 cup finely grated fresh coconut

Cream butter and shortening at medium speed of electric mixer. Add sugar very slowly, creaming until light and fluffy.

Sift together flour, baking powder and salt. Reduce speed to low. Add dry ingredients to creamed mixture alternately with milk, beating well after each addition. Stir in vanilla. Fold egg whites into batter. Pour into 3 greased and floured 8-inch cake pans. Bake at 350 degrees for 20 to 30 minutes. Turn onto wire racks; cool completely.

Filling: Combine sugar and cornstarch in saucepan; gradually stir in water. Cook over medium heat, stirring constantly, until mixture boils and thickens; boil 1 minute. Slowly stir small amount of hot mixture into egg yolks; gradually add egg yolks to hot mixture in saucepan. Boil 1 minute longer, stirring constantly. Remove from heat; continue stirring until smooth. Stir in butter, lemon juice and rind. Cool. (Add 1 to 2 drops yellow food coloring for rich, yellow color, if desired.) Stir in coconut. Spread on 2 layers.

For icing: In top of double boiler place sugar, egg whites, water and cream of tartar; beat until thoroughly blended. Place over rapidly boiling water; beat with electric hand mixer for 7 minutes. Remove from heat; add vanilla. Continue beating until icing is of spreading consistency. Frost top and sides of cake. Sprinkle with fresh coconut. Refrigerate.

PIES, CAKES AND ICINGS

DELICIOUS HOLIDAY FRUIT CAKE

I was minding my own business, not exceeding the speed limit or doing anything wrong. All of a sudden I turned my car around right in the middle of the deserted highway and made a bee line back to the house where I had just seen the most spectacular flowers blooming close to the house. With some trepidation I knocked on the door to inquire about the lovely flowers, at the time unknown to me. I met Mrs. Nettie Sammons who welcomed me in and told me all about the Confederate Rose and also about a holiday fruit cake that she was cooking at the time. She shared the recipe that seemed sort of weird to me because you stir it while it's cooking but there's nothing weird about the taste. It's one of the most delicious fruit cakes ever. And perhaps one of the most expensive. At last count, it was about a $50 production, not counting if you want to pour a little spirits over it.

1	pound butter	1	pound red crystallized cherries, cut into small pieces
4	cups sugar		
1	dozen eggs	1	pound package grated coconut
4	cups self-rising flour	3	pounds nuts, chopped
1	pound crystallized pineapple, green and yellow, cut into small pieces	½	pound dates, chopped

Cream butter and sugar in an aluminum dishpan. Add eggs one at a time beating after each addition. Sprinkle about 1 cup flour on fruit and nuts. Fold remaining flour into batter. Fold in fruit. Bake in the dishpan in a 350 degree preheated oven. Stir with a large spoon every 15 minutes for 1 hour and 15 minutes. Remove from oven-leave oven set at 350. Pack the cake into a large Bundt pan which has been greased or into 2 medium-size greased tube pans. (You may arrange pecan halves and cherries on top.) Return cake to oven. Turn off heat. Let stay in oven for 15 to 20 minutes. Remove. Cool on rack. Wrap tightly and store in closed container until ready to use.

BEST WHITE FRUIT CAKE

An elderly lady, Mrs. P. C. Price, was my across-the-street neighbor at one time in Wrightsville. She was a wonderful old-fashioned cook and I was just beginning housekeeping, trying to learn everything I could about cooking. I probably worried Mrs. Price to death for her recipes but she never indicated any displeasure; she always smiled and apparently with pride. One day she brought me this wonderful fruit cake and I followed her home for the recipe. This is my favorite and the fruit cake I have made every Christmas since the '50s.

½	pound butter	¾	pound glacé cherries, chopped
1	cup sugar	1	pound glacé pineapple, chopped
5	large eggs	4	cups shelled pecans, chopped
1¾	cups flour	½	ounce vanilla extract
½	teaspoon baking powder	½	ounce lemon extract

Cream butter and sugar until fluffy. Add eggs one at a time. Chop nuts and fruits and mix with ¾ cup flour. Sift remaining flour and baking powder together. Fold in. Add flavorings and mix well. Fold in nuts and fruits. Pour into greased, paper-lined tube pan or small loaf pans. Place in cold oven and bake at 250 degrees for 3 hours. Small loaves may be done in 2½ hours. Keep at least 24 hours before slicing.

ORANGE SLICE CAKE

If you are one of those who malign fruit cake, you might like this as a substitute. Most often I stay with my old tried and true recipes for cakes but one holiday season I saw this and thought it sounded good. I tried it and it turned out to be a great hit. Now I make it often for special occasions. It's a great Halloween cake and of course always tastes good at Christmas.

½	pound butter	1	(8-ounce) dates, chopped
2	cups sugar	1	pound candy orange slices, chopped
4	eggs	2	cups chopped pecans
1	teaspoon soda	1	can coconut (3½-ounces)
½	cup buttermilk	2	tablespoons grated orange rind
3½	cups flour		

Cream butter and sugar, add eggs. Put soda in buttermilk and add to butter mixture. Add flour to dates and orange slices. Add to batter. Add nuts and coconut and orange rind. Makes rather stiff batter. Put in round tube pan. Bake at 250 degrees for 2½ or 3 hours.

PIES, CAKES AND ICINGS

JAPANESE FRUIT CAKE

My friend, Reba Hatcher, shared with me years ago her wonderful recipe for Japanese Fruit Cake which I made almost every Christmas. One year when I reached for the recipe it was gone-nowhere to be found. I wasn't too upset though because I knew the recipe would be in any cookbook I happened to lift from the shelf. Not true at all. I searched through hundreds of books and couldn't find the recipe. Then, just like the nose on my face, Reba's recipe was right before me where it always had been. I never want this outstanding recipe to get away from me again. I'll hang on tight this time.

1	cup butter	1	teaspoon vanilla
2	cups sugar	1	teaspoon cinnamon
4	eggs	1	teaspoon allspice
3¼	cups flour	½	teaspoon ground cloves
3	teaspoons baking powder	¾	cup chopped raisins
1	cup milk		

For Filling:

	Juice of 3 lemons	3	cups sugar
	Grated rind of 2 lemons	3	tablespoons cornstarch
1	large coconut, grated		

For cake, cream together butter and sugar. Add eggs, one at a time, to sugar mixture, beating well after each addition. Sift flour and baking powder together. Fold in flour and milk, beginning and ending with flour. Add vanilla. Divide batter into 3 parts and to 1 part add cinnamon, allspice and ground cloves. Add chopped raisins. Put batter into 3 (8-inch) cake pans and bake at 325 degrees until cake tests done.

For filling: Put first 4 ingredients in a saucepan and place on medium heat. Mix cornstarch with ⅔ cold water and stir into lemon mixture. Cook, stirring until mixture drops in a lump from spoon. Stack cake while filling is still warm; being sure to put spiced layer in the middle. Cover tops and sides with filling.

TRULY DIFFERENT CUPCAKES

Joyce Vickers has always been the Susan Hayward of Wrightsville. A beautiful red head and a sweet neighbor to me, Joyce shared a recipe one time long ago that I still treasure and use frequently. The next time you need cupcakes, this is the recipe to use. These are the favorite of Grandson II, Guyton Porter.

4	squares semi-sweet chocolate	1	cup flour
2	sticks margarine or butter	4	large eggs
1½	cups chopped pecans	1	teaspoon vanilla
1¾	cups sugar		

Melt chocolate and margarine. Add pecans and stir. Remove from heat. Combine sugar, flour, eggs and vanilla; mix only until blended. Do not beat. Add chocolate-nut mixture and again mix carefully. Put into 18 muffin cups; bake at 325 degrees for about 30 to 35 minutes. Frost with chocolate fudge frosting.

JUNE'S CARAMEL ICING

My good friend, June Daley, in Wrightsville, says that she makes no claims about cooking. But she is too modest. June's Caramel Cake gets rave reviews whether she takes it to a church supper or to a holiday get together with her nieces and nephew. There's never any cake left. June uses a sour cream pound cake, with almond and vanilla extract cooked in a 9x13x2-inch pan and ices it with this wonderful caramel icing . I've always said there's an art to making caramel icing. June is Michaelangelo!

3	cups sugar	¾	cup milk
1½	sticks butter	1	teaspoon vanilla

Mix 2⅔ cups sugar, butter and milk in a bowl. Pour gently into a large saucepan. Do not splash against side of pot and do not stir while cooking. In an iron skillet brown ⅓ cup of the sugar. Add ¼ cup hot water and cook until sugar is melted. When first mixture begins to boil over medium heat add melted brown sugar. Do not stir. Cook for 3 minutes and 15 seconds. Remove from heat; add vanilla and cool slightly. Beat to spreading consistency. Ices a 13x9x2-inch pound cake or 3 layers.

PIES, CAKES AND ICINGS

BROWN SUGAR CARAMEL FROSTING

In December of 1992, I wrote myself this note on a large legal pad, yellow sheet of paper. "After making many caramel cakes this season with none of them being truly wonderful, I ran out of sugar. With one more cake to go, and only brown sugar (light) on hand, I tried this and it was just "perfect." Caramel Icing is tricky to me and I vasciliate between the many recipes I've collected. This is just one of many.

3	cups brown sugar	1	teaspoon vanilla
1	cup water		Cream or rich milk
1	tablespoon butter		

Boil the sugar and water until the syrup reaches 238 to 240 degrees. Add the butter and vanilla, remove from heat. Cool, then beat until thick and creamy. Add cream only if necessary.

CARAMEL ICING

Jan Smith of the Dublin Service League wowed us all one year with her absolutely delicious caramel cake. Of course I added this recipe to my caramel cake file. Jan makes a pound cake in 4 layer pans and uses this yummy, rich, creamy icing.

1	box light brown sugar	½	cup sugar
½	pint whipping cream	1	stick butter
1	cup sweetened condensed milk	1	teaspoon vanilla

Combine all ingredients except vanilla and cook on medium heat, stirring frequently, until soft ball stage. Remove from heat and cool completely. Add vanilla and beat until spreading consistency.

FUDGE FROSTING

This is a delicious Fudge Frosting that I acquired somewhere along the way. I like it because you know exactly how long to cook it to get perfect results. No candy thermometer is required.

3	tablespoons shortening	10½	tablespoons milk
2¼	cups sugar	3	tablespoons butter
1½	tablespoons corn syrup	⅛	teaspoon salt
3	squares semisweet chocolate	1	teaspoon vanilla

Combine all ingredients except vanilla in a heavy saucepan. Place over low heat and allow to come to a rolling boil. Cook exactly 1 minute. Cool before beating. Add vanilla. Beat until smooth.

CAROLYN JACKSON'S
ONE MINUTE NEVER FAIL CHOCOLATE ICING

Carolyn Jackson was one of my Wesleyan buddies in Wrightsville, a good friend and a smart friend. My collection of recipes includes several from Carolyn who was a good cook in addition to all her attributes. This is the chocolate icing that really never fails.

3	cups sugar	¾	cup milk
⅓	cup cocoa		Pinch of salt
1½	sticks butter	1	teaspoon vanilla

Mix first 5 ingredients and bring to a boil over medium heat. Boil 1 minute. Remove and add vanilla. Beat immediately-do not cool first. Spread on cake.

PIES, CAKES AND ICINGS

COCONUT FROSTING

This is an old, but good, recipe for Coconut Cake Icing. I always use this on 1-2-3-4 Cake.
Since "a handful" is so inexact, I just use ½ cup of marshmallows.

2   stiffly beaten egg whites
     Pinch of salt
     Pinch of cream of tartar
1½ cups sugar

¼   cup water
     Handful miniature marshmallows (½ cup)
2   packages frozen coconut

Beat egg whites with salt and cream of tartar. Boil sugar and water until it spins a thread, stir in marshmallows. Pour over beaten egg whites until all used. Put icing between the layers and sprinkle with coconut. Ice cake all over and sprinkle on the coconut.

LEMON CHEESE CAKE FILLING

Lemon Cheese Cake has been in my family much longer than I have. Grandmother made it;
Mother made it; and I make it. Lemon Cheese Cake is not cheesecake as most people think of
cheesecake. There's no cheese in it at all. I really wish I knew how it got its name. I know how it
gets its flavor, though and that's what counts. This filling goes on a 1-2-3-4 cake.

2   cups sugar
2   whole eggs   .
     Grated rind of 2 lemons

     Juice of 1½ lemons
½   stick of butter

In a heavy saucepan combine sugar, eggs, lemon juice and rind. Mix thoroughly then add the butter. Cook over low heat stirring constantly until thick. Remove when thick enough for spreading. Beat until creamy and spread between layers and over cake.

SEVEN MINUTE ICING

I have about as many white icing recipes as I have places to put them but this one is a keeper. It glazes over real well and holds up well.

1½ cups sugar	Pinch of cream of tartar
2 egg whites	6 large marshmallows or 60 small ones
5 tablespoons water	

Put all ingredients into top of a double boiler over simmering water. Cook, beating constantly with an electric mixer at high speed for about 7 minutes or until icing becomes stiff and glossy. Remove from heat and add vanilla. (This holds up very well, even in damp weather.)

WHITE MOUNTAIN ICING

This recipe is as old as the hills but is one that I use a lot and always have good results. It almost got away from me one time but after a diligent search through hundreds of books, I found it and intend to preserve it for posterity. There are several versions of this frosting but this is the easiest and perhaps the best.

3 cups sugar	3 egg whites
1 cup water	Dash of salt
¼ teaspoon cream of tartar	Flavoring (vanilla, orange extract, etc.)

Cook together sugar, water and cream of tartar until candy thermometer reaches 238 degrees or until syrup spins a long thread when dripped from a spoon. Pour a thin, slow stream of the syrup into stiffly beaten egg whites, beating constantly until frosting stands in peaks. Stir in salt and flavoring to taste. Spread on cake.

PIES, CAKES AND ICINGS

Food prepared on
site for movie
"Fried Green Tomatoes"

Chef Tell presents
diploma to Louise

Louise visits the
Culinary Institute of America
in Hyde Park, N.Y.

CANDIES
AND
COOKIES

SUPPLY-SIDE ECONOMICS FUDGE

One of the thrills of my writing career was receiving a hand written letter from the great, distinguished William F. Buckley, The Editor-in-Chief of National Review, *a syndicated columnist, author and host of the TV show,* Firing Line. *It seems that I wrote that "All those who wanted could have Paul Newman or Robert Redford. If I were to be stranded on a desert island, I'd take William Buckley."*

I never knew how Buckley saw the column unless he had a clipping service but he answered in his own inimitable style, "And I would take you." Isn't that priceless? I love it! And just because I wanted to call up that story I'm including his recipe for Supply-Side Economic Fudge, not your conventional recipe for sure. It's from The Great American Writers' Cookbook.

1½	cups milk	½	pound butter
4	squares of Baker's chocolate	2	cups sugar

Stir until you see what looks like discrete goblets. Test these by dripping, by teaspoon a drop or two. If they come down fragmented, you must leave the mixture under boil. If they come down whole, you are ready to lift the mess off the stove. On no account should you pass stage two from inattention, because the effect of this is a granular fudge. At this moment, you should add a teaspoon full of salt, and 2 or 3 teaspoons of vanilla extract. The point of waiting this long is that you should have not allowed the vanilla to evaporate. If you are living in the post-industrial revolution, you may submit the whole to a blender, adding nuts or not, according to market demands, always assuming you are not a supply-sider: in which case you should add the nuts *malgré-soi*. The beating should continue until the stuff is very nearly cool. And only then poured into a plate.

RICH COCOA FUDGE

Don't ever take for granted that a certain recipe will always be there for you. Not even the old, old recipe for Chocolate Fudge that for as many years as I can remember was always right there on the side of the Hershey's Cocoa box. I nearly panicked when I realized it was no longer there.

Searching through all the cookbooks was to no avail. There were fudge recipes, lots of them, but not the old classic that I always used.

Word went out that I was on a search for the recipe. I even went to one person's house who thought she had one of the old cans but it was gone when she started to reach for it.

Since that time I have received several copies of the recipe from friends through the mail. One even sent me the recipe from an old box. I am so grateful to all who helped me and I vow never to let it slip away again.

3	cups sugar	1½	cups milk
⅔	cup Hershey's Cocoa	¼	cup (½ stick) butter or margarine
⅛	teaspoon salt	1	teaspoon vanilla extract

Line 8-or 9-inch square pan with foil, extending foil over edges of pan. Butter foil. In heavy 4-quart saucepan, stir together sugar, cocoa, and salt, stir in milk. Cook over medium heat, stirring constantly, until mixture comes to a full rolling boil. Boil, without stirring, until mixture reaches 234 degrees F on candy thermometer or until syrup, when dropped into very cold water, forms a soft ball that flattens when removed from water. (Bulb of thermometer should not rest on bottom of saucepan.) Remove from heat. Add butter and vanilla. DO NOT STIR. Cool at room temperature to 110 degrees (lukewarm). Beat with wooden spoon until fudge thickens and just begins to lose some of its gloss. Quickly spread into prepared pan, cool completely. Use foil to lift fudge out of pan, peel off foil. Cut into squares. Store in tightly covered container at room temperature.

Nutty Rich Cocoa Fudge: Beat cooked fudge as directed. Immediately stir in 1 cup chopped pecans.

DOOTSIE'S DIVINE DIVINITY

In my entire career of food writing I have never referred to a recipe as "divine." Miss Kitty got me straightened out on that years ago. "Nothing is divine, Louise, except the Deity." Well all right. I'll go along with that out of respect to my Mother.

This recipe, however, is so special and since calling it Dootsies with Divinity makes perfect alliteration I just had to call it "Divine." Not only that if you could have seen our little Dootsie (Carol's nickname when she was an adolescent) with her pony tail flopping, stirring up a batch of divinity, you too could have thought it was "divine. "

Carol always could beat me by a country mile making candy. It's really not my forte but it certainly is hers. I never knew her to have a failure with this "divine" recipe and I'll have to admit I've had several.

3	cups sugar	1	teaspoon vanilla
½	cup white corn syrup	1	cup chopped nuts (optional)
½	cup hot water		Food coloring (optional)
3	egg whites, beaten stiff		

Combine sugar, corn syrup and hot water in saucepan, cook to soft ball stage–238 degrees. Add one half of the syrup gradually to egg whites, beating constantly. Continue cooking other half of syrup until it reaches the hard ball stage–250 degrees. Keep beating the first mixture, then add remaining syrup gradually. Add vanilla. Beat until cool. Add any of the optional variations you so desire. Drop from teaspoon onto greased pan or waxed paper.

BUTTERMILK PRALINES

This might not be your typical N'awlins Pralines (pronounced praw-lines in N'awlins), but it certainly is a good recipe. This makes about 1½ pounds but won't last long.

2	cups sugar	1	teaspoon soda
1	cup buttermilk	1	teaspoon vanilla
2	tablespoons light corn syrup	⅛	teaspoon salt
1	cup butter or margarine	1	cup coarsely chopped pecans

Butter sides of 4-quart saucepan. Combine sugar, buttermilk, syrup, butter and soda. Cook and stir over low gas flame until sugar dissolves. Without stirring, boil over medium flame until a small amount dropped in very cold water forms a soft ball. Turn off flame. Add vanilla and salt, beat until mixture thickens and begins to lose its gloss. Stir in pecans, drop from teaspoon onto waxed paper. Cool.

CANDIES AND COOKIES

HEATH BAR CANDY

When my friend Othine Garner, of Dublin, puts out information I always listen because she knows what she's talking about, whether it's style, theology, cooking or child rearing. Othine and I have swapped a lot of recipes through the years and one day she asked me if I had Moore and Moore the cookbook put out by Moore Street School in Dublin.

When I told her that I do have it, she said, "Be sure to try the Heath Bar Candy that is Martha Touchberry's recipe." She didn't need to say another word because Heath bars are perhaps my favorite candy and I was off and running.

One tip: Have your pan buttered and the Hershey bars grated before you start to cook the candy.

1	pound margarine		6	Hershey bars (plain)
2	cups sugar		½	cup pecans (ground)
1	cup pecans (ground)			

Slowly melt margarine. Add sugar and 1 cup of pecans. Cook on high until it boils. Reduce heat to low and continue to cook to hard crack. Butter pan (14x10-inch cookie pan) and spread mixture in pan. Grate Hershey bars in food processor and add to top of candy mixture. Then sprinkle with ½ cup of ground pecans. After 30 minutes roll pecans with small water glass. When cool break in pieces.

PEANUT BRITTLE

My cousin, Mary Warren Johnson in Albany used to play hostess at some of the plantations in Albany where the quail hunters would come from all over the country. Mary had wonderful recipes and put them to good use entertaining the hunters. Since Albany is right down in peanut country, she liked to serve this Peanut Brittle that is a very good introduction to Albany and plantation life.

1½	cups sugar		2	cups raw shelled peanuts
½	cup white Karo syrup		½	teaspoon soda
¼	cup water		½	teaspoon salt

Bring to a rolling boil sugar, syrup, and water mixed together. Slowly add raw peanuts to keep a rolling boil until peanuts pop and brown. (Hard Crack state 290 degrees.) Remove from heat and add soda and salt. Pour onto a foil lined, buttered cookie sheet.

CHOCOLATE MINT BROWNIES

My neighbor in Wrightsville, Mary Ann Norris, gave me this wonderful recipe just as we were getting ready to go to Florida to visit some friends. I decided to give it a try and it turned out beautifully. Thus I took a box of these brownies along to my friends and they thought they were great. Everybody always does-and they're pretty too.

2	cups sugar	1	cup flour
4	eggs	2	sticks butter (melted)
1	cup cocoa	4	drops peppermint oil

Beat eggs and sugar until thick. Add cocoa and flour. Next add melted butter and peppermint oil. Beat thoroughly. Pour mixture into a long greased cookie pan and bake at 350 degrees for approximately 12 minutes. It will be gooey cool.

First Icing:

3	cups confectioners' sugar	10	drops peppermint oil
1	stick softened butter		

Mix ingredients until creamy. Spread over cooled brownie mixture. A little milk on spatula will help in spreading. A few drops of green food coloring make it very appealing.

Second Icing:

1	stick butter	8	squares semi-sweet baking chocolate

Melt ingredients and spread over top of brownies. Let cool in refrigerator 15 minutes and cut to desired size.

JOHN HUSTON BROWNIES

We were thrilled to be able to have several very special encounters with the great Hollywood producer, John Huston, when he was in Macon filming Flannery O'Connor's Wise Blood. *Once we attended a party for him at what is now the Crowne Plaza Hotel. Another time he invited us to sit in the directors' chairs as he filmed a scene in a historic home on Bond Street. I remember it was supposed to be raining so the Macon Fire Department was supportive with great drops of water from their fire hose. Another time we spent a Sunday afternoon with him in the basement of his hotel where he was viewing film flicks. I'm reluctant to say that we really didn't realize what a truly great man he was until much later. I did find out right away that he liked Brownies and thus I made these available to him on two occasions.*

½	cup butter		¾	cup chocolate-flavored syrup, canned
1	cup sugar		2	teaspoons vanilla extract
3	eggs		¾	cup chopped walnuts or pecans
	Dash salt			Pecans or walnuts, for garnish
1	cup all-purpose flour			

In a bowl, cream together butter, sugar and eggs until very creamy and well blended. Add salt. Stir in flour, mixing to blend well. Add chocolate syrup, vanilla and chopped nuts. Turn mixture into well greased and lightly floured 9-inch square pan. Smooth top. Bake at 350 degrees for about 35 minutes or until a cake tester inserted near center comes out clean. Cool in pan on wire rack but loosen cake at edges. Cut into squares. Garnish with pecan or walnut halves or dust with powdered sugar.

TAFFY BARS

A recipe contest seemed like a sterling idea for our newspaper to sponsor. And indeed, it turned out to be such an overwhelming success that we did one every year for several years.

This recipe was one that was entered in 1985 and when the judges declared it a winner I seconded the decision over and over again.

This is one of the tastiest bars or cookies that I know. I like it so much that it has become one of my favorite confections to make. It's easy, it's quick, it's foolproof and best of all it's super delicious. Everybody loves it. You may use club wafers if you prefer, instead of saltines. Strangely enough a stack pack of either one perfectly fills a jelly-roll pan.

1	stack-pack saltine crackers	1	cup chopped pecans, optional
1	cup brown sugar	1	package (12 ounces) chocolate chips or 4 to 6 milk chocolate bars
2	sticks (½ pound) butter		

Line jelly-roll pan with aluminum foil. Cover with rows of saltines. Boil sugar and butter for 3 minutes stirring constantly. Pour over crackers. Nuts may be added. Bake for 7 to 8 minutes at 400 degrees. Immediately put on top the chocolate chips or bars broken into small pieces. Spread at once. Cut or break into pieces.

JOYCE'S EASY COOKIE/CANDY

While I was in a perfect frenzy one holiday season, baking as fast as I could clean up the mixer and get some more going, my darling friend, Joyce Clay, who was my roommate at Wesleyan, called in her always calm and serene manner.

When she sensed that I was only six inches away from climbing the wall, she said, "Why don't you do it the easy way? My boys love this recipe that you don't even bake." And she proceeded to give me the recipe over the phone.

All the ingredients happened to be right in the pantry and I quickly took her advice and started doing it the easy way. It was a life saver and not only that the children really liked the easy cookie/candy.

1	cup sugar	12	ounces smooth peanut butter
1	cup Karo syrup	4	cups corn flakes

Bring sugar and syrup to a boil to dissolve the sugar. Stir in 12 ounces smooth peanut butter and 4 cups corn flakes. Drop by teaspoonfuls onto waxed paper.

CANDIES AND COOKIES

REMELLE'S OATMEAL COOKIES

Oatmeal Cookies have always been a standard at my house. My Grandmother made them. My mother made them. I make them and my daughter makes them. Until several years ago I would just go with the first recipe I could put my hands on. It might have been on the oatmeal box or even the first cookbook I happened to grab off the shelves.

Now all that has changed. One day the book I just happened to grab off the shelf to use for making oatmeal cookies was "Perennial's" by the Junior Service League of Gainesville and the recipe was called Remelle's Oatmeal Cookies. Although I really don't know Remelle I really know this recipe—almost by heart.

When I lift this book off the shelf it automatically turns to my favorite cookie recipe because I have used it so much. I use all the optional ingredients, sometimes not the coconut, and it makes a truly delightful morsel.

½	cup firmly packed light brown sugar		½	teaspoon baking powder
½	cup sugar		½	teaspoon baking soda
½	cup shortening		½	teaspoon cinnamon (optional)
1	egg		¼	teaspoon nutmeg (optional)
1	tablespoon water		1½	cups rolled oats
2	teaspoons vanilla extract		½	cup chopped nuts (optional)
1	cup flour		½	cups raisins (optional)
½	teaspoon salt		½	cup shredded coconut (optional)

Cream sugars and shortening. Add egg, water, and vanilla; blend well. Combine flour, salt, baking powder, soda, and desired spices. Gradually blend into creamed mixture. Fold in oats and any remaining optional ingredients. (Mixes well in food processor.) Drop by teaspoonfuls onto greased baking sheets. Bake at 375 degrees for 10 minutes.

SEVEN-LAYER COOKIES

Although we always had a good cook in the kitchen when I was growing up, I never had that luxury when I became the homemaker. Actually, it was a role reversal because many times I would cook special recipes for those who worked for me.

Cilla Mae Marshall was the nurse when the children were little and I bet she rolled them a thousand miles in that stroller. One day she rolled our baby boy, named William Asa, out to the health department to visit one of her friends who worked there. One of the nurses said to her, "Cilla, what did the Dodds name the baby?"

"I doesn't rightly know," she replied. "They calls him Bill but I think he's really named Willie Azer." Ever since we teasingly called Bill, Willie Azer. Cilla loved these Seven Layer Cookies so much and would occasionally ask me if I was planning to make some. I always took it as a gentle nudge.

½	cup stick butter	1	(6-ounce) package butterscotch chips
1	cup graham cracker crumbs	1	can sweetened condensed milk
1	(7-ounce) can flaked coconut	1	cup chopped pecans
1	(6-ounce) package chocolate chips		

Melt butter in a 9x12-inch baking pan. Add ingredients by layers, in order listed. Bake at 325 degrees about 30 minutes. Let cool in plan, then cut into small squares.

TEA CAKES

Mrs. H. G. Lane of Thomson was the mother of our dear friend George Lane who was at one time a surgeon at the VA in Dublin and later a radiologist and practicing in Thomasville. Although Mrs. Lane was a southern lady of impeccable distinction, I shall never forget the picture of her in my mind, riding up to George's front door on the back of a motorcycle hanging on for dear life and evidently trusting in her grandson's driving. She was only 80 at the time. Mrs. Lane gave me this recipe, written by hand, and I shall always treasure it.

1	stick butter	2	tablespoons milk
1	cup sugar	½	teaspoon vanilla
1	egg	1¾	cups self-rising flour (if plain flour add 1¾ teaspoons baking powder)

Cream butter, sugar, eggs, milk, vanilla. Add flour last. Roll and cut into circle. Bake at 375 degrees for 8 minutes.

CANDIES AND COOKIES

PEANUT BUTTER GEMS

I Love Lucy. Lucy McMichael, that is. She was my lovely neighbor in Wrightsville, where she taught school for many years. She adored little children and fortunately the neighborhood was full of them to love. I called them alphabets. We had A through G—Allen, Bill, Carol, Dickey, Emory, Freddie and Greg. And that wasn't all. She was always sweet to share her recipes. This is one of hers that is a real keeper. It's really easy but so-o-o good.

Melt in top of a double boiler, 2 cups semisweet chocolate pieces (12 ounce package).

While it is melting, mix together 1 cup peanut butter (crunchy or creamy), 1½ cups graham cracker crumbs, 1 cup (2 sticks) melted butter, ¾ pound confectioners' sugar, preferably sifted. Put this into 13x9-inch pan. Spread melted chocolate on top. Chill 30 minutes. Cut into small squares. These freeze well.

GOOD FRUIT CAKE BARS

Mary Jo Fennell of Wrightsville once made fruit cake bars that were sensational. They were the hit of the holiday season. My late friend, Betty Stephenson of Wrightsville, also made a fruitcake bar that was out-of-this world. I really don't know which one of them this recipe belonged to but I do know it's delicious. This really is a lot easier to deal with than fruit cake and less expensive to make.

1	pound light brown sugar	3	cups pecans, chopped
1	cup butter	1	pound mixed fruit
4	eggs	1½	cups shredded coconut
2	cups flour		

Cream butter and sugar. Add eggs one at a time; then add flour. Add fruits, nuts and coconut. Spread in jelly-roll pan. Bake at 350 degrees.

CHERRY CREAM LOGS

Suzanne Moody came into my life via the Writers Club and then I discovered we were down-the-street neighbors. She's an excellent writer and a good cook too. Her Cherry Cream Logs not only taste delicious, they are fun to create, and excellent to serve for Washington's Birthday or when cherry blossoms are in all their glory.

1	can (1 pound) red sour pitted cherries	2	tablespoons sugar
2	tablespoons cornstarch	1	teaspoon almond extract
¼	teaspoon cinnamon	¼	cup chopped almonds, optional
¼	cup sugar	1	package refrigerated crescent rolls
1	cup whipping cream		

Cherry Cream: Drain cherries reserving ¼ cup liquid. In saucepan, combine cornstarch, cinnamon, sugar and cherry liquid. Cook until thick. Add drained cherries. Chill.

Whip Cream: Blend in sugar, extract and almonds. Gently fold cherries and whipped cream together. Set aside.

Logs: Divide package of crescent rolls in to 4 rectangles; smooth out diagonal markings. Cut each rectangle in half making a total of 8 squares.

Roll 2 (12x12-inch) pieces of aluminum foil "log fashion" to form a tube 1½ inches in diameter. Wrap each square around foil log, sealing seam, thus making 8 logs.

Bake at 375 degrees for 10 minutes (seam down). Place Cherry Cream filling in hollow of each log. May sprinkle each log with powdered sugar for garnish.

YUMMY COOKIES

Louise Sikes Bryant said that when she and Sweeny were doing a psychiatry residency at Yale, this recipe was given to her by another resident's wife and with it she said, "Guard this with your life." She did and all these years (50 something) later they are still friends and still guarding this recipe with their lives.

1	cup butter	½	teaspoon soda
½	cup brown sugar	½	teaspoon salt
½	cup sugar	1	cup pecans
1	egg	1	teaspoon vanilla
2	cups flour		

Cream butter and sugar. Add egg and beat well. Combine flour, soda, and salt and add to butter mixture. Add pecans and stir in vanilla. Roll and refrigerate and slice. Place on baking sheet and bake at 350 degrees for 5 minutes. Turn pan and cook 5 minutes more.

PRALINE COOKIES

It was one of those made-to-order spring days when Ethel Ann Kibler entertained the Medical Auxiliary at her lovely country home near Dudley. Because Ethel Ann is a marvelous cook and had a good committee of cooks helping her, they had truly memorable refreshments. One thing that I especially remember is the Praline Cookies for which I requested the recipe to put in the newspaper. Ethel Ann was sweet to share and these are sweet too—not too sweet—but just right.

1⅔	cups sifted flour	1½	cups brown packed sugar
1½	teaspoons baking powder	1	egg
½	teaspoon salt	1	teaspoon vanilla
½	cup butter	1	cup pecans

Sift flour, baking powder and salt together. Cream butter, add sugar—blend in egg—vanilla and pecans and dry ingredients. Drop by teaspoonfuls on ungreased sheet. Bake at 350 degrees for 10 minutes.

Frosting: Combine 1 cup brown sugar and ½ cup cream in small saucepan. Bring to boil, stirring constantly. Boil 2 minutes. Remove from heat. Blend in 1 cup 4X sugar-beat until smooth. Place several pieces of pecans on each cookie and drizzle praline frosting over top.

LYNDA'S LEMON LOVE NOTES

When Lynda Colston was a beautiful little girl in the sixth grade, she used to frequently bring these cookies to me, her teacher. One day at my request her mother sent me the recipe. Years later when Lynda married, I decided there would be nothing more appropriate to serve at the tea for Lynda than the Lemon Love Notes. It has become one of my traditional wedding shower, tea or reception sweets.

2	cups sifted plain flour	¼	cup plain flour
½	cup confectioners' sugar	⅓	cup freshly squeezed lemon juice
1	cup butter, softened	½	teaspoon baking powder
4	eggs, slightly beaten		Confectioners' sugar
2	cups sugar		

Preheat oven to 350 degrees. In medium mixing bowl, combine 2 cups flour and ½ cup confectioners' sugar. Cut in butter with a fork. Pat this mixture into the bottom of an ungreased 13x9-inch pan. Bake at 350 degrees for 25 to 30 minutes.

In another bowl combine eggs, 2 cups sugar, ¼ cup flour, lemon juice and baking powder; beat until ingredients are mixed thoroughly. Pour over the cooked crust and bake 25 minutes or until edges are brown. Cool the cookies and sprinkle with confectioners' sugar.

HELLO DOLLIES

It was so long ago that the blue bank check on which this recipe was written has turned yellow and green. We were up at Lake Sinclair vacationing and swapping recipes and my sister-in-law, Sybil, had just found out about Hello Dollies that went on to become a classic.

All of us were so anxious to try this new recipe that we went straight to the grocery store, bought the ingredients and had the cookies in the oven in less that an hour.

1	block butter	1	cup chocolate chips
1	cup graham cracker crumbs	1	cup chopped nuts
1	cup coconut	1	can condensed milk

Melt butter in 9x9-inch pan and layer other ingredients in order as named. Bake at 350 degrees for 25 to 30 minutes.

CANDIES AND COOKIES

MAGIC MARSHMALLOW CRESCENT PUFFS

I'll never forget the night that Betty Hatton Young of Wrightsville brought these delicious puffs to a covered dish supper at our school. I thought they were absolutely delicious and of course just had to get the recipe. The next time I saw Betty she handed me the neatly copied recipe that I still treasure to this day. She said it was a grand prize winner at the Pillsbury Bake-Off® contest and I certainly see why.

¼	cup sugar	16	large marshmallows
1	teaspoon cinnamon	¼	cup butter or margarine (melted)
2	cans (8-ounces) each refrigerated Quick Crescent Dinner Rolls	¼	cup chopped nuts

Glaze:

½	cup powdered sugar	2-3	teaspoons milk
½	teaspoon vanilla		

Combine sugar with cinnamon. Separate crescent dough into 16 triangles. Dip a marshmallow in butter, roll in sugar-cinnamon mixture. Wrap a dough triangle around each marshmallow, completely covering marshmallow and squeezing edges of dough tightly to seal. Dip in butter and place buttered-side down in deep muffin tins. Place on foil or cookie sheet during baking to guard against spill overs in oven.

Bake at 375 degrees for 10 to 15 minutes until golden brown. Immediately remove from pans and drizzle with glaze, sprinkle with nuts. Serve warm or cold.

Tips: Reheat wrapped in foil for 5 to 10 minutes at 375 degrees. To make ahead, prepare, cover and refrigerate for 2 to 3 hours, bake as directed. Puffs may be frozen and reheated from frozen state, wrapped in foil for 10 to 15 minutes at 375 degrees.

$250 COOKIE RECIPE

We've probably all heard the story about the retail store that charged the customer $250 for a cookie recipe that she casually requested in their tea room and later found charged to her bill.

The store denies the story. The customer declares it's true. Since the customer could produce the recipe I tend to lean toward her story. But it really doesn't matter. Although I would never pay $250 for it, it is a mighty good recipe and it makes an enormous number of cookies.

2	cups butter	1	teaspoon salt
2	cups sugar	2	teaspoons baking powder
2	cups brown sugar	2	teaspoons soda
4	eggs	24	ounces chocolate chips
2	teaspoons vanilla	1	(8-ounce) Hershey bar, grated
4	cups flour	3	cups chopped nuts (your choice)
5	cups oatmeal		

Cream the butter and both sugars. Add eggs and vanilla, mix together with flour, oatmeal, salt, baking powder, and soda. Add chocolate chips, Hershey bar and nuts. Roll into balls and place 2 inches apart on a cookie sheet. Bake 10 minutes at 375 degrees.

JOSEPHINE BAILEYS' INSTANT OATMEAL COOKIES

This delicious and easy-to-make cookie that requires no baking was an absolute favorite of my children when they were growing up. I'll have to admit I like it a lot myself.

This was given to me by Josephine Bailey who lived at Donovan with her husband Cecil and all the boys. We used to make house calls up there whenever one of them was sick and I always enjoyed going in and visiting with Josephine. Maybe it was on one of those visits that she gave me this recipe because it's written on a prescription pad. I consider it a very special keepsake.

Into 1 bowl measure 3 cups minute oatmeal. Add 1 teaspoon vanilla. Shake on dash of salt. Add 1 cup nuts. Cook 2 cups sugar, ½ cup evaporated milk, 1 stick butter, 2 tablespoons cocoa. Bring to boil. Stir oatmeal mixture in and drop on waxed paper.

SNICKERDOODLES

For years and years Mrs. Ruth Hicks operated a small grocery store in Wrightsville and lived in a big old two-story house on Elm Street—the trademark of which were two enormous Boston ferns on the front porch.

My friend Mary Ann Norris, secured this recipe from Mrs. Hicks so many years ago that we cannot remember. The irony of the story is that Mary Ann and Joe bought the old Hicks house, have restored it in perfect taste that Mary Ann is well known for—and the very same ferns are still on the porch. I wonder if Mary Ann still has the Snickerdoodle recipe too.

1	cup soft shortening (butter)		1	teaspoon cream of tartar
1½	cups sugar		1	teaspoon baking soda
2	eggs		¼	teaspoon salt
2¾	cups all-purpose flour		2	teaspoons vanilla (optional)

Mix shortening, sugar and eggs. Sift dry ingredients together. Add to sugar mixture and blend. Add vanilla. Roll in balls and roll balls in this mixture:

4	tablespoons sugar		4	teaspoons cinnamon

Bake at 375 degrees or 400 degrees on ungreased baking sheet for 8 to 10 minutes.

MIM'S COOKIES

This wonderful recipe that I use over and over again came a long route from Henning, Tennessee which is the home of the noted author of Roots, *Alex Haley. Henning is also my friend's, Sally Shurling's, hometown and it was she who gave the recipe to my friend, Mary Ann, who gave it me.*

These cookies are so delicious that I never take them anywhere that someone doesn't request the recipe. Please don't take any liberties with it—it's perfect like it is. Note that it says "butter" and also that you leave it out to soften before you proceed. Raspberry jam is just a must—mainly because it's my favorite fruit flavor. This makes about 4 dozen cookies which won't be enough no matter how many you are having to share them with.

1	cup sugar		
2	sticks butter (do not use margarine)	2	cups grated pecans
1	teaspoon vanilla		Raspberry jam
2½	cups flour		

Leave butter out overnight. Cream butter with sugar. Add vanilla, flour and pecans.

Make into small balls, about size of large marbles. Place on ungreased cookie sheet, about 1-inch apart. Press with thimble or index finger to make indentation in center. Fill with jam. Bake at 300 degrees for 20 to 25 minutes. Roll (lightly) in powdered sugar when slightly cool.

PICKLES AND PRESERVES

McJaals Bridge Club
in Mardi Gras Masks.
Ann Wall, Ann Oxley, Louise,
Clare Dodd and Joyce Clay.

GREEN TOMATO PICKLES

Grandmother Eva Shearouse should really be remembered for her great faith in the Lord and her ability to "hang in there" with never any complaints when Life dealt her some almost insurmountable obstacles. She had six children and another one on the way when my grandfather died. Although they had lived rather well when he was living, it all came to an abrupt halt when the young father died. Grandmother rolled up her sleeves and got to work—when she wasn't on her knees praying. She opened her home to school teacher boarders, made a garden, raised some chickens and didn't complain—ever. That's what she should always be remembered for but let's do slip in her unbelievably memorable Green Tomato Pickles that generations after her still savor with great delight. She always referred to this as "pickles" but it really seems like more of a relish. Who am I to question this old, highly prized, heirloom recipe.

1	bucket green tomatoes	Vinegar
6	good sized bell peppers	Sugar
6	medium onions	Pickling spices
	Salt	

Peel and slice tomatoes thin. Cut peppers and onions in small pieces. Salt as you slice and alternate with tomatoes. Let stand about 8 hours. Drain and squeeze. Put in container you are going to cook them in and pour vinegar until it just shows. Keep an account of cups of vinegar and put in equal amount of sugar. Put spice in a clean cloth, tie and put in pot. Cook until tender (not long). Stir. Put into jars and seal.

SQUASH PICKLES

This is one of the fine recipes of all times. Given to me by Nelly Veal of Wrightsville, these pickles are so good they are addictive. You can just stand at the fridge and eat them out of the jar. Good idea—I'm going for some now.

8	cups yellow squash, thinly sliced	2	cups vinegar
2	cups onions, thinly sliced	2	cups sugar
2	bell peppers, finely chopped	2	teaspoons whole celery seed
¾	cup salt	2	teaspoons mustard seed

Soak squash, onions and peppers in icy water with salt for 1 hour. Wash thoroughly. Bring vinegar, sugar and spices to a boil. Add squash, onions and peppers. Bring to a boil and boil 3 to 5 minutes. Seal in hot jars.

PICKLES AND PRESERVES

MAMA GORDY'S CRISPY PICKLES

My friend, Madge DeMay of St. Simon's Island, sent me her recipe for Crispy Pickles that are delicious. Try this—you'll be glad you did.

1	gallon dill pickles, drained and sliced to desired thickness (hers are thin)	2	tablespoons whole black peppercorns
5	pounds sugar	1½	tablespoons cloves
2	tablespoons garlic–chopped or already in jar	2	tablespoons mustard seed

In large container, crock or glass or plastic, layer half of pickles then half of spices, then rest of pickles, then rest of spices. Cover with sugar. Let it stand until sugar has melted, then stir often for 10 days. If container has no lid, cover tightly with plastic wrap. Put up in jars.

OKRA PICKLES

John LaRowe, who edited a great cookbook and guide to Northeast Georgia called Something's Cooking in the Mountains *sent me an autographed copy which I treasure. The LaRowes converted an old grist mill into an interesting craft shop where they make and sell their own pottery. They interestingly added a lovely porch that is over the beautiful Soque River and visitors can see mountain trout in their own habitat. This recipe was submitted to LaRowe's book by Babyland General Hospital which made a national reputation by making doll babies that had to be "adopted" by their owners.*

3¼	pounds small okra pods (3 to 4 inches)	1	pint white vinegar (5% acidity)
5	cloves garlic	⅓	cup pickling salt
5	small fresh red peppers	2	teaspoons dill seed
1	quart water		

Pack okra firmly in hot sterilized jars, leaving ¼-inch head space. Place a garlic clove and a hot pepper in each jar. Combine remaining ingredients in a saucepan and bring to a boil. Pour over okra in jars and seal. Process in boiling water bath 10 minutes.

QUICK PICKLED PEACHES

This is an especially nice recipe that I like a lot. Since early childhood, I have adored Peach Pickles. Mother used to put one on the salad plates she served at bridge and I always sneaked one—or two. Not off the plates, of course—too obvious! Now we can make our own peach pickles very simply. And if you use peach halves, they are lovely to place around a meat salad or meat platter. They're also nice if you use cling, whole peaches or even slices. Great with ham or chicken salad.

2	(No. 2½) cans cling peach halves	1	teaspoon allspice
¾	cup brown sugar	1	teaspoon whole cloves
½	cup cider vinegar	2-3	cinnamon sticks

Drain peaches. To peach syrup, add sugar, vinegar and spices. Boil 5 minutes. Add peaches and simmer 5 minutes. Allow fruit to stand in syrup overnight. Serve chilled.

WATERMELON RIND PICKLES

My grandmother made Watermelon Rind Pickles with the rinds left from a watermelon cutting. I always felt she was a bit cheated with the rind I left because I ate the watermelon and then some.

7	pounds watermelon rind	1	pint vinegar
1	tablespoon slaked lime	2	sticks cinnamon or tablespoons mixed pickle flavorings
1	gallon water		
4	pounds sugar		

Peel and cut rind in 1½-inch pieces; soak overnight in mixture of lime and water. Wash several times; place in large cooking pot. Cover with clear water; cook until tender. Drain. Boil sugar, vinegar, and cinnamon together; cool. Pour over rind; let stand overnight. Bring to a boil; boil until rind is transparent. Pack into fruit jars; pour in hot syrup. Seal jars.

BABY ZUCCHINI PICKLES

On a trip to Martha's Vineyard one summer, I acquired a handsome cookbook of the island that featured this interesting recipe for Zucchini Pickles. It only makes a quart—I know you'll want many more.

Enough tiny (3 to 4-inch) zucchini squash to fill quart jar

1 teaspoon salt

¼ teaspoon cayenne pepper (optional)

2 cloves garlic, peeled and sliced

1 teaspoon olive oil

Sprig of fresh tarragon, dill, or basil

1 cup vinegar

1 cup water (approximately)

Allow 2 or 3 extra squash as they should be well forced into the jar when packed. Wash squash well, remove stems and blossom ends, let soak in a bowl of hot water while you assemble other ingredients, then pack carefully and neatly into clean hot quart jar. Add salt, cayenne (if used), garlic, and olive oil. Heat vinegar and water almost to boiling and pour over zucchini. Use a knife if necessary to remove any air at bottom of jar. Place sprig of tarragon, dill, or basil on top of squash, seal, and process 10 minutes in hot water bath.

SYBIL'S CUCUMBER PICKLES

Sybil's, my sister-in-law's introduction of this delicious, crisp pickle caused a stampede among the family's pickle lovers with Carol Dodd at the head of the pack. This is truly a wonderful pickle, made from those huge, old cucumbers that are too large for ordinary use.

7 pounds cucumber

2 gallons water

2 cups lime

2 quarts vinegar

5 pounds sugar

1 teaspoon salt

⅓ box whole cloves

1 box stick cinnamon

1 cup raisins

Green food coloring

Cut cukes in half lengthwise and scrape out seeds with a spoon. Cut in cubes. Soak in 2 gallons water and lime for 24 hours. Drain; soak in clean water for 3 hours. Mix and boil vinegar, sugar and salt. Tie cloves and cinnamon in a clean cloth bag. Add to vinegar, soak cukes in vinegar overnight. Boil 30 minutes next morning. Add 1 cup of raisins and boil 5 minutes. If desired add food coloring at beginning of cooking. Put in sterilized jars and seal.

MOTHER'S BREAD AND BUTTER PICKLES

All I have to do is say it's Mother's recipe—the rest is a given. This is just one of the many, many marvelous recipes that Mother has collected in almost a century of good cooking.

25-30	medium cukes	5	cups sugar
8	large white onions	2	tablespoons mustard seeds
2	large sweet green peppers	1	teaspoon turmeric
½	cup salt	½	teaspoon cloves
5	cups cider vinegar		

Wash cukes and slice as thinly as possible. Chop onions and pepper. Combine with cukes and salt. Let stand 3 hours and drain. Combine vinegar, sugar and spices in large preserving kettle; bring to boil. Add drained cukes, heat thoroughly but do not boil. Pack thoroughly while hot into sterilized jars and seal.

CORN RELISH

This recipe is from a lovely old Gloucester, Virginia home, Lisburne, that was built around 1810. Somewhere in my travels in Virginia I managed to acquire their wonderful recipe for Corn Relish. It's delicious—try serving it on fresh greens or on a relish tray. You'll love it.

5-6	ears corn	1½	cups vinegar
3	bell peppers, chopped	1	cup sugar
¾	cup sweet red pepper, chopped	2½	teaspoons salt
1	cup ripe cucumber, peeled and chopped	1	teaspoon mustard seed
½	cup celery, diced	¾	teaspoon turmeric
1	cup onions, chopped	2	teaspoons celery seed
3	cups ripe tomatoes, seeded and diced	¼	teaspoon dry mustard

Wash and drain all vegetables. Cut corn from cob, scraping well. Combine all vegetables except tomatoes. Turn into colander to drain thoroughly. Add tomatoes. Combine with remaining ingredients in 3 quart pot, heat to boiling. Reduce heat and simmer for 40 minutes until vegetables are just tender. Pour at once into hot sterilized jars. Seal.

CUCUMBERS

This is not really a pickle in the true sense of the word but it comes close enough to satisfy me. These cucumbers keep well in the refrigerator—no, not really. They're so good that they'll soon be all gone.

7	cups cucumbers, slice very thin with peels on	1	tablespoon salt
1	cup onions, slice thin	2	cups sugar
1	cup bell pepper, slice thin	1	teaspoon celery seed
		1	cup vinegar

Sprinkle salt on vegetables, let stand 30 minutes. Mix sugar, celery seed and vinegar. Pour over vegetables; put in refrigerator.

VIDALIA ONION RELISH

Anything with Vidalia onions is good. I believe they'd be good in a cake. Try this recipe for Vidalia Onion Relish that is in a cookbook The Joy of Sharing, *given to me in October '93 by the Baptist Young Women of Rock Springs Baptist Church in Dublin. I thank them over again every time I make this delicious relish.*

1½	gallons ground Vidalia onions (16 or 18)	1	teaspoon pickling spice (tied in a bag)
½	cup salt	1	teaspoon turmeric
1	quart apple cider vinegar	1	small jar pimento, chopped
4½	cups sugar		

Grind onions to yield 1½ gallons, add ½ cup salt and let stand 30 minutes. Squeeze juice from onion salt mixture and discard juice. Add vinegar, sugar, spices, and pimento. Bring to a boil and cook 30 minutes, stirring often. Pack both onions and cooking liquid to cover in hot jars leaving ½-inch head space. Remove air bubbles, wipe jar rims clean. (Use large mouth funnel to fill jars.) Screw on rings adjusting lid, process 10 minutes in boiling bath.

PEAR RELISH

Granted—pear relish is trouble to make—especially if you peel the pears which in my opinion is a must. Anything this good is worth the trouble, though, so when pears are ripe, roll up your sleeves and get going with this wonderful keepsake recipe that was given to me by the Glenwood Methodist Church in their cookbook A Little Taste of Heaven.

1	peck pears	5	cups vinegar
5	medium onions	1	tablespoon salt
6	bell peppers (3 green and 3 red)	1	tablespoon mixed spices
2	pounds sugar	1	tablespoon turmeric

Put peeled pears, onions, and peppers through a food chopper; add other ingredients and cook 30 minutes after the mixture comes to a boil. Remove from heat; put into jars and seal.

APPLE-CRANBERRY CHUTNEY

In 1958, when traveling the 120-mile trip back and forth to the obstetrician, I always looked forward on the way home to seeing the little man who had set up a very small produce stand on Highway 57. I always bought Rome Beauty Apples and ate them all the way home.

Now, anytime I see a recipe with Rome apples, my interest is piqued. This chutney recipe doesn't make a great amount but it surely is delicious.

2	cups, peeled, chopped Rome apples (about 2 medium)	1	tablespoon grated orange rind
1	cup cranberries	2	tablespoons cider vinegar
¼	cup golden raisins	¼	teaspoon ground cloves
2	tablespoons brown sugar	¼	teaspoon ground nutmeg
		¼	teaspoon ground cinnamon

Combine all ingredients in a non-aluminum saucepan. Place over a high heat. Bring to a boil; stirring constantly. Reduce heat and simmer, uncovered, for 15 minutes or until apples are tender. Remove from heat, and let cool. Position knife blade in food processor bowl; add cranberry mixture. Top with cover and process, until combined. Place in a medium bowl; cover and chill.

FIG PRESERVES

A toasted English muffin with Fig Preserves is one of the world's great breakfasts. It's even more grand if you have homemade preserves. I hope you have a fig source—I don't

4	pounds ripe figs	2	cups water
½	teaspoon baking soda	4	pounds sugar

Wash figs in mixture of baking soda and water. Rinse in clear water. Place figs in heavy saucepan. Pour sugar over figs and let stand 2 hours or until syrup begins to form. Cook fig mixture over medium heat until figs are brown in color and syrup thickens. Stir occasionally at start of cooking process and as preserves begin to thicken. Pack into hot sterilized jars and seal.

UNCOOKED PEACH JAM

Mother introduced me to this delicious jam many years ago. It's the only peach jam I know that tastes exactly like delicious, fresh, Georgia peaches.

2¼	cups ripe peaches	5	cups sugar
2	tablespoons lemon juice	1	box Sure-Jell

In large bowl put lemon juice, sugar and peaches. Put Sure-Jell in ¾ cup water. Boil 1 minute. Pour over fruit and stir 10 minutes. Put in containers and freeze.

SYRUP FOR FRESH PEACHES TO FREEZE

Not every idea for freezing fresh peaches works well. But this one, from my sister-in-law Sybil, I have found to be very satisfactory. Use the syrup hot and pour over the sliced peaches and seal well.

1¾   cups sugar to 1 pint water

Bring to a boil. Cool. Slice fruit. Cover with syrup. ⅓ to ½ cup syrup to 1½ cups fruit. Can be made ahead of time and kept in refrigerator.

WATERMELON RIND PRESERVES

My paternal grandfather who fought in the Confederate Army in the War Between the States, Abram Futrelle, was a mover and shaker in the New Providence Baptist Church in Guyton, now almost 200 years old. They have recently published a nice cookbook called Breaking Bread Together *and from it comes Louise Bath's, (a school friend when I was growing up) good recipe for one of my favorite preserves—Watermelon Rind. It's easy, uncomplicated and delicious.*

Watermelon rind

Sugar

Peel and cube white part of watermelon. Place in boiler. Cover with water. Boil until melon looks clear. Drain. Place in thick boiler to prevent sticking, 2 cups watermelon to 1 cup sugar. If you prefer more sugar to make them thicker and sweeter, add more. Cook over low heat until thick. Put in sterilized jars and seal.

PEACH AND ORANGE JAM

Years ago we started out to Birmingham to a Dodd family reunion. Although a strong suggestion was made by my husband that we make hotel reservations, I assured him and reassured him that it wouldn't be necessary because the traveling salesmen never were in hotels on the weekend and there'd be more than ample room. After going through Atlanta, cars began to pass us with stickers all over them. More and more frequently the flag-waving drivers came until I was beginning to think we were the only people on the road not going to Talladega. You know the rest of the story. They all spent the night in Birmingham—with reservations—and there wasn't a hotel nor motel room in the entire city. We ended up spending the night in the hospital of all places. They had guest rooms and we were lucky to be thought of as guests. It was a crazy weekend but worth it all. This recipe alone given to me by one of the relatives, was worth the trip.

12	medium-sized oranges		Sugar
1	lemon	1	cup drained, sliced maraschino cherries, if desired
12	large peaches		

Cut lemon and oranges in half and remove seeds. Coarsely grind. Scald, peel, and pit peaches; slice. Measure fruits; add an equal amount of sugar, about 6 cups. Divide mixture in half. Cook each portion until thick, stirring frequently. Add cherries. Seal in hot, sterilized glasses.

PICKLES AND PRESERVES

INDEX

❧✦❧

INDEX

D

INDEX

INDEX

INDEX

LOUISE DODD

Courier Herald
115 South Jefferson Street
Dublin, GA 31021

Please send me _____ copies of
Eating from the White House to the Jailhouse   @ $25.00 each _____

Sales tax   @ $ 1.50 each _____

TOTAL _____

Name _____

Address _____

City _____ State _____ Zip _____

Please make check or money order payable to Louise Dodd.

- -

LOUISE DODD

Courier Herald
115 South Jefferson Street
Dublin, GA 31021

Please send me _____ copies of
Eating from the White House to the Jailhouse   @ $25.00 each _____

Sales tax   @ $ 1.50 each _____

TOTAL _____

Name _____

Address _____

City _____ State _____ Zip _____

Please make check or money order payable to Louise Dodd.